J. Harris Sculp.

y Andrew Archer and
es for Building St Philips Church
st obedient humble Servt W: Westley.

3. The Rector's house.
4.4. Temple Row.
. St Martin's Church

A HISTORY OF
BIRMINGHAM

The Bull Ring in the 1820s, with St Martin's church and Digbeth behind.

A HISTORY OF
BIRMINGHAM

Chris Upton

Phillimore

1993

Published by
PHILLIMORE & CO. LTD.,
Shopwyke Manor Barn, Chichester, Sussex

© Chris Upton, 1993

ISBN 0 85033 870 0

Printed and bound in Great Britain by
BIDDLES LTD.,
Guildford, Surrey

To Fiona, Olive and Jeff
(for much patience and encouragement)

Contents

List of Illustrations ix
Illustration Acknowledgements xi
Introduction xiii

1   Beginnings 1
2   A Town on the Move 8
3   A Walk Around the Town 14
4   A Brush with History 20
5   Preparing for the Revolution 28
6   A Town on the Move 35
7   Entertaining the Town 42
8   Radicals and Rioting 50
9   A Little Philosophical Laughter 58
10 The Golden Boys 65
11 Steam Power for the World 71
12 Cleansing, Paving, Lighting 78
13 A Transport Revolution 85
14 The Railway Age 93
15 New Settlers 100
16 King Tom and the Democrats 107
17 The Far Side of Newhall Hill 114
18 The Musical Town 121
19 From Ballads to Bhangra: Birmingham's Popular Culture 128
20 Matters of Life and Death 135
21 Libraries, Baths and Parks 142
22 Municipalisation 150
23 Schools and Hospitals 159
24 Entertainment Without Music 167
25 City of a Thousand Trades 173
26 The Changing Bull Ring 180
27 Greater and Greater Birmingham 188
28 Homes for Heroes 195
29 What Went Wrong with Tomorrow? 203
30 The Rebuilding of Birmingham 210

Index 215

List of Illustrations

Frontispiece: The Bull Ring in the 1820s

1. Site of the Roman fort at Metchley 2
2. Extract from Westley's map, 1731 5
3. The village pump in the 18th-century Bull Ring 7
4. The guild hall and school, 1931 10
5. Sketch of the moat and buildings 11
6. Half-timbered house, Digbeth 13
7. St Martin's Lane, 1840 15
8. The chamber over the Old Cross 16
9. View of the Bull Ring from New Street, from an 1827 engraving 18
10. Aston Hall in Victorian times 20
11. The lodge, Aston Hall 21
12. The long gallery, Aston Hall 23
13. Frontispiece to *Burning Love*, 1643 24
14. Birmingham's first map 26
15. Birmingham bedstead-makers 29
16. Owen's Farm, Sparkbrook 32
17. Charles Lloyd the elder 33
18. Old Square, engraving 36
19. North-east side of the Old Square 37
20. The New Theatre before the fire 43
21. John Baskerville 46
22. Bradford's map of the town, 1751 48
23. The Old Meeting House 50
24. James Gillray's cartoon of the Birmingham banquet 52
25. The assault on the Old Meeting House 53
26. Looting at Priestley's House, Fair Hill, 1791 55
27. Withering's monument in St Bartholomew's church, Edgbaston 60
28. Joseph Priestley 62
29. Matthew Boulton 65
30. Soho Manufactory, Handsworth Heath 68
31. Watt's discovery of steam power, engraving 72
32. William Murdock 75
33. Looking south from the tower of St Philip's, 1850s 79
34. The Bull Ring, 1812 82
35. The Public Office, Moor Street 84
36. The *Stork Hotel*, Old Square 86

37.   Advertisement for Rothwell's coach services 87
38.   The B.C.N. Canal Offices, Paradise Street 89
39.   Old Worcester Wharf, 1913 91
40.   The Curzon Street portico 94
41.   The *Queen's Hotel* 97
42.   Joseph Wright's works, 1859 99
43.   The staff of the Electric Theatre, Station Street, 1911 101
44.   Cannon Street, 1892 102
45.   The Murphy Riots in Park Street, 1867 104
46.   Thomas Attwood 109
47.   Attwood and Spooner's Bank, New Street 110
48.   Cartoon satirising the Reform meeting of 1836 113
49.   The gathering on Newhall Hill, 1832 115
50.   View of the town from St Philip's, painting by Samuel Lines, 1821 116
51.   An incorrect version of the borough arms 118
52.   Peel's statue moving to Pershore Road 121
53.   Designs for the new General Hospital, Steelhouse Lane, ... 123
54.   The Town Hall during a festival 125
55.   The Symphony Hall in the International Convention Centre 127
56.   The Imperial Theatre, Bordesley High Street 130
57.   Advertisement for picture shows at Curzon Hall 131
58.   Advertisement for the Theatre De Luxe 133
59.   The temporary village for workers and their families at Elan Valley 138
60.   The General Cemetery, Key Hill 139
61.   Warstone Lane Cemetery 140
62.   Bird's eye view of Birmingham, 1887 144
63.   Allin's eccentric Cabinet of Curiosities, watercolour by Paul Braddon 145
64.   The Industrial Exhibition, Bingley, 1865 147
65.   The School of Art, Margaret Street 148
66.   Artist's impression of the new Council House 150
67.   Joseph Chamberlain 151
68.   The corner of Newton Street and Corporation Street 153
69.   The Victoria Law Courts 154
70.   A cartoon from *The Dart*, 1882 155
71.   *The Dart*'s cynical view of the 'new Birmingham' 156
72.   Lancastrian Free School, Severn Street 160
73.   Josiah Mason 163
74.   Birmingham Workhouse 164
75.   Birmingham and Midland Homeopathic Hospital 165
76.   Birmingham and Midland Eye Hospital 166
77.   The *Dog and Duck* 168
78.   Charity fête at Aston Hall 171
79.   Birmingham Super Prix 172
80.   Advertisement for Bird's blancmange 174
81.   Advertisement for Kynoch's cycles 175

82. Elkington's Works 177
83. Advertisement for the Austin Motor Car Co. 178
84. The Market Hall 181
85. The Bull Ring 182
86. King Kong in Birmingham 184
87. The Beehive Warehouse, Albert Street 185
88. Aerial view of Birmingham, 1970s 186
89. A steam tram on the Stratford Road line 189
90. The Chamberlain family 192
91. Tank Bank Week 194
92. Rejected design for the Hall of Memory 196
93. Advertisement for Birmingham Corporation's outer-circle bus service 197
94. W. Raymond's proposed Council House, Broad Street 198
95. Broad Street between the wars 202
96. High-rise homes 204
97. Birmingham Central Mosque, Belgrave Road 207
98. Jamaican baptism, 1956 208
99. Chinese restaurant 209
100. Lucas Works, Great King Street 211
101. Birmingham of the 1990s 214

Illustration Acknowledgements

Birmingham Central Library: 4, 6, 15, 36, 39, 44, 59, 65.
Birmingham Post & Mail: 43, 86, 95, 98.
Birmingham Museum and Art Gallery: 50, 77.

Introduction

In July 1938 many of the people of Birmingham had their first experience of what we now call 'living history'. For two short weeks the fields around Aston Hall rang with the sound of prehistoric monsters, medieval knights and Georgian rioters. The occasion was the 100th anniversary of the city's Borough Charter and, in one of the largest pieces of community drama ever seen, over 6,000 Brummies re-enacted their city's history from the Druids (not very historical) to Queen Victoria's visit (almost living memory).

Birmingham believed it had risen to the top. It had its very own prime minister (Neville Chamberlain) and for 20 years had been the second city in the kingdom. The whole Pageant of Birmingham cost £31,000 and entertained over 130,000 people, including the Australian cricket team (I wonder what they made of it!). The romance of history led to many an off-stage romance, as human sacrifice from Saltley met medieval priest from Harborne. And on that memorable last performance, the Battle of Crécy lost its grip of historical authenticity as the French pelted the English with flour, eggs and rotten apples. They were knights to remember.

During the Pageant preparations, the Minister of War visited the makeshift 'armaments factory' in Cambridge Street to watch the making of bows and arrows and cavemen's clubs. Sad to realise (as the newsreels used to say) that a few months later there would be need of the real thing. All that living history would be forgotten, as the erstwhile actors began to live history in a very different sense. Once the war was over, a new age would be beginning.

Ask a stranger what he or she knows of Birmingham now and the catalogue is sadly familiar: Spaghetti Junction, endless subways and a round skyscraper called the Rotunda. Hardly the stuff that dreams are made of. And hardly the rich tapestry of history either. That Birmingham was the cradle of the Industrial Revolution in the 18th century, or cradle of local government and state education in the 19th, may have escaped the notice even of Brummies themselves. All this is not surprising.

At some point in the early 20th century, Birmingham decided to abolish the past. It was not a decision ratified by the City Council, but it was entirely in harmony with an image cultivated over a century or more. Here was a city and people more interested in tomorrow than yesterday: brash, energetic, financially astute and innovative. Even her coat of arms bore the legend 'Forward'.

As the new ideas and technologies of the century advanced—internal combustion engine, aeroplane, shopping centre—Birmingham was first on the bandwagon, energetically moving forward. Many of those symbols of the new age are still with us, at least at the time of writing—Spaghetti Junction, Bull Ring Shopping Centre, Ring Road and Rotunda—and each step into the future erased a little more of the past. The past needs time and contemplation, and Birmingham was in too much of a hurry for such niceties.

Birmingham's first historian, William Hutton, would have understood the problem perfectly. After all, his description of his first impressions of the place in 1741 rings as true today as it did then.

> I was much surprised at the place, but more at the people. They were a species I had never seen; they possessed a vivacity I had never beheld: I had been among dreamers, but now I saw men awake: their very step along the street shewed alacrity. I had been taught to consider the whole twenty-four hours as appropriated for sleep, but I found a people satisfied with only half that number.

It was not long before William Hutton became one of them. Unusually for a historian, he was more at home with the present than the past, and not the most reliable witness of either. But we should be grateful to him; it would be a hundred years before Birmingham produced any more historians. The Industrial Revolution intervened, and there was no time for looking back.

Perhaps what links the town that Hutton visited with the city of today is its earning capacity, the over-riding desire to make an honest buck. Birmingham abolished the past because it was not marketable: there was no money in history.

But times and attitudes change. We are now in a world of conferences, service industries and tourism. Selling the city is a means to survival in a changing world, and the past is part of the package. In the 1980s, Birmingham looked below the surface of its brave new world, and found half a dozen brave old worlds still there. It was a rediscovery and a past of which to be proud. The Industrial Revolution of Boulton, Watt and Murdock; the canal age; the surprisingly unspoilt Jewellery Quarter; the terracotta palaces of the late Victorians; the Chamberlains' city state.

Suddenly the past is highly marketable. Any newspaper editor will tell you that an old photo is worth more than a thousand words; it is worth a few thousand on the circulation too. Cities and nations may have histories, but people have memories. Memories of the old Bull Ring, of immigration in the 1950s, of the lost cinemas and dance-halls of youth.

There's a tendency now for history to divide in two about 1930. After that date the evidence is still walking around the streets, just waiting to be asked! It's immediate, alive and very collectable. But the distant past is no less alive or exciting. Chartist riots, the arrival of the first trains, discovering oxygen: they're all Birmingham stories. It would be sad if the 'story' fell out of 'history', and the first part should certainly be 'his and hers'.

Dr. Johnson once said that he found the history of Birmingham dull. I suppose it was old William Hutton he was reading. Johnson did, however, enjoy reading the Latin poetry of 16th-century Scotland. Having done the latter I can only say his tastes are somewhat peculiar. It's a personal challenge anyway. Let's try to brighten up his posthumous reading!

Chapter One

Beginnings

Now where do we begin? The Normans? Or perhaps the Romans? The history of the place now known as Birmingham does not begin with Domesday Book, though the problems of finding, let alone interpreting, earlier evidence might make us wish it did. Even if we take the Romans as our starting point, we would be doing less than justice to the prehistoric inhabitants who eked out a living on the Birmingham plateau thousands of years before the city of Rome was even a glimmer in Romulus' eye.

The problem is that they have left us so little, an axe head here and a burial mound there, and Birmingham has become so big and blotted out so much of the archaeological record. That there was prehistoric activity in the area is undeniable: hand-axes made of local quarzite pebbles have been uncovered from as early as the Palaeolithic period (beginning at 10,000 B.C.). But finds turn up only sporadically and by chance: a jigsaw scattered over a wide area.

Sutton Park, because relatively undisturbed, has yielded the most, particularly from the Bronze Age (1500 B.C. onwards). There's what looks like a timber trackway and a burial mound, excavated as early as 1859. More impressive is a mound at Kingstanding, virtually on the route of the Roman road, though it may have been rebuilt early in the last century. From the top of it, according to tradition, Charles I reviewed his troops before passing through Birmingham on the way to Edgehill.

Palaeolithic, Mesolithic, Neolithic and Bronze Age have all left their puzzling examples of primitive tools but, with the Middle Bronze Age, there is a little more to go on. Burnt mounds of broken pebbles and charcoal have turned up in a number of places, such as Kings Heath, Bournville and Northfield. Usually they are beside streams; indeed, it is the water's erosion that has usually uncovered them. The pebbles were heated in charcoal fires to heat water, perhaps for cooking or even bathing. The burnt mounds date to around 1100 or 1000 B.C. What we might call an early bath.

In the absence of more interpretable data, we must, regrettably, leap forward a thousand years.

The curious native, peering out of the forests that once covered the West Midlands, could witness an activity that would continue unabated in Birmingham for a couple of thousand years: road building was in progress. It was about A.D. 48 and the Romans were pushing north-westwards. There might even have been a sign that read: 'Forest of Arden By-pass. Due for completion 50 A.D.'.

Those earliest roads were military routes, enabling the Romans to force a passage into the Celtic hinterland. Near to the intersection of Watling Street and Rycknield Street

1. The site of the Roman fort adjoining Queen Elizabeth Hospital at Metchley.

stood Letocetum, now called Wall, where the Romans could take a bath on the edge of civilisation as they knew it. Further south, where Rycknield Street was joined by a road leading south-west to Droitwich (roughly the route of the A38), the invaders also set up a large fortress at a place called Metchley. It was probably part of the campaign by the new governor, Ostorius, against the Welsh tribes. The 18th-century historian, William Hutton, thought the site too big to be a Roman settlement and instead associated it with 'those pilfering vermin, the Danes, more acquainted with other people's property than their own'.

Compared to the surrounding sites of Wall, Wroxeter or even Droitwich, Metchley Park is indeed no major attraction, but it does represent Birmingham's earliest brush with the occupying powers that would dictate the nation's history for the next thousand years. It is also an interesting example of Birmingham's 'casual' attitude to its past. Part of it was cut away to build a canal; another section was lost to the railways, and a third to the expansion of the Queen Elizabeth Hospital. For a time in the 1950s it was even a Roman theme park. Now it's a series of uneven banks beside the University Medical School.

What excavation has taken place on Metchley suggests that the camp was not in continuous occupation. It was built, extended and then abandoned around A.D. 70. A few years later, the Romans returned, before leaving it for good about A.D. 120.

Much as Metchley has claimed the historians' attention, it is not the only Roman site within Birmingham, though new ones are slow to appear. Parson's Hill, on the route of Rycknield Street through Kings Norton, and Mere Green have yielded something, the latter revealing a Roman kiln site.

Following Rycknield Street north through Birmingham is not easy today, though we can pick it up on the west side of Sutton Park. No doubt the Romans found it easier, but they seemed to pay little attention to the view on either side. They appear to have left the forests well alone. Another invader, seven centuries later, would begin to explore more thoroughly. But first we need a little geological scene-setting.

What has a large city to do with geology? All the features seem to be man-made; the high-rise mountains and the subway valleys create their own geography. But if you were in charge of a runaway carriage rolling down to the old Bull Ring, or herding cattle across the River Rea in flood, or even taking a roller-coaster ride on Newhall Hill in the 1820s (and you could), you would know that there was a real landscape there somewhere.

When the Anglo-Saxons picked their way along the river valleys to Birmingham, they discovered a ridge of Keuper sandstone. The ridge runs from Sutton Coldfield in the north to Northfield in the south. To the south-east of it lay the valley of the Rea; to the west the poorer soil called Bunter marl. The latter was not a problem for the handful of farmers first on the ridge. Later on it would be a real barrier to agricultural expansion, and up to the 18th century it would be the nearest local equivalent to Desolation Row. It was known, affectionately or otherwise, as the Heath.

Around A.D. 700 the Anglo-Saxon tribes, in their endless pursuit of new land to settle in, were homing in on the Birmingham Plateau from a number of directions. Not that it was prize farming land—it was just that their momentum was taking them that way. The southern villages, like Yardley and Kings Norton, were probably settled by a group called the Hwicce. The northern ones, such as Birmingham itself, were occupied by Anglian Mercians, working their way along the tributaries of the Tame, with Tamworth as their power base.

The 'dual settlement' theory is supported by the evidence of the ecclesiastical boundaries that divided Birmingham even into this century. Until Greater Birmingham came into existence, the villages of the south, such as Yardley, Kings Norton or Northfield, were part of the diocese of Worcester, roughly corresponding to the sub-kingdom of the Hwicce. Those to the north formed part of the vast diocese of Lichfield. Later on, county boundaries were introduced to muddy the waters, creating the geographical nightmare that was once the West Midlands. Modern Birmingham contains lands that were once part of three counties, and Edgbaston, the county ground of Warwickshire Cricket Club, is only in that county by the width of the River Rea. The practice ground was once part of Worcestershire! And the inhabitants of Smethwick must be even more confused—they have lived in three counties in the last 40 years.

In the absence of documentary evidence or good archaeological remains to tell us the story of those early Saxon settlements, we can go a long way with place-names. The suffix '-ley' refers to a clearing in a forest. Thus Selly, Yardley, Moseley or Weoley show the Saxons clearing, or making use of a gap in the tree cover, to put down roots. Other place-names reflect the name of the original settlers. Birmingham itself means a hamlet (ham) of the followers (ingas) of Birm or Beorma. It was a name that underwent numerous changes of form and spelling, and the local name 'Brummegum' is a legacy of the medieval form. There is still a Castle Bromwich and a West Bromwich nearby. The names Northfield and Norton show that these were originally northern offshoots of settlements further south, probably around Bromsgrove.

The sandstone ridge above the River Rea made adequate rather than good farmland. But what it lacked in fertility, it made up for in the excellence of the water supply. Even in Victorian times the Digbeth area was famous for its springs and is still riddled with long neglected wells. Water-carriers once loaded their carts here before transporting and selling it to the drier parts of the town. And at Ladywell, now the site of the Arcadian complex, were Birmingham's first swimming baths in the 18th century. Only the pollution of the wells in the 19th century forced the closure of one of the town's few natural resources.

From the ridge the land sloped rapidly down to the Rea valley. This was no Thames or Tiber, but in time of flood could be a considerable obstacle. The name Floodgate Street, a road running north off Digbeth, testifies to the need to control its force. But it was rarely a raging torrent, tending to spread rather than deepen, and it was easily forded where Digbeth crosses it. It also marked the boundary between the parishes, and then the boroughs, of Birmingham and Aston even into this century.

We will see that much of Birmingham's early history revolves around that short stretch of land between the Rea and the Bull Ring. But there's no real reason to assume that the pre-Conquest settlement was there. The early settlements were often scattered and unfocused, as Edgbaston is today. The idea of an Anglo-Saxon village around the Bull Ring, complete with church and green, in the style of *The Archers*, is probably erroneous. There may have been groups of settlers over a wide area. But leaving speculation aside, let us use what we have.

Following the early history of Birmingham and the surrounding villages is a little like catching a train from New Street to Wolverhampton: from a dark tunnel the train emerges momentarily into daylight and then plunges into another tunnel. The first shaft of documentary light comes with Domesday Book. From it we can make guesses at what lies in the tunnel, but cannot know for certain.

At some point between the early settlement of the area and Domesday, the small independent villages lost their independence and fell under the control of large landowners, forerunners of the feudal system that would control England for centuries. Men like Earl Edwin, who held Aston and Erdington, and Ulwin or Wulfine, who held Birmingham and Selly Oak.

But even Edwin and Ulwin were only intermediate steps on the feudal pyramid; ultimate control lay with William Fitz Ansculf of Dudley Castle. His arrival in the area pre-dated the Conquest, but his Norman origins and allegiance to the Conqueror safeguarded his possessions.

The Domesday Survey of 1086 is not the most reliable of evidence, but for many places, including Birmingham, it is the first documentary source, the first shaft of light, and with it the little village of Birmingham enters historical record: 'Richard holds of William four hides in Birmingham. Land for six ploughs; one is in the lordship. There are five villagers and four smallholders, with two ploughs. Woodland half a mile long and two furlongs wide. It was and is worth 20s. Wulfine held it freely'. The Domesday Survey presents problems of interpretation to the historian and comprehension to the non-specialist, so technical is the vocabulary and many the omissions. So a little explanation is called for.

The valuation of the manor of Birmingham, famously only £1, is a rough estimate of what the whole estate, both goods and land, could expect to bring in as rent in a year. The manor lacked rich agricultural land, a fact reflected in the low price. There is no mention of a church, but the commissioners were not particularly interested in churches unless they owned land. It does not rule out the possibility of St Martin's having a Saxon or early Norman predecessor. We simply do not know. The William referred to in the

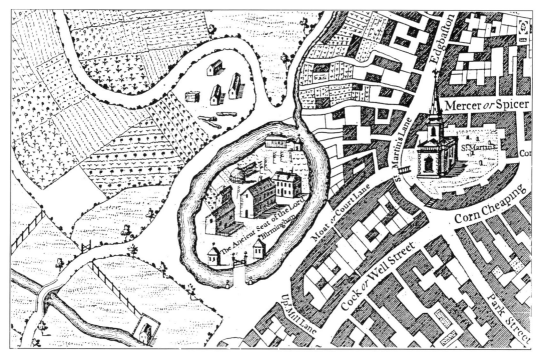

2.   Extract from Westley's map of 1731, showing the moated manor house site. At this date the Bull Ring is known as Corn Cheaping.

Survey is William Fitz Ansculf of Dudley. The absence of a surname for Peter has led historians to christen him Peter de Birmingham, first named holder of the manor of Birmingham and a line that would last, with interruptions, for 500 years.

The Survey has much to tell us of the surrounding manors too, areas that would later become suburbs of the city. Birmingham was one of the poorest manors in the Domesday Survey, but then the Survey reflects both the size of the manor and the current state of its agricultural development. Handsworth, Northfield and Yardley were each worth five times that sum. Indeed that of Yardley is recorded as having previously been worth £8.

Let us look at what the Survey has to say of Aston:

> William Fitzansculf holds Aston from the King and Godmund from him. There are eight hides there. Land for twenty ploughs. In the lordship land for six ploughs, but ploughs are not there. Thirty villagers with a priest, one slave and twelve smallholders have eighteen ploughs. A mill at 3s; woodland three leagues long and half a league wide. The value was £4; now 100s. Earl Edwin held it.

At Aston the Survey records 43 adults (not a total population), making it the most populous manor in the area. Hardly crowded, though. In fact, the population of Aston remained greater than Birmingham for much of its history as a separate borough. The Survey records the presence of a priest both at Aston and Northfield, suggesting that there may already have been churches in these two villages. There is some confirmation of this at Northfield, where the Norman doorway in the north wall, with its rounded arch and 'beak' ornamentation, is the oldest standing structure in the whole of modern Birmingham.

(There are also two Norman windows at King's Norton.) The presence of a corn mill would add to the value of the manor (others are recorded at Erdington and Handsworth). These were water-mills; that of Aston standing on the Tame, which runs diagonally to the north of Aston Hall.

Essentially Domesday was a 'land use' survey, recording arable land, pasture and woodland. The latter was no impenetrable jungle, but contributed to the local economy in a number of ways. Had it not done so, the commissioners would not have been interested in it. Birmingham, along with Witton, Erdington, Aston and Edgbaston, was in the Coleshill Hundred, a subdivision of the county or shire of Warwick.

Selective (whether by accident or design) as Domesday was, it does show that many of the Birmingham manors were the Norman equivalent of 'one horse towns' without the horses. Compared to nearby places like Bromsgrove, they were poor and under-developed. The largest populations, and therefore the highest turnover, lay to the south in the Vale of Evesham or south of Stratford. But Birmingham's fortune would not lie in the soil, and the lord of the manor would soon be making the kind of shrewd business deal that would lay the foundation of growth and success for centuries.

Within a couple of centuries the place that was one of the least developed in Warwickshire had become one of the biggest. At the same time many of the villages around it had declined. The question 'Why did Birmingham grow?' is almost as old as the place itself. Some of the proposed solutions have mixed up cause and effect. Certainly there was migration from surrounding villages, and Birmingham's central position in the communication system became important, but this was only important if it were a place worth communicating with. For the want of any better explanations we are left with the market charter.

It may well be that the lords of the manor of Birmingham were entrepreneurs in the best Brummagem tradition. Deprived of great income by the unimpressive nature of the agricultural land, they put their trust in the market, as it were. Quite when the first unofficial trading began there we do not know, but in 1166 Peter de Birmingham bought from the King the right to hold a weekly market in his castle. Twenty-three years later a confirmation charter places it in the 'villa' of Birmingham. Business, it seems, was already booming.

Markets were a lucrative industry and Peter was shrewd to petition for one so early. Not only could he levy tolls on the traders, once the stick of the tolls was in place, the carrot of freedom from tolls and privileged access to the new market could be offered to potential settlers. Birmingham was soon in the position to exploit the growth in population and activity in the surrounding area. If we accept the idea that the early settlement of Birmingham was scattered, then Peter was effectively building (or sponsoring) a completely new town, centred on his market.

The growth of Peter's town in the next century or so is surmised rather than proved, but there is enough evidence from scattered documents to show that a mercantile sector had also grown up to service the new town and its passing trade. In 1232 a group of 16 townsmen negotiated an agreement with William de Birmingham freeing them from the obligatory haymaking duties. Their trades show them to be a mixture of merchants and tradesmen: purveyor, merchant, smith, tailor and weavers.

As the agreement with William shows, Birmingham was making an early name for itself in the cloth industry, probably second only to Coventry in the county. And the cloth

3.   The village pump in the 18th-century Bull Ring. The spire of St Martin's can be seen on the extreme left.

industry involved a series of activities. The first name on the Lay Subsidy Roll for Birmingham in 1332 is 'Adam the dyer'. Evidence from a less likely source shows that the future 'metal-bashing' town was involved in metal manufacture of a different kind as early as 1308. In that year the Knights Templar were subjected to mass arrests in England as they were in France. The master of the Order, William de la More, was imprisoned and the contents of his house examined and catalogued. The inventory includes the item 'eleven Birmingham pieces' (pecie de Birmingham), which were subsequently delivered to him in prison. Quite what these 'pieces' were we do not know, but their high value suggests something involving precious metals. Is this the first indication of the town's pre-eminence in the jewellery trade, or of the production of plate? Posing more questions than it answers, this note at least suggests that Birmingham was recognised nationally for the production of something. The beginnings of a wide trading influence were just around the corner.

Chapter Two

A Town on the Move

The early history of Birmingham is a series of unrelated facts and guesses, not a continuous story. What we have are pieces of the jigsaw, without any hope of seing a complete picture. One piece of evidence, the Lay Subsidy Rolls of 1327 and 1332, a tax on movable goods, suggests that the town had risen to third place in the county of Warwickshire, behind Coventry and Warwick. By the middle of the 14th century the population had probably reached four figures. (Aston, which had been the larger settlement at the time of Domesday, had now become Aston-juxta-Birmingham; Aston beside Birmingham.) But another document suggests that such growth was not without its drawbacks. A reference in the court rolls of Halesowen of 1313 shows that within recent memory there had been a large fire ('magnam combustionem') in the town of Birmingham. The medieval towns, built mostly of wood, were frequent victims of minor conflagrations, but this must have been a bigger affair altogether. For a fire to spread far enough to become a 'great fire' implies close-knit building on a relatively large scale. We must be grateful for such incidental references, for no documents survive from the manorial court of Birmingham to shed light on its early history.

Around the nucleus of the market and the manorial castle had grown a town of burgesses and traders, specialising in cloth and perhaps metalwork. If the church of St Martin had been there since Norman times, by the end of the 13th century it no longer reflected the rising status of a market town. Since this was where the lords of the manor had their last resting place, it was incumbent on the present occupant of the castle to provide funds for its modernisation. After all, it might be a long wait until the Last Judgement. In fact, it may be that the first St Martin's dates from this time. The new church had north and south aisles and a clerestory, together with stained glass and murals. The 19th-century restoration of St Martin's riefly uncovered some of the wall paintings, but now all that remains of the old church are the tombs of the early lords. No doubt the old lords would feel that this was how it should be.

Another foundation of the 13th century has also left a faint impression on the town. The Hospital of St Thomas of Canterbury has left its legacy in various street-names of the city centre. Priory Queensway, formerly Upper and Lower Priory, marks the site of the Hospital, while Congreve Street, which disappeared under the Paradise Circus complex, recalled the presence of the warden's rabbit-warren (coningre). But the activities of the priory are somewhat mysterious; it does not seem to have been a very efficient or effective organisation.

More important was the Guild of the Holy Cross, established in 1392. The Guild performed both religious and charitable functions. It maintained four almshouses and other tenements where poor members could live rent free, as well as with two priests at St Martin's church to ease their path into the afterlife. As the report of Henry VIII's Commissioners phrased it: 'Also, there be dyvers pore peaple ffounde, ayded, and suckared, of the seyde Gylde, as in money, Breade, Drynke, Coles; and, whene any of them dye, thay be buryed very honestlye at the costes and charges of the same Gilde, with dyrge and messe ...'.

The Guild's activities (particularly the feasting) centred upon the hall and gardens at the foot of New Street, later the site of King Edward's Grammar School, where a clock and chimes helped passers-by with their time-keeping. It also maintained a common midwife. But the Guild's most useful social function was its maintenance of two stone bridges across the Rea, key elements in Birmingham's transport network, together with 'divers ffoule and daungerous high wayes' in the town.

The problem of the Rea crossing led to another religious foundation about this time. Around 1380 a chapel of St John the Baptist was built on Deritend, just across the river. Deritend was a curious settlement, originally part of the manor of Aston, but by this date part of the manor but not the parish of Birmingham. Since the Rea marked the boundary between the parishes of Birmingham and Aston, the inhabitants of Deritend and Bordesley had to face a long journey to their parish church. An agreement was reached:

> That the seyd inhabitans of Deretende myght have one Chapeleyne to celebrate Dyvyne servyce within a Chappelle there of Saynt John, newleye erected and mayde, and also to mynyster unto them all Sacramentes and Sacramentalls, Beryinges except; by-cause they be ii myles dystaunt ffrom there parisshe churche, so that, in wynter season, the seyde parisshyoners coulde not go to there parisshe churche without great daunger of perysshyng.

So the new chapel fulfilled a vital social need and reflected Deritend's quasi-independent status. From the outset St John's, Deritend, was almost a separate parish church. In a move that almost prefigures Birmingham's radical free-church attitudes of the 19th century, the parishioners negotiated in 1382 the right to elect their own priest and manage their affairs independently of the mother church.

Between 1450 and 1500 the Guild of St John built a new guildhall to include both a residence for the priest and a school for the children of members. Remarkably, for a city that has never gone overboard on its medieval heritage, the building still remains. Evidence is not conclusive, but the *Old Crown* in Deritend seems to fit the bill. If this is true then the *Old Crown* public house (as it became later) was Birmingham's first school, distant ancestor of nearly 450 schools and three universities in the city today.

But of all the buildings that were rising or renewing in the town, the manorial castle must still have dominated. At some point, perhaps in the early 14th century, a moat was constructed with a drawbridge. If this was for defensive reasons, it was not entirely successful, for in 1476 the castle was broken into and the occupant beaten up. But even by 1528, when the manor was surveyed, the decline of the moat and the manor house had set in, together with the family that owned it:

> The manour place ys moted rounde about and hath a drawbrygge to the same and the mote is sore ovdr growen with wedes and full of mudde and ash Robbush and the moste parte of the manor place fallen downe and the Resydew that standyth ys sore decayed so that no man wyll hyre hit.

Probably one of the reasons for the low water level was the lord's mill, called Malt Mill, which was powered by a mill-race off the moat. Below it, on the same stream out of the moat, was the Town Mill. Yet the moat itself survived into the last century, though there had been so many changes of use of the site, from private residence to factories to market, that even the careful excavations of the 1970s revealed little of the medieval buildings that stood within it.

Still the moat outlasted by far the family that had built it. The history of the de Birmingham family reflects the changeable nature of the times they lived in. (The one thing that did not change was that almost every lord of the manor was called William!) One William supported Simon de Montfort in the civil war against Henry III and lost his life at the Battle of Evesham in 1265. But his descendants were not long out of favour: his grandson served Edward I in France, and the next William, despite being up to his neck in debts, was knighted in 1306. After all, financial problems have never stood in the way of nobility.

And so we pass, through a 'Forsythe Saga' of lunacy, intermarriage and legal disputes to Edward de Birmingham in the 1530s, who finally lost the manor for good. Edward made enemies at court who secured his arrest and the confiscation of his property. From 1533

4. By 1931, when this photograph was taken, the guild hall and school had become a pub and restaurant.

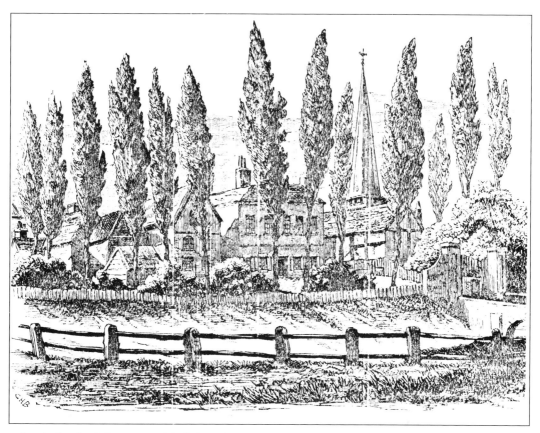

5. A sketch of the moat and buildings by the historian, Thomas Hamper, early in the 19th century.

to 1537 he was in the Tower of London, but even his eventual release did not save his possessions in Warwickshire. By 1538 he was dead and the manor of Birmingham was in the tight grip of the Crown, though his widow, Elizabeth, probably continued to live in the town for some years after. This was the end of the de Birminghams in England and their connection with the manor of the same name.

Looking at the history of the lordship of the manor of Birmingham in the 16th century, it is hard to avoid the impression that there was something of a curse upon it. Edward having gone to join his ancestors, the manor was given in 1545 to Lord Lisle, a member of the Dudley family. Lisle rose to become Duke of Northumberland, the most powerful man in England during the later years of Edward VI. The latter's premature death led the ambitious Duke to go for broke and attempt to place his daughter-in-law, Lady Jane Grey, on the throne of England. The nine-day coup took both Jane and her father-in-law to the Tower and the block. That Northumberland's lands reverted to the Crown because of his treason was the least of his problems. He may not have even had time to visit the manor he had held for just eight years.

The saga of Edward de Birmingham and Northumberland makes exciting reading, but probably had no more than superficial effect on the life of the town. Lords of the manor continued to have importance into the 16th century, but their influence, particularly in an industrialising town like Birmingham, was waning. After all, they were absentee landlords most of the time. Having been kick-started into life by the market charter and the privileges attached to it, the town had gained a momentum of its own. The officials that ran the town, and the court that appointed them, were still under manorial control, but they had little direct control over trade and manufacture.

It was in 1538 that John Leland, the wandering scholar, visited the town and recorded his impressions in his *Itinerary of Britain*. Since it was the first description of Birmingham not made for tax purposes, it merits recording in full:

> I came through a pretty street as ever I entred, into Bermingham towne. This street, as I remember, is called Dirtey [Deritend]. In it dwell smithes and cutlers, and there is a brooke that divideth this street from Bermingham, and is an Hamlett or Member, belonginge to the parish therebye.
>
> There is at the end of Dirtey a propper chappell, and a Mansion house of tymber hard on the ripe [bank], as the brooke runneth downe; and as I went through the ford, by the bridge, the water ran downe on the right hand, and a few miles below goeth into Tame, ripa dextra [right bank]. This brooke, above Dirtey, breaketh into two armes, that a little beneath the bridge close again. This brooke riseth, as some say, four or five miles above Bermingham, towards the Black Hills.
>
> The beauty of Bermingham, a good markett towne in the extreame parts of Warwikshire, is one street goinge up alonge, almost from the left ripe of the brooke, up a meane hill, by the length of a quarter of a mile. I saw but one Parroch Churche in the towne. There be many smiths in the towne that use to make knives and all mannour of cuttinge tooles, and many lorimers that make bittes, and a great many naylors. Soe that a great part of the towne is maintained by smithes, who have their iron and sea-cole out of Staffordshire.

Leland's entry into the towns was from the south-east, as we would expect. The 'Mansion house of tymber' that took his attention is probably the Old Crown, already mentioned. In Leland's time it was presumably still the guildhall. The 'propper chappell' of St John, Deritend, survived until the bombing of the Second World War. The visitor was not impressed by Birmingham's river, which he calls a brook, and found no difficulty in riding through it.

Leland's visit was evidently a brief one, and he did not stop to explore the area behind the one street that he travelled down. Doubtless he turned right into High Street, rode along Dale End, and off into the countryside again. But many of his impressions are confirmed by his fellow antiquary, William Camden, who called in on the town almost 50 years later. In 1563 Camden found the place 'swarming with inhabitants and echoing with the noise of anvils'.

From Leland and Camden onwards, every visitor to the town remarked on how busy it was and the deafening sound of its metal-bashing. Another Elizabethan visitor, William Smith, described 'a proper town with a spyre steeple, where great store of Knyves are made, ffor allmost all the townes men are cutlers or smithes'.

There seems no doubt that Birmingham was now exploiting the geographical position that had led the Saxons to settle there and a market to be established. Its proximity to the South Staffordshire coal and iron seams, noted by Leland, gave it both the raw materials and the fuel for the metalwork on which its later reputation was forged. And the convergence of roads from the south-east to cross the Rea at Digbeth established the place as both a manufacturing centre and a trading route.

Birmingham's reputation for metalwork had already spread far and wide before Leland and Camden called in. In 1511, and again two years later, the Clerk of the Ordnance had ordered horseshoes, bits and weapons for the royal army. The suppliers were all from Birmingham: John Coke, John Ripton and Richard Russell. There was also trade with East Anglia and probably, via the River Severn, with Bristol too. Nor was this metalwork limited to Birmingham. The surrounding villages too were involved in the trade. There were scythe smiths in Erdington, Bordesley and Kings Norton; and nailers in Moseley, Harborne and Handsworth, to name but a few. It would appear that the metal trades had begun to supplant cloth as the town's major industry. There were still seven fulling mills within four miles of the town in the early 16th century, such as Holford, Bromford and Pebble Mill, but they would soon be converting to iron mills.

But Birmingham had not yet put all its eggs into one metal basket. Had Leland used his eyes less and his nose more, he would surely have noticed

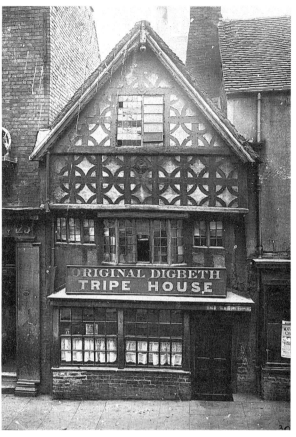

6. One of a number of half-timbered houses that stood on Digbeth until this century. Victorian Birmingham was a voracious consumer of tripe.

another industry that dominated Birmingham life. This was tanning. As with the smiths, the tanners were concentrated in Deritend beside the river. This was an industry benefiting from the importance of Birmingham's cattle market, whose attraction was probably felt as far away as the Welsh Marches.

No doubt both Leland and Camden were noting what was distinctly different about Birmingham, and it was the smiths and their anvils that made the town special. Camden had similar things to say about Sheffield.

Another industry with a long history ahead of it was also invisible to Leland and almost to us as well. A goldsmith is referred to as early as 1406, and again in 1524 Lord Middleton paid a Birmingham goldsmith for making nine spoons and repairing two cups. One named jeweller at the end of the 1500s, Roger Pemberton, was beginning to establish his family as important property owners in the town.

Already by the middle of the 16th century a number of familiar names are appearing that will dominate the town in the centuries to follow: Vesey, Smallbrook, Holte, Phillips, Colmore and Russell. Such families, with substantial holdings in property and land, were a far cry from the burgage holders of two centuries before.

Chapter Three

A Walk Around the Town

What was Birmingham like at this time? I have avoided posing this obvious question until now: before the 16th century an answer is just as likely to be wrong as right. After all, the first map of the town was not produced until 1731.

But the problems faced by the manorial lords of Birmingham in the 16th century had a useful spin-off for historians. Every time the manor was up for grabs (1528, 1534 and 1553), a survey of the estate was drawn up. Using these surveys, along with travellers' tales and other sources, we can for the first time get some clear idea of what the town of Birmingham was like at the beginning of what is called 'the early modern era'.

The population of the town in the 1520s was probably around 1000, roughly what it had been two hundred years before. Not the kind of statistics you might expect of a growing town, but the population of England in general had so declined during this period that such stability was unusual. Migration into Birmingham from the surrounding areas, a phenomenon that would last well into this century, was already underway.

The lower part of the town around Digbeth was the Tudor equivalent of an industrial park. Industries that needed water collected around the many streams and brooks that collectively were known as the Rea. The woollen industry used water in the fulling process; tanning too required vast quantities of water and a group of workshops, known as Tanners Row, occupied a stretch of water half-way up the hill. Metalwork needed water for cooling and for driving the bellows. Many had workshops facing onto Digbeth and consequently attracted the eyes and ears of early visitors, riding up to the Bull Ring.

Deritend had once been an outlying hamlet, but a combination of workshops and private houses along the main road now bridged the gap. The Old Crown is the last representative of Leland's 'pretty street' still in place, though another house, later known as the *Golden Lion*, was removed to Cannon Hill Park in 1911. A number of others, including the *Old Leather Bottle*, were still there in Victorian times. The water meadows either side of the road were still largely agricultural. Ringing the town were three manorial parks, long ago enclosed by the de Birminghams, but by the 16th century these were feeling the neglect inevitably caused by the decline of the lordship. The one at Rotton Park was certainly living up to its name: 'Item. Ther ys a perke belongynge to the same manor wherin ys a great ponde whych ys overgrowen with wedes and rede and littel fyshe er now therin and the logge ys sore decayed ...'.

Either side of Digbeth were Holme Park and Little Park, giving the lower part of the town a remarkably rural appearance, even when the first prospects of Birmingham were drawn in the early 18th century. Between Holme Park and the town stood the moated site

7. St Martin's Lane ran to the west of the parish church. This sketch of 1840 shows the church wall on the extreme right.

of the manor house, whose decay has already been described. A little to the west, marking the end of Edgbaston Street, was another moated building, the Rectory or Parsonage House of St Martin's. With its ring of water and willow trees, the Parsonage remained an obstinate thorn in the side of urban expansion until the Street Commissioners demolished it in the 1820s.

At the top of Digbeth, where the road took a sharp turn to the right, the spire of St Martin's church towered above the confusing huddle of streets around it. The open market-place that lay in front of it until the notorious Bull Ring development of the 1960s did not appear until the energetic Street Commissioners cleared the area in the 1820s. To the left of the church ran Mercer or Spicer Street, no doubt named from the traders who used it. Later still it became Spiceal Street. To the right the road was known as Corn Market, or Corn Cheaping, the first of the straggling sequence of market areas running into High Street.

If ever Birmingham had possessed an open market area, such as it has today, it had long gone by the 16th century. The area must have felt claustrophobic even on days when the market was not in operation. As Hutton wrote: 'The space now used as our market was in 1769 completely choked with buildings and filth; the shambles, the round house and the cross nearly filled the area'. The 1528 Survey gives us an idea what the place was like:

Item. Ther ys ii Fayres holden every yere upon Holy Thursdaye and the other upon Mychelmas daye and merkett ones a weke upon Thursdaye and hit bygynnyth at x of

the clok before none and lastith unto iii of the clock at after none and ther ys shewe
of all maner of Bestes and every straunger beyng not fre of the markett doth paye Tolle
for every iii bestes that they bye a i d and for every score iii d and for every C shepe
ii d and so doth the seller in lykewyse and every straunger beyng fre of the markett
doth paye for the same tolle but i d a yere and the Burgeyses and commoners of the
Town pay no tolle.

8. The chamber over the Old Cross was built in 1703. It
was demolished in 1784.

These tolls were collected at the
toll-house, at the junction of New
Street and High Street. In the next
century it was used for the stamping
of leather and became known as
Leather Hall. Like the Parsonage,
Leather Hall occupied an awkward
site, almost entirely blocking the
entrance to New Street. In 1728,
according to Hutton, it was demolished
by the lord of the manor 'while men
slept' and three houses built in its
place. It was not until 1776 that the
thoroughfare between High and New
Street was finally secured.

The demolition of the Leather
Hall also spelt the end of the town's
dungeon which lurked in the basement.
This was the town's first lock-up, but
although it was no place for a picnic,
it could hardly have been worse than
the building which replaced it. On
9 September 1733 a public meeting
above the Old Cross declared its intention of erecting a new bridewell or
prison in Peck Lane, where New Street
Station now stands. Hutton called it
'of all bad places, the worst', and his
feelings were echoed by John Howard,
the prison reformer, who visited the
place in 1779:

The court is only about 25 feet square. Keeper's House in front; and under it two cells
down seven steps: the straw is on bedsteads. On one side of the court two night-rooms
for women, 8 feet by 5 feet 9 inches; and some rooms over them; on the other side
is the gaoler's stable, and one small day-room for men and women; no window ...

In this small court, besides the litter from the stable, there was a stagnant puddle
near the sink, for the gaoler's ducks. [Gaoler's poultry is a very common nuisance; but
in so scanty a court it is intolerable.] The whole prison is very offensive. At some
particular times here are great numbers confined. Once in the winter of 1775 there were
above 150, who by care of the magistrates had a supply of proper food, broth &c.

When Howard re-visited in 1788 he noted: 'The court is now paved with broad stones, but dirty with fowls. There is only one day room for both sexes, over the door of which there is impudently painted, *Universal Academy*'.

One of the problems was that the gaoler was not paid a salary, and therefore earned his self-sufficiency by other means, usually as a publican. Both the Birmingham bridewell, which served as an off-licence, and the Aston prison, which was a tavern on High Street, Bordesley, fulfilled this curious dual role. It was not unusual for the carousing at the front to be accompanied by the mass exit of prisoners from the back. One could hardly blame them: the Aston Prison was one of the worst in the country, consisting of two subterranean dungeons reached through a trap-door. Prisoners received an allowance of 4d. a day, plus a rug to cover them.

In Peck Lane conditions were marginally less primitive, and in some ways extraordinarily lax. Since the keeper was also a beer-seller, he increased his trade by allowing customers to drink with his inmates. Stop-overs with a difference. There was even an alternative to damp nights in the straw: 2s. 6d. got you a bed in the gaoler's house, though you had to put up with being manacled to the bedstead.

William Hutton suggested as early as 1780 that the Peck Lane prison ought to be demolished and a new one built at what is now the corner of New Street and Colmore Row, but the Street Commissioners had grander plans for this site. Instead they built a new lock-up in Moor Street, which opened in 1806. Here a 26-ft. wall prevented the kind of unauthorised absences seen in Bordesley. The prisoners' allowance was a pennyworth of bread and a slice of cheese twice a day, together with use of the pump. Beer was no longer on the menu. Moor Street remained the town's prison for almost forty years, before the final move to Birmingham Heath. Of the great borough gaol built at Winson Green, we will have more to say in a later chapter.

Let us return to our walk. Between the toll-house and the shambles stood the market cross, roughly where Nelson's statue was originally sited. It continued to be called the Old Cross even when it had been replaced by a two-storey hall. The upper storey, built in 1702-3, was Birmingham's first place for public meetings; the lower arcaded floor provided the driest place for street trading in town.

Further along High Street stood the Welch Cross, which in the 18th century looked like a miniature version of the Old Cross. In the 16th century it was marked by a single pillar in the middle of what was called the Welsh Market. Birmingham has long had connections with Wales, from the attractions of its north coast as a Victorian holiday resort to the drovers' roads of the late Middle Ages. Both cattle and sheep faced the long journey from the Welsh Marches to Birmingham, with the herdsmen traditionally staying at the *Bull Inn*, kept in the 16th century by Henry Sedgwick. This was on Chapel Street, though after the disappearance of the Priory chapel it was renamed Bull Street.

The lack of an accommodating open market-place meant that the Birmingham markets had spread through the surrounding streets. Nearest the church was the Cornmarket; next was the English or Rother Market, primarily for cattle, followed by the Welsh Market. There was also a butter and cheese market, centred on the Old Cross, which later moved to the Welch Cross. A painting of the early 19th century shows geese and fowl being sold at the bottom of New Street. Non-agricultural produce was also for sale: as early as 1403 there are records of the sale of brass and iron.

9.   The Harborne artist, David Cox's view of the Bull Ring from New Street. From an engraving of 1827. The church of Holy Trinity, Bordesley, can be seen on the horizon.

The further one walks from the Bull Ring, the sparser the buildings become. New Street begins well, with the Leather Hall and the Guild Hall at its foot, but dwindles away to a trackway further up. Park Street is there, skirting that part of the lord's demesne known as Little Park, as is Moor or Molle Street.

It was on Moor Street that one Wiliam Lench had dwelt, forever associated with a string of almshouses in Birmingham that bear his name. By a deed of 1525, Lench had placed various properties in the hands of feoffees to ensure that the rents from them were directed towards the upkeep of roads and bridges in the town and other charitable work. Throughout this century and the next other gifts of property were added to the pool, such that by the early 17th century an almshouse could be built on Digbeth, followed by others elsewhere in the town. The largest was that on Steelhouse Lane which contained 42 rooms.

Of all the institutions of late-medieval Birmingham, Lench's Trust is the only one to survive today. Had Lench linked his bequest to the Church, or instituted a chantry at St Martin's to ensure the good health of his soul in the after-life, his charity would have fallen victim to the ideological changes that were the English Reformation. The state civil servants, bent upon reform and the redistribution of Church wealth, fell upon Birmingham, and everywhere else for that matter, in two waves.

In 1536 the monasteries of England were dissolved, from the mighty foundations of Fountains or Reading, to smaller ones such as St Thomas's Priory in Birmingham. Its lands, most of which lay beyond the Welch Cross on the edge of town, fell into private hands. Nine years later, Henry VIII's commissioners arrived to assess the value (financial and otherwise) of the remaining religious foundations. This was not always the act of destruction that it is often portrayed as. To their monetary valuations the commissioners appended an assessment of each institution's value to the social life of the town. On this they clearly took evidence from the townspeople themselves. Of the Guild of the Holy Cross, for example, they wrote:

> Allso theare be mainteigned, with parte of the premisses, and kept in good Reparaciouns, two greate stone bridges, and divers ffoule and daungerous high wayes; the charge whereof the towne of hitsellfe ys not hable to mainteign; So that the Lacke thereof wilbe a greate noysaunce to the kinges majesties Subiectes passing to and ffrom the marches of wales, and an utter Ruyne to the same towne,—being one of the fayrest and most proffittuble townes to the kinges highnesse in all the Shyre.

If this was diplomatic prose, designed to engineer a sympathetic response from the Crown, it was unsuccessful: the Guild was written off, along with the smaller Guild of St John on Digbeth. With it went the town's first school, though it would not have to wait long for another one. But it appears that the commissioners' report was not entirely ignored, as their following recommendation was accepted: 'The said Towne of Brymycham ys a verey mete place, and yt is verey mete and necessarye that theare be a ffree Schoole erect theare, to bring uppe the youthe, being boathe in the same towne and nigh thereaboute'.

At a stroke the Guild Hall of the Holy Cross on New Street became the Grammar School of King Edward VI, and the sound of feasting was replaced by the sound of latin verbs and the catechism. The new school had to make do with its second-hand buildings for over 150 years, until the timber-framed Guild Hall was finally demolished in 1707. On this issue the Free School, as it was known, was shackled by the terms of the original foundation, whereby that part of the Guild's endowment which was earmarked for the School could only pay the salary of a master and usher. None could be used for the maintenance of the building. Over half of the former Guild's endowment was retained by the Crown: royal foundations are not necessarily rich foundations!

Still the creation of the Free School more than compensated for the loss of the school attached to St John's, and the institution descended from it is still Birmingham's foremost secondary school. This was the first of many complex changes to overtake Birmingham's oldest educational institution. By 1911, as well as the first King Edward's, there was a High School for Girls on New Street, as well as five grammar schools at Aston, Camp Hill (Boys and Girls), Five Ways and Handsworth. These five became voluntary-aided schools after the 1944 Education Act, the other two becoming direct grant schools in the following year. In 1993 the grammar schools too became grant-maintained. However, it has to be said that the early history of the Free School can hardly be said to have been progressive: the pupils were all boys, and the curriculum was all classics.

Chapter Four

A Brush with History

During the 1620s a large country-house was under construction to the north of Birmingham. Travellers on the Aston Expressway can see it still, as then, hard by the old church of SS Peter and Paul. High Jacobean windows lead to a skyline bristling with chimneys, pinnacles and lead-capped turrets. When the owner moved into his completed mansion in 1634, it was a powerful symbol of the wealth and status of Sir Thomas Holte, Lord of the Manor of Aston.

The Holte family of Birmingham had been in the business of accumulating land and estates in the area since the 14th century. Here was a family that had done very nicely out of the Reformation. Thomas Holte, grandfather of Sir Thomas, had been an agent of Thomas Cromwell's and was in a perfect position to profit from the dismantling of religious property. In the south the Holtes were leasing land to feed the industrial expansion of Birmingham; in the north the old manor of Aston was being enclosed to create the park in which Aston Hall would proudly sit.

10. Aston Hall in Victorian times, but little changed today. It is still a museum owned by the city.

11. A visitor passing through the lodge in 1793 wrote: 'I found my entrance as difficult as into a garrison town, from the sulkiness of the porter'.

Until 1603, Sir Thomas had been plain Thomas Holte. In that year he had benefited from the royal progress from Edinburgh to London of James VI of Scotland (and James I of England), when knighthoods were being showered like confetti on almost anyone who could pay for one. As a man, Sir Thomas was not an easy character to deal with, quite prepared to disinherit his son when he made a marriage that the father disapproved of. Locally, though the allegation was never proved, he is remembered as the master who took a cleaver to his cook, thus investing Aston Hall with the ghost that somehow it was always going to attract.

The Holtes' chief seat was at Duddeston Hall, a couple of miles to the south, but Sir Thomas made the decision to re-build on a new site. Thus Aston Hall had been begun in 1618, but the work continued almost to Sir Thomas's death in 1654. The whole project probably cost him upward of £60,000. It was only half used in Sir Thomas's lifetime, and the owner himself spent little time in it. He was, of course, decidedly in residence when the King came to call in October 1642, but more of that anon.

The Holtes and their successors remained owners, and sometimes occupants, of the Hall until the estate was dismantled, and the house sold, in 1818. It was a sign of the changing times that the old mansion fell into the hands of the nouveaux riches, in the form of James Watt Jnr., son of the steam giant. He elected to rent the place at £358 12s. a year, and began the work of restoring the hall to its former grandeur. In addition to his appreciation of the hall's antiquity, Watt welcomed the opportunity to do some gardening on the grand scale.

James Watt was in residence in 1830 when the hall received its second royal visitor, the future Queen Victoria. But when Victoria returned to Aston Hall in 1858, a sea-change had taken place. The old industrialist was dead, and the hall had been taken over by the

Aston Hall and Park Company, along with much of the land. The Queen had been called upon to give the new enterprise a suitable gala opening. The new company would have little to learn from the Disneyworlds and theme-parks of recent years, and they presided over the most extraordinary period of the hall's history.

To the ancient edifice was added a miniature Crystal Palace and aquarium, and the Jacobean rooms were given a new lease of life as Chinese streets or underground caverns. Outside, Aston Lower Grounds became a kind of Tivoli Gardens, with live music, skating, circuses and themed historical revels. In short, it was Birmingham's chief entertainment centre, despite not even being in Birmingham. But in July 1863 the Aston Hall and Park Company finally overreached itself. An acrobat, known as the Female Blondin, fell to her death during a tightrope walk. Victoria voiced her disapproval that the enterprise she had blessed had fallen so far, as it were. There was nothing for the company to do but skulk quietly away, and Aston Hall finally became the property of Birmingham Town Council. It was the town's first museum, and the first time such a building had been opened as a municipal museum and art gallery.

The Lower Grounds continued to be dominated by sporting entertainment, and here in 1879 one of the world's first floodlit football matches was played between teams from Birmingham and Nottingham. Reports suggest that the phosphorescent flares did not quite reach the midfield, and Wimbledon-style direct football was employed to bypass it. The Grounds were also used for cricket and cycling events, as well as for skating when the lake froze over. The place's sporting connection has been continued to this day by Aston Villa Football Club whose ground now stands on the site.

Which all takes us a long way from Sir Thomas Holte's magnificent mansion and its royal guest, who spent a troubled night there on 18 October 1642.

The reasons behind Charles I's visit to Aston in that month take us for the first time right into the mainstream of English history. The causes of the division between Crown and Parliament that would soon be turning to blows 27 miles away at the field of Edgehill are long and complex. Suffice it to say that the Midlands were as ideologically divided as the rest of the country. In the south, Oxford was a royal stronghold; in the north, Coventry and Birmingham had very different allegiances.

The latter's disaffection with royal policies doubtless had a long history. Puritanism and Presbyterianism, two strands of Christianity that contributed so much to the Parliamentary cause, had long been growing in the town and its neighbours. The radical English clergy had long resented royal meddling in their internal affairs, and many perceived in Stuart Anglican reforms a slow drift back to Catholicism.

Thomas Hall, the curate of Kings Norton who fulminated on the local practice of erecting maypoles, had a reputation for radically 're-defining' the limits of Anglicanism. Of him it was said that 'maintained and held up by the old Puritans, they so operated on his spirit that he relinquished his former principles and adhered to the party, and in many respects became an enemy to the Church of England'.

The rector of Sutton Coldfield, John Burgess, was a Doctor of Medicine of Leyden, from which hotbed of Calvinism he had no doubt also picked up political doctrines unacceptable to the English Crown. And two of the curates or lecturers at St Martin's, Josiah Slader and Francis Roberts, fitted very uncomfortably into their Anglican pulpits.

When Charles I refused a petition sparing Warwickshire its contribution to a ship-building tax on the grounds of recession, Roberts openly criticised the Crown. Clarendon,

12. The magnificent long gallery at Aston Hall.

the great historian of the Civil War, described him as 'the principal governor and incendiary of the rude people of that place against their sovereign'.

Once war broke out, the gun-makers of Birmingham also began to put their money where the curate's mouth was. A Royalist tract, called *A Letter Written from Walshall*, notes the despatch of 15,000 swords to the Earl of Essex. In addition, they 'not only refused to supply the King's forces with swords for their money, but imprisoned diverse who bought swords, upon suspicion that they intended to supply the King's forces with them'. So long before nonconformity came officially to Birmingham, there were nonconformist tendencies in place; and long before Charles made his visit to Aston Hall, there were many there who did not wish him well.

Royal visits were not a thing to be regarded lightly. While the King was dining in style as the guest of some local magnate, his troops were just as likely to be staging an impromptu 'take-away' in town, plundering what they could through a combination of threat and intimidation. It was just one of the perks of the job. This had already happened at Wolverhampton, prior to Charles' arrival at Aston. Thus his march through Birmingham was hardly anticipated with the kind of relish with which a royal parade would be welcomed today. Having paused at Kingstanding to address new recruits, Charles entered Birmingham on 19 October 1642.

What followed was to have serious repercussions for the town. However much the royal soldiery exercised their usual predatory instincts, this hardly justified the assault on the royal baggage-train that followed. Goods were looted for the Parliamentary cause and guards were captured and literally 'sent to Coventry', reputedly the origin of that popular phrase. Birmingham was noted for its 'peremptory malice to his majesty' and its card marked for future retaliatory action.

At the same time, the King's nephew, Prince Rupert, was similarly having good reason to regret his presence in the area. On his way to meet the King at Solihull, Prince Rupert had passed through a 'pratty uplandyshe town' called Kings Norton, where sympathies, fostered by the rector, were with the Parliamentarians. This in itself would not have unduly disturbed him, but the presence of a small Parliamentary force did. According to one source, Rupert lost around fifty men, with a further twenty taken prisoner.

It was in the Spring of the next year that Birmingham paid dearly for its earlier inhospitality. Charles I's Queen, Henrietta Maria, had returned from the Low Countries after a successful shopping-trip. The sale of the crown jewels had procured her an impressive array of munitions for the Royalist army. If the weaponry was to be successfully transferred from Bridlington to the King's army at Oxford, it was essential that the unsympathetic Midland towns in between were kept in check. Prince Rupert was despatched north to carve a passage and 'remind the Midlanders of their duty'.

The most Illuftrious and High borne PRINCE RUPERT, PRINCE ELECTOR, Second Son to FREDERICK KING of BOHEMIA, GENERALL of the HORSE of His MAJESTIES ARMY, KNIGHT of the Noble Order of the GARTER.

13. The frontispiece to *Burning Love*, a Cromwellian account of the Battle of Birmingham, printed in 1643.

It was on Easter Monday afternoon, 3 April 1643, that Rupert and a force of 2,000 men hit town. Having tested the goodwill of the locals with a request for lodgings, and found it wanting, the Prince prepared for a direct assault instead. We could hardly call it a siege, since Birmingham was 'built in such a form as was indeed hardly capable of being fortified'. Using earth barricades, the defenders had endeavoured to block the obvious routes into town, principally along Deritend. But Birmingham was no medieval walled fortress and the meadow-lands provided an easy, if soggy, alternative entrance.

The inhabitants used a mixture of bad language and guns to welcome them, calling them 'cursed dogs, develish Cavaliers, Popish traytors'. Unable to stage a genuine defence of the town, the defenders waged a short-lived guerrilla campaign, before escaping 'over hedges and boggy meadows and hiding their arms'.

Once the Royalist forces had gained possession of the town, they fell upon it with relish. A Parliamentary pamphlet, entitled *Prince Rupert's Burning Love to England, discovered in Birmingham's Flames*, made the most of their savagery:

> They ran into every house cursing and damning, threatening and terrifying the poore Women most terribly, setting naked Swords and Pistols to their breasts, they fell to plundering all the Town before them, as well Malignants as others, picking purses, and pockets, searching in holes and corners, Tiles of houses, Wells, Pooles, Vaults, Gardens and every other place they could suspect for money or goods, forcing people to deliver all the money they had ... They beastly assaulted many Womens chastity, and impudently made their brags of it afterwards, how many they had ravished; glorifying in their shame especially the French among them, were outrageously lascivious and letcherous ... That night few or none of them went to Bed, but sate up revelling, robbing, and Tyranising over the poore affrighted Women and Prisoners, drinking drunke, healthing upon their knees, yea, drinking drunk Healths to Prince Rupert's Dog.

If Rupert's assault on Birmingham did nothing else, it handed the Parliamentary propaganda machine a huge publicity coup, and the pamphleteers handled it with righteous indignation. Only the above mentioned *Letter from Walshall* attempted to present an alternative picture of the events. A good example of the two views can be seen from the accounts of the death of a man called Whitehall.

Burning Love describes it thus:

> Mr Whitehall a Minister, who hath bin long Lunatick, held Jewish opinions, and had layn in Bedlam and other prisons (some say) 16, some 22 years, and was lately come out; they comming to him asked him if he would have quarter, he answered to this (or like purpose) he scorned Quarter from any Popish Armies or Souldiers, whereupon they supposing him to be Mr Roberts Minister of Birmingham, did most cruelly mangle and hack him to death, and found certain idle and foolish papers in his pocket, which they spared not to divulge (as they thought to the Roundheads infamy ...)

The author of the *Letter from Walshall* has a very different interpretation:

> One thing more I heard of at this taking of Burmingham, which made some Impression with me, which was the death of a minister killed presently after the entry of the souldiers into the Towne. But it is alleadged that he told the souldier who killed him, that the King was a Perjured and Papisticall King, and that he had rather dye than live under such a king, and that he did and would fight against him; and in his pocket after his death were found some papers sufficient to make mee to beleeve the man was either mad, or one of the new Enthusiasts. It burdens my modesty to repeat them, but the truth (which you will desire to know) extorts them from mee, some of which were to this effect, that the 23 of March last he had a comfortable Kisse from Mris. E. with some moystnesse, and another day a cynnamon Kisse from another woman, and another from one of 14 yeares old, with much more such like stuffe which I blush to write.

Whatever the truth of the events of Easter Monday 1643, it was generally felt that raping and pillaging were not the way to win the hearts and minds of the people. The

The PLAN of BIRMINGHAM, Survey'd in the Year 1731.

In the Year 1700 Birmingham Contained 30 Streets, 100 Courts and Alleys, 2504 Houses, 15032 Inhabitants, one Church dedicated to S.t Martin & a Chappel to S.t John & a School founded by Edward 6.th also a Dissenting Meeting Houses.

To the Honourable Edw.d Digby & Will.m Peyto Esq.rs Members of Parliament for the County of Warwick this Plate is humbly Dedicated by their most obed.t humble Serv.t W. Westley
The Plate in the Possession of Thos.s Hutton in the Year 1789. Nephew to M.r Westley.

the Increase of this Town from 1700 to y.e Year 1731 is as follows 25 Streets, 50 Courts & Alleys, 1215 Houses, 8254 Inhabitants, together with a new Church, Charity School, Market Cross, & 2 Meeting Houses, for a further account See y.e next page.

14.   Birmingham's first map of 1731, made soon after the completion of St Philip's. The plan has unfortunately been reversed: Digbeth should enter the town from the south-east.

defenders may have been more than 'poore unarmed inhabitants ... whose trade was to make nails, sythes and such like iron commodities', but they were civilians. And righteous indignation is not an emotion that subsides quickly. It is reported that a song called 'The Armourers Widow' was still being sung into Victorian times:

> When Rupert came to Byrmingeham
>   We were in a sorry plyght,
> Our blood God's earth ystained by daye,
> Our homes in blazing ruins laye
>   And stained the skye at night.

With matchlock and with culverin,
    With caliver and drake,
He battered down our ancient town,
He shot our sons and fathers down,
    And hell on earth did make.

Our children's cries, our widows' prayers
    Ascended with the flame,
And called down the wrath divine
Upon the Royal Murderer's line,
    And brought his kin to shame.

But just as the accounts of the Battle of Birmingham vary depending on the orientation of the writer, the subsequent propaganda had two sides to it. A pamphlet of 1682, for example, describes Satan himself as 'that Brummigham Uniter of Mankind'. The Battle of Birmingham may only have been a minor skirmish in the early days of the English Revolution, but it helped forge for the town a reputation of dissent and unorthodoxy that would last long after the Restoration, a reputation that the good townsfolk would spectacularly reverse in 1791. But more of that later.

This would not be the last time that Birmingham saw violence on its streets, but for the time being, once the Civil War had run its course, it was to be a period of tranquil expansion. Some sign of the increasing wealth of the town can be gauged from the value of the lands appropriated for the Grammar School. In 1552 the former Guild properties and land brought in rents of £20. By 1654 the rent-roll was worth £73, rising to £302 by the end of the century. Even allowing for additional properties, this was something of a property boom. What frustrated the headmaster was the mysterious disappearance of this additional revenue. In 1633 the salaries of the master and usher were still pegged at £20 per annum, leaving a large sum which could not, by the terms of the original foundation, be allocated to maintenance or expansion of the buildings. Someone, somewhere, was making a lot of money out of education.

Chapter Five

Preparing for the Revolution

Sometime soon after the Civil War, Birmingham's population overtook Coventry's to leave it as the largest town in Warwickshire. In the 1670s the total must have been approaching 7,000, doubling again before the beginning of the next century. William Westley, who drew the first plan of the town, calculated that the population in 1700 was 15,032. In 1731, when he sat down to engrave his map, he estimated it at 23,286.

The rapid growth was not without its slumps, as disease sporadically took hold, particularly of the young. But this was more than compensated by immigration into the town. Most of this, on the evidence of settlement certificates, came from the area around Birmingham, as we would expect. New legislation made it easier for noncomformists to settle and thrive in an un-chartered town than in one that had a charter, and this may have been an inducement to some. But this is a factor that is easily exaggerated.

What is equally likely is that an atmosphere of entrepreneurship was beginning to pervade the town. More than anything, Birmingham probably had a reputation of a place that was 'going somewhere', with a variety of trading and manufacturing opportunities. In 1835 Alexis de Toqueville wrote that 'its inhabitants work as if they must get rich by the evening and die the next day'. Could there have been a large sign on Digbeth that read 'Birmingham welcomes small businesses'?

The energy of Birmingham's traders, and its virtual monopoly in much of the iron trade, was already apparent by the middle of the century. In 1650 it was observed that 'all or most of the London ironmongers buy all or most of their nails and petty ironwork either from Birmingham, almost a hundred miles from London, or at London as brought from thence ... all England ... supplied from a single market'. The good value of Birmingham-made goods was appreciated in Europe too. The traveller, Francois Maximilien Misson, wrote of the artifacts he had seen in Milan in 1714: 'Fine works of Rock Crystal, Swords, Heads for Canes, Snuff Boxes, and other fine works of steel,' but added dismissively, 'they can be had better and cheaper at Birmingham'.

The steel trade was already an international one by the end of the 17th century. Steel could be imported directly, or the iron converted on site. For the latter, Swedish iron was widely considered the best. Steelhouse Lane in the city centre owes its name to Kettle's Steelhouses on what was then Whitehall Street, engaged on the conversion of iron by the early 18th century. By 1710 there were three 'sellers of steel' in the town, one of whom, Sampson Lloyd, imported his iron through Hull.

Sporadic disruption of the Swedish trade led manufacturers to look even further afield. By 1715, Russian iron had begun to enter the country, considerably undercutting English prices. There's nothing new about these kinds of trade wars. In 1737 Abraham

Spooner, a Birmingham ironmaster, estimated that 9,000 tons of iron per annum were being used in the Birmingham area, of which almost a third was imported. This, he thought, accounted for the employment of around 45,000 men. Spooner himself was importing various types of Russian iron by the 1730s. Imported along with the iron were Russian apprentices to learn their trade from the Birmingham masters, perhaps the first foreign migrants to arrive in this multi-cultural city.

For the Birmingham manufacturers, Europe was not the only source of cheaper iron. By the early 18th century iron was being shipped in from the American colonies, particularly from plantations in Philadelphia and Maryland. As early as 1717, Joseph Farmer, a Birmingham ironmonger and gunmaker, visited the plantations to assess the quality of the ore. From its origins in New England, the raw material began a long circular journey. The importer bought it directly from the American factor, shipped it to Bristol, and sold it to the bar ironmonger, conveniently situated near to the factory. The latter sold it to the ironmaster, at whose factory it was worked, before sale to the ironmonger in London. From him the exporter sent it back to the Colonies.

Given the nature of the plantations from which the iron originated, and the likelihood that the final product returning thither might be guns or chains, we might well have doubts

15.   Birmingham bedstead-makers. The town became the centre of the whole brass industry.

as to the morality underlying such trade. But such moral sensibility would not develop in England for another couple of generations. By then Birmingham merchants like Joseph Sturge, Quaker abolitionist and peace campaigner, were well aware of the immoral trading system in which they were enmeshed. Sturge founded the British and Foreign Anti-Slavery Society in 1839 and campaigned for discriminatory tariffs against slave labour products like sugar.

As the Birmingham economy continued its switch from agricultural to industrial, the mills of the area steadily converted to slitting and rolling metal. Rolling mills begin to appear in Birmingham in the middle of the 18th century, the first being Thimble Mill on Hockley Brook, converted from a blade mill in the 1740s. There were soon others at Sarehole and Sparkbrook.

By this time, the slitting process was only one of a series of operations that could be performed at these new super-mills. The old Town Mill, near the Moat, shows this change of usage. Built in the mid-16th century, it continued to grind corn until early in the next century, when it converted to blade manufacture. Its reputation as supplier of swords to the Parliamentary forces in the Civil War led to its destruction by Prince Rupert in 1643. Rebuilt, it returned to life as a corn mill, before converting to a slitting mill in the early 18th century. Sampson Lloyd II acquired it in 1728 as both a corn and slitting mill. In 1755 a London tourist described the work going on there:

> Next morning we went to see Mr L——'s Slitting Mill, which is too curious to pass by without notice: its use is to prepare iron for making nails; the process is as follows: they take a large iron bar, and with a huge pair of shears, worked by the water-wheel, cut it into lengths of about a foot each; these pieces are put into a furnace, and heated red-hot, then taken out and put between a couple of steel rollers, which draw them to the length of about four feet, and the breadth of about three inches; from thence they are immediately put between two other rollers which, having a number of sharp edges fitting each other like scissors, cut the bar as it passes, into about eight square rods; after the rods are cold they are tied up in bundles for the nailers' use.

In addition to the slitting, Lloyd was using the excess capacity for milling flour, though this was a line that he later discontinued. As far as Lloyd's customers, the nailmakers, were concerned, their relatively unskilled trade was increasingly being relegated to the poorer quarters of the outlying villages. Nailmaking was still being pursued at Northfield Workhouse well into the 19th century.

The constant change in the use of mills is not surprising: since the driving power was running water, there was a finite number of mills possible on Birmingham's crowded watercourses. It was not always possible to squeeze in a new mill, though Nechells Slitting Mill at the confluence of the Tame and the Rea was built in 1746 at a cost of £1,212. Even here the site had been formerly occupied by a blade mill. With mills required in the production process of corn, blades, sheet metal and cloth, Birmingham was rapidly reaching full capacity by the middle of the 1800s. This, as much as anything, led to the exploration of new forms of energy which we call the Industrial Revolution.

If water drove the mills, it was credit that drove the entrepreneurial economy. Industrial expansion or diversification, such as was involved in the building or conversion of a mill, depended upon a credit and loan system to fuel it. Birmingham's 18th-century historian, William Hutton, wrote that 'every tenth trader was a banker, or a retailer of cash. At the head of whom were marshalled the whole train of drapers and grocers'. Many of the probate inventories of the period show that manufacturers were constantly indebted to bankers. Of course, this does not necessarily imply that they were hopeless bankrupts; simply that their everyday trade relied on the give and take of loan and repayment. Even a relatively successful firm like Boulton & Fothergill were continually sailing close to the wind as far as debts were concerned. Then, as now, the interest rate was seen as one of the principal engines of the economy.

The constant to and fro of loan, repayment and debt can be seen in the establishment, in 1752, of a Court of Requests. This was a small debts court, allowing for the recovery of debts under 40 shillings. The court sat weekly in the chamber over the Old Cross to examine the hundred or so cases before it. Later the commissioners moved into a purpose-built building on High Street.

Birmingham's banking tradition would have a national impact in the next century, but in those final years of the 1680s, another local industry was making its presence felt. With England at war both with France and in Ireland, the demand for guns was outstripping the London gunsmiths' ability to supply. The Office of Ordnance commissioned a supply of the new flintlock muskets from a Birmingham gunsmith, and followed this up with two further orders. The monopoly of the London Gunmakers' Company was broken, but they hung on tenaciously to their monopoly in the proving of weapons. Guns still had to go to the capital to be tested. Despite their lobbying of Parliament, it was not until 1813 that a Proof House was finally authorised in Birmingham.

A key moment in the trade war between Birmingham and London was in 1698, when the African market was opened up, in spite of objections by the Royal African Company in London. This would become a highly lucrative market for the Birmingham gunmakers, such that by 1766 over 150,000 guns were despatched annually to the coast of Africa. But the trade was not without its critics. A Spanish visitor to Birmingham in the early 19th century, prior to the establishment of the Proof House, described the industry in hostile terms:

> A regular branch of trade here is the manufacture of guns for the African market. They are made for about a dollar and a half; the barrel is filled with water, and if the water does not come through, it is thought proof sufficient: of course they burst when fired, and mangle the wretched negro who has purchased them upon the credit of English faith, and received them most probably as the price of human flesh!

Gunmaking was not the only example of trade diversification. Toymaking, an area that Birmingham made its own, was making headway by the early years of the 18th century, and by 1759 was employing around 20,000 people. The manufacture of the small metal objects known as toys—buckles, buttons, snuff boxes and the like—show that Birmingham was no longer confining itself to one kind of metal or one kind of expertise. This was a lucrative but shaky market, subject as it was to sudden changes in taste and fashion, and manufacturers had to be prepared to adapt or perish. A change in dress, such as the replacement of the buckle by the shoelace, or Victoria's rejection of jewellery after the death of Prince Albert, could at a stroke swell the ranks of the unemployed or the bankrupts. At one of the Triennial Musical Festivals smartly dressed concert-goers, sporting their new shoe-laces, were picketed and jostled by resentful buckle-makers, who turned up to express their opinion of the new fashion!

Undoubtedly the 'king of the button-makers' was John Taylor, called by Hutton 'the Shakespeare or Newton of his day'. On his death in 1775, the former cabinet-maker left an estate upwards of £200,000. The turnover of buttons alone from his factory near the present Union Street was valued at £800 a week, though his innovations in the production of painted and enamelled snuff-boxes were just as considerable. The work was highly labour intensive. Around 500 hands were employed in the factory, the majority of whom were women. A visitor to the works in 1755 was told that a single gilt button went through 70 separate operations, involving 70 different employees.

Business undoubtedly was booming, and some individuals, like John Taylor, were becoming very wealthy men indeed. Most of the elements that would characterise the economy of Victorian Birmingham were already in place a century earlier. Predominantly reliant on metalwork, whether steel, iron or brass, it was the ability to manufacture skilfully and cheaply that singled out the Birmingham craftsman. And the products were diverse, from the ornaments and decorative goods suitable for the home and European market, to hardware items such as guns for the world market.

On the downside, Birmingham's wholehearted integration into the global market left it vulnerable to global changes and foreign wars. The French wars at the end of the 1700s would precipitate an appalling slump in the local economy, on top of a national depression. The world was a dangerous and precarious place. In 1755, for example, the extensive trade links with Portugal were threatened by the Lisbon earthquake, which 'hath very affectingly alarmed the inhabitants of this town, a great quantity of our manufacturing being sold there'.

Similarly, the training of Russian apprentices, or too close cooperation with American ironmasters, might be the very kick-start that these economies needed to go it alone. It was certainly true that the Americans soon found that they would be better served manufacturing their own products.

Of the families that had found in Birmingham the perfect spring-board to fame and fortune, the Lloyds are a perfect example. Sampson and Mary Lloyd moved to Birmingham from their farm at Leominster in 1698. A Quaker couple, they moved to a town that was not antagonistic to dissenters; indeed a Quaker meeting house had recently been established there in Bull Lane. But as important as was the

16. Sampson Lloyd II bought Owen's Farm in Sparkbrook in 1741/2. He planted an avenue of elms and built the Georgian mansion that the family simply called 'Farm' in 1750.

religious atmosphere, the move also took the Lloyds into a close family circle of manufacturers. Sampson's wife was a Crowley; a well established family of ironmongers in the area. And Sampson's brother was another Quaker ironmonger, John Pemberton, who owned the land on which another meeting house was built in 1703.

Sampson and Mary moved into a newly-built town house in Edgbaston Street, on a site originally intended for two houses. It was described as having 'two staircases of the superior kind, panelled rooms, and decorated door-frames on the upper floor'. After Sampson's death in 1725, his two sons, Charles and Sampson II, bought the Town Mill, enabling them to combine both the selling of iron and its milling as well. Later still, Sampson II purchased a forge at Burton on Trent, and thus controlled the whole production process from ore to rod.

Sampson II's personal wealth rose considerably after his brother's death in 1741, and the following year he bought the country estate he had long contemplated. The Elizabethan

17. Charles Lloyd the elder (1748-1828). He was a leading anti-slavery campaigner, as well as a poet and translator of the classics.

house and grounds in Sparkbrook were known as Farm and cost him £1,290. A decade or so later he added the elegant Georgian house that still stands there, though most of the out-buildings have now gone. Sampson never moved into his new estate, preferring to continue life in Edgbaston Street, with occasional forays out to Farm to indulge his love of garden-ing and planning the estate. It was almost as if the family had gone full circle.

Recognising the importance of a stable system of business loans in the development of Birmingham's industry, his son, Sampson III, formed a company with the button manufacturer, John Taylor, to set up the town's first bank. Taylor's and Lloyds Bank opened on Dale End in 1765, ancestor of the Lloyds Bank we have today.

Another generation would produce Charles Lloyd the banker, who lived (and died) in a house off Broad Street called Bingley. Charles spent the spare time that was now his due translating Homer and Horace. Such literary pretensions were passed on to his son, another Charles, romantic poet, arch-miserablist and one-time friend of Coleridge and Charles Lamb. This Charles Lloyd, of whose obscure and not desperately successful poetry Lamb wrote that it was 'not to be understood reading on one leg', moved to Versailles, where he died in 1839. By this generation the steel seems to have been bred out of the family sinews.

Unofficial Quaker alliances were to have important social results in the generations to come. In 1825 the Birmingham Female Society for the Relief of Negro Slaves was founded by women like Mary Samuel Lloyd, Maria Cadbury and Mary Sturge, eight years before the Emancipation Act. They campaigned for the boycott of 'slave produce' and to improve the lot of 'the unhappy children of Africa, who receive from British hands their lot of bitterness'.

By the mid-1700s, the foundations for Birmingham's economy for the next two centuries had been laid. But what effects were increasing wealth and population having on the town itself? The next chapter will take us out of the factories and into the streets of the growing town.

Chapter Six

A Town on the Move

The chief impression 18th-century Birmingham left with its visitors was of almost continuous building work. Not that different from today, in fact, except that this Birmingham was still creating itself, rather than re-creating. Hutton thought there was nowhere in the country, outside London, where more buildings were being erected. The 18th century saw the high town being claimed for superior housing, together with a string of public buildings such as theatres, hospital, workhouse, churches and chapels.

One of the earliest new developments was initiated by John Pemberton the ironmonger, the brother-in-law of Sampson Lloyd. Here was one of the last beneficiaries of that religious realignment of the 16th century. The lands formerly occupied by the medieval Priory of St Thomas had fallen into the hands of the Holtes of Aston, as we have seen. From the Holtes they passed to the Smallbrookes and then, in 1697, to John Pemberton. The latter recognised the lucrative potential of a piece of controlled estate planning, targeted at the wealthier families. The centre-piece of the new Priory Estate was to be Old Square, with streets radiating from it. In the centre of the Square was a tree-lined garden, surrounded by iron railings, more of which stood in front of each house, 'that boys should not creep in or through the same'.

The development followed a common pattern for the period: Pemberton conveyed building plots to developers, who borrowed capital (not surprisingly from Pemberton's brother-in-law) to pay for construction. They were then sold leasehold to the prospective occupants. In order to maintain the exclusive nature of the area, occupants were forbidden from keeping pigs, dumping muck or opening butchers' or blacksmiths' shops. All the houses in the Square were built by Thomas Kempsey. Pemberton reserved the corner house for himself, the other occupants being a mixture of doctors, business men and gentlemen. They included Henry Bradford, himself a prominent Quaker and property developer, whose name is preserved by a street on his estate in Digbeth.

Old Square was for many years Birmingham's most prestigious address and Pemberton's house alone boasted a number of famous occupants. In 1747 it became the residence of Edmund Hector, the surgeon. Hector was a life-long friend of the century's greatest literary figure, Samuel Johnson, who frequently visited him there. In the next century it was the home of Joshua Scholefield, who in 1832 became one of the town's first members of Parliament. Joshua's son, William, continued the reputation of 1 Old Square by becoming the borough's first mayor, and subsequently following his father into the Commons.

18.   An engraving of Old Square by William Westley, shortly after its completion. It dates from *c*.1730.

If Pemberton had been striving to maintain the decorum of the Square, this was not always successful. At the end of the 18th century, nos. 3 and 4 were converted into a hotel. But worse was to follow, for the enterprising owner of *The Stork Hotel* used the extensive stableyard to hold a circus in. It was known as the Amphitheatre, Stork Tavern Yard, and staged everything from equestrian events and acrobatics to lectures and demonstrations of science and new inventions.

Almost all the important pre-Victorian names of Birmingham seemed to spend some of their lives in the Old Square, from the Quaker, Sampson Lloyd III, to the soldier, Thomas Unett, whose death at the siege of Sebastopol is commemorated by the distinctive obelisk in the grounds of the cathedral.

It was soon after the members of Birmingham's Shakespeare Club had erected a plaque on Hector's House to remember its literary associations that the end came. Old Square's final demise was suitably spectacular: it fell victim to Joseph Chamberlain's bulldozers, as the great Birmingham visionary carved his grand boulevard through the heart of the town in the 1870s.

The Priory Estate was one of the first stages in the gentrification of Birmingham. Standing on or near the top of the sandstone ridge, it looked down geographically and psychologically on the remains of the medieval town down by the Bull Ring. Hutton said that there were remains of the old Priory buildings in the cellars of the Old Square houses.

19. The north-east side of the Old Square looking along Lichfield Street. The last houses were demolished in 1896.

But it was only one of a series of developments that created an upper (class) quarter of the town, not unlike the new town of Edinburgh. Not surprisingly, it was known as the High Town Quarter. Another was the area around St Philip's church.

The need for a new Anglican church in Birmingham had long been felt. St Martin's, the only such establishment since the middle ages, had become so overcrowded that 'every recess capable of admitting the body of an infant, was converted into a seat'. The petition presented to Parliament in 1708 claimed that the one church was 'not sufficient for a 5th part of the inhabitants'. This presented not only a problem for the living, but also for the dead, since the old church in the Bull Ring possessed the only Anglican cemetery in town, though of course it made life, or rather death, a lot easier for the body-snatchers. (Additional space was later made available in Park Street in 1807.)

Land, of course, was not a particular problem and two local landowners, William Ing and Penelope Phillips, had given enough space to build a new church. It was the latter's surname that gave the church its dedication. A curiously secular decision this, but then the building of St Philip's had as much to do with status and economics as it had to do with religion. But finding enough money to finish the building was not so easy, and a gift of £600 by the King was a key factor in its completion.

The new church, dedicated but not completed in 1715, was built of brick, faced in stone and marks the beginning of Italianate design in the town. The designer was Thomas Archer and its baroque style is unique among the English cathedrals, though it would be almost two centuries before St Philip's would be raised to that status. It is also the smallest of the English cathedrals; indeed its size has been something of a problem to the present day. When St Philip's was the venue for concerts in the early days of the Triennial Music Festivals, concert-goers frequently abandoned their dignity in an unseemly struggle for seats. And in recent years, building work has gone on in the crypt to extend the building's working space.

Standing at the highest point on the ridge, St Philip's symbolised the new age of Georgian Birmingham. Certainly it made an immediate impression on William Hutton:

> When I first saw St Philip's, in the year 1741, at a proper distance, uncrowded with houses, for there were none to the north, New Hall excepted, untarnished with smoke, and illuminated by a western sun, I was delighted with its appearance, and thought it then, what I do now, and what others will in future, the pride of the place.

As was the case with St Paul's church a generation later, the new church became a focal point for new domestic building, too. There was nothing quite as grand as a view onto the local church, and its presence guaranteed that it would not be a view shortly to be interrupted by other domestic or industrial developments. By 1762, when William Toldervy visited the town, St Philip's and its surroundings had become Birmingham's architectural high point:

> I entered the Town on the side where stands St Philip's ... This is a very beautiful modern building ... There are but few in London so elegant. It stands in the Middle of a large Church-Yard, around which is a beautiful walk ... on one side of this Church-Yard the buildings are as lofty, elegant, and uniform as those of Bedford Row, and are inhabited by People of Fortune, who are great wholesale Dealers in the Manufactures of this Town. These buildings have the Appellation of Tory-Row (*Temple Row*); and this is the highest and genteelest part of the Town of Birmingham.

These 'lofty, elegant' buildings may have been town-houses, but they did not lack for country pleasures either. One house in Temple Street was advertised in 1743 as having 'an entire Garden walled, and the walls covered with Fruit Trees'. At the end of the terrace walk was a summer house, 'adjoining to the open Fields, and commanding a Prospect of four Miles Distance'.

Westley's 1731 map (see p.5) shows the sudden transition from town to country on this side of Birmingham. On the far side of St Philip's churchyard ran New Hall Lane (now Colmore Row). Beyond it lay the estate of the Colmore family, offering the unrestricted views boasted of by the estate agents of the day. The line of Newhall Street roughly follows the main entrance to the estate; iron gates opening onto a broad avenue of elms leading up to New Hall itself. It was wooded, well-watered, and destined to disappear.

It was in 1746 that Ann Colmore obtained a private act of Parliament allowing her to carve up the estate and profit from the land-hungry town to the west. This was to be the most significant of the redevelopments of 18th-century Birmingham, for the size of the plots and their cost allowed for a mixture of industrial and domestic use. Birmingham was given on a plate the opportunity to expand its business sector, moving away from the old base around Digbeth. The pattern it set was of wealthy industrialists living round the corner from skilled craftsmen and unskilled labourers. Small family businesses could live and work in the same place, much as they had done in the overcrowded quarter near the Rea.

In particular, it allowed cooperation between small workshops specialising in different parts of the manufacturing process, with metal items passing through a series of hands, before emerging as a finished product. The development made particular sense in the toy and jewellery industries, and the foundation was laid for the specialised Jewellery Quarter that still dominates the area.

New Hall itself was not long to survive the industrial tide that enveloped it. By 1787 it was up for sale, and there was nothing sentimental about the terms of its disposal: 'The whole to be pulled down, and the Materials carried away within 1 Month from the Time of Sale'. The old family home was now simply standing in the middle of progress road.

The building work in Birmingham was not limited to new workshops and houses. In 1724, just as the finishing touches were being put to St Philip's, another building was going up on the north side of the churchyard. This was the Blue Coat Charity School, an Anglican foundation to provide education for the children of poorer families in the town, who could not afford the fees of King Edward's. Essentially its purpose was to provide the growing town with a small army of apprentices and domestics, raised in godliness and good learning. And as the latter category implies, unlike the school in New Street it opened its doors to girls as well.

The school provided bed, board and uniforms for its small inmates, and for two centuries lines of children in their distinctive blue uniforms could be seen trooping across St Philip's churchyard for the daily service. A further distinction was the presence over the entrance of two statues showing a girl and boy in school dress. Discounting the monuments in the parish churches, these were Birmingham's first statues, executed in 1770 by Edward Grubb. When the school moved to Harborne in 1930 the statues moved with it and now stand in the assembly hall.

Blue Coat marks the beginning of the slow extension in the elementary education of the town beyond the limited scope of King Edward's and the small private schools of the rich. But the opportunities offered by Blue Coat and King Edward's were restricted to children of Anglican parents. Indirectly they led to establishment of the Protestant Dissenting Charity School in Meeting Street in 1760. Although founded to accommodate 18 boys and eight girls, it later became a school for girls only, generally between the ages of nine and fifteen. As with Blue Coat, its principal output inevitably was domestic servants. This allowed the institution to make considerable savings on the wages bill by not employing a domestic. Such work was all part of the girls' training.

The rules of the Dissenting School suggest an arrangement that was disciplined, but not devoid of sensitivity. Day began at six in morning and ended by nine at night, 'but such of them as choose it may go to bed sooner'. Lessons, meals and prayers were time-tabled, but so too was play: 'At eight they are to breakfast, and after breakfast they may play till nine; the Master taking care that they do not exceed their bounds, nor use profane, or any indecent Language, or be otherwise guilty of Rudeness or Immodesty'.

In the case of both the Blue Coat and the Protestant Dissenting School income was entirely reliant on charity, either from bequests or the proceeds from annual charity sermons. Both were later able to increase their intake and move to larger buildings. In 1791 the Dissenting School moved into a building in Park Street, and in 1840 to newly-built premises in Graham Street. But in this century the two schools have gone in decidedly different directions: Blue Coat has become a wealthy and well-respected private school, while the Dissenting School became an asylum.

If the Church of England was gradually losing its exclusive grip on the education of the town, it still remained at the centre of the system of poor relief. The obligation to support those unable, through age or infirmity, to support themselves, fell fairly and squarely on the parish authorities. As the numbers of poor increased in the 18th and 19th centuries, central government and the local parishes sought ways to lessen the burden on the rate-payer by increasing the efficiency of poor relief. Parliamentary acts empowered parishes to reduce the spiralling costs of out-relief by erecting workhouses, thereby concentrating resources in one place. Aston parish built its workhouse at Erdington soon after 1700, when a rate was levied to raise the finance. This building, added to and adapted until the original core was unrecognisable, remained in use till the 1860s, when a new union workhouse was constructed at Gravelly Hill. This now forms part of Highcroft Hospital.

The parish of Birmingham did not act with quite the same alacrity as Aston. It was not until 1733 that a workhouse was erected, at a cost of £1,173, on Lichfield Street, near to the present Victoria Law Courts. Later in the century two wings were added, one as an infirmary and the other as a place of labour, giving the building the distinctive façade often seen on workhouse tokens and early maps. But although it contained around six hundred paupers, the bill for out-relief continued to rise. In 1781 the cost of poor relief to the parish exceeded £11,000 when a total of 5,240 persons were in receipt of it. Numbers in the workhouse too continued to grow, even after the removal of 300 children to an Asylum for the Infant Poor on Summer Lane in 1797.

Various means were found to subsidise the system, chiefly by the introduction of profitable labour into the workhouse. The overseers plied the inmates with mop-yarn and pack-thread with limited success. Attempts to increase the self-sufficiency of the place by keeping pigs or grinding corn were of similarly limited effect. By 1783 the proposal to solve Birmingham's poor law problems 'at a stroke', by building a massive new workhouse on the Heath, had reached the ears of Parliament. Even Hutton, whose loyalties were torn between rate-payer and pauper, thought the measure misguided and short-sighted.

Nevertheless the proposal became bricks and mortar in 1852 with the opening of a new workhouse for 1,160 persons in Winson Green. This forms a now disused part of Dudley Road Hospital. We will have more to say of the complex of Victorian institutions in Winson Green in a later chapter. Suffice it to say here that the Victorians were more than grateful that the old manor and parish of Birmingham had stretched so far. The empty heathland to the west, once cursed as unfit for agricultural use, became an ideal location for those growing institutions that could no longer be accommodated in the town centre.

It is no coincidence that three of the city's great hospitals are currently using sites that were laid out as workhouses. As we have said, Birmingham Union Workhouse stands next to Dudley Road Hospital. Kings Norton Union Workhouse has become Selly Oak Hospital, while Highcroft was once the workhouse of Aston Union. Poverty could be the result of unemployment, but also of infirmity, and the latter required on-site medical facilities. The workhouse in Lichfield Street had an infirmary wing added in 1766, but being a parish institution, it was limited to parishioners of Birmingham. John Ash, an eminent local physician, observed in a letter to the town's newspaper in November 1765: '... More than half the Manufacturers in the Town of Birmingham are not Parishioners of it, and cannot be entitled to any Relief from the present Infirmary: Many of them are Foreigners, but the greatest Part belong to the Parishes of the neighbouring Country'.

Ash's rallying call for a General Hospital was answered by many, and industrialists, gentry and ordinary people raised around £2,000. It was an impressive effort, but well short of the £3,000 needed to build it. The shell of the new hospital on Summer Lane languished, hardly yet in a state to receive patients. It seems that the wealthier citizens of the town had found in the newly announced canal undertaking a more profitable place to invest their spare cash.

But in May 1768 the Hospital Board hit upon the perfect solution to their cash-flow problems. An announcement appeared in the local press: 'On Wednesday, Thursday, and

Friday, the 7th, 8th, and 9th of September, the Oratorios of L'Allegro, &c, Alexander's Feast, and the Messiah will be performed here'.

The solution was a kind of 18th-century Live Aid, a series of charity concerts, from which the profits would go to the General Hospital. It would be too much to say that three concerts built the hospital, and it took another musical event in 1778 to consolidate its success. In September 1779 the General Hospital finally opened its doors, complete with 40 beds, four nurses and physicians, and a barber.

But the Hospital Board had created more than a place to house the sick. The musical festivals put Birmingham, for the first time, on the cultural map. From the fund-raising event of 1768, music and charity took each other's hand and walked into the next century. Together they would make beds for the sick, build churches and a town hall.

Chapter Seven

Entertaining the Town

In 1733 a humble mechanic from 'the busy town of Birmingham' wrote a verse letter to a craftsman 'in the sleepy Corporation of Warwick':

> Here Guns and Swords Cyclopean hands divide,
> And here with glittering Arms the World is still supply'd.
> Here Implements and Toys for distant Parts,
> Of various Metals, by mechanic Arts,
> Are finely wrought, and by the Artists sold,
> Whose touch turns every Metal into Gold;
> But 'tis in vain, alas! we boast our Skill;
> Wanting thy Arts, we are deficient still.

Impressions of the place would be no different a century later. De Toqueville stopped by in June 1835 and wrote: 'These folk never have a minute to themselves. They work as if they must get rich by the evening, and die the next day. They are generally very intelligent people, but intelligent in the American way'. A translation of Toqueville's last phrase might be 'street-wise'.

Birmingham has had to bear such comments through the ages. From the impressions of visitors who only scratched the surface of the place it would seem to be 'an immense workshop, a huge forge, a vast shop'. But, as the fund-raising initiative to support the General Hospital indicates, by the second half of the 18th century a veneer of culture had begun to stick to the old metal vessel. There was enough surplus cash in the hands of the industrialists and artisans to demand a little entertainment at the end of a hard day. This might be a stand-up comedian, a play or a cock-fight: all tastes were catered for.

The first theatrical entertainments in the town were from travelling companies or performers. Hutton mentions a shed in the fields that were to become Temple Street. By the 1730s this had graduated to a stable in Castle Street. A decade later, and a theatre had appeared in Moor Street. In July 1747 *Hamlet* was performed there. But running a theatre in 18th-century England was not easy. They were generally felt to be a corrupting influence on the morals of society, and in theory all theatres had to be licensed, though in practice this was often ignored. Proprietors were able to get round the blanket ban by calling their shows 'A Concert of Music' and then slipping in a play after the music. The authorities were usually prepared to turn a blind eye unless there was strong local opposition.

Birmingham, being a predominantly nonconformist town, was tough on corrupting influences. This was a tradition that was slow to change. Even in the 1930s the uncompromising attitudes of the licensing magistrates to shows and films that they felt to be unsavoury gave Birmingham the nickname of the 'holy city'. Resistance to the Moor Street theatre was strong, particularly from the Methodists. There may have been an ulterior motive here for, when the place was closed down, it was converted into a Methodist chapel. 'Happy would it be, if all the playhouses in the kingdom were converted to so good a use', preached Wesley in the newly-converted building in 1764.

But a tide was growing that was becoming difficult to resist. Another playhouse had appeared in Smallbrook Street, and a third opened in King Street in 1752. Again no licence was sought, presumably because of the risk of having it turned down. The King Street theatre was content to peddle its low-brow entertainment of rope-dancing, puppet shows and the like, all under the cover of 'a concert of music'. This venue too was to be brought down from behind, and in 1786 became another Methodist chapel. There was clearly something morally satisfying in the re-occupation of a place of entertainment. Half a century later, in 1834, the building known as Ryan's Amphitheatre in Bradford Street was taken over by the Baptists and re-named the Circus Chapel in memory of its previous attraction.

In 1774 yet another theatre opened on New Street with the usual 'Concert of Music' concealing a performance of *As You Like It*. But such furtive activity hardly befitted a town with artistic pretensions. The moves to set up a genuine licensed theatre for the town were long and complicated. There was strong support from among the leading intellectuals of the town (men like Boulton, Watt and Small) for the idea of one licensed theatre of good reputation, instead of two or three playhouses of dubious artistic merit. But there was strong opposition, too. It was an issue that cut across long-standing alliances: the Lloyds opposed it, though their business partner, John Taylor, was a supporter. A bill was presented to Parliament in 1777, in the course of which Edmund Burke famously described Birmingham as 'the great Toy Shop of Europe'.

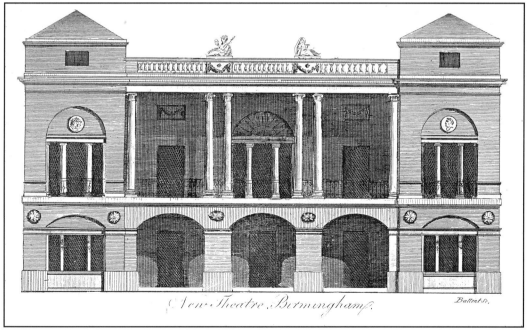

New Theatre, Birmingham.

20.   The New Theatre, later Theatre Royal, in New Street as it stood before the fire of 1820. All that survives of the theatre are two medallions of Shakespeare and Garrick, now in the Central Library.

Other than that, the bill was a unremarkable failure. It was not until 1806 that a licence was granted, and the institution known as the Theatre Royal became an established part of Birmingham life for a century and a half. That is, when it was not being rebuilt. Two disastrous fires, both of suspicious origins, brought the house down in 1792 and 1820. There were many other disruptions caused by riots, unruly behaviour and low attendance figures. Added to that, the Birmingham theatres were only active during the summer months and reliant on visiting companies from London, together with occasional stars like Garrick, Kean and Mrs. Siddons. As far as the stage went, Birmingham could hardly be said to be undergoing a cultural renaissance yet.

In the second half of the 18th century, Birmingham's chief centre of outdoor entertainment was at Duddeston. After the Holtes moved their family seat from Duddeston Hall to Aston, the grounds of the old manor were used for a variety of sports, including cock-fighting and bowling. In 1758 the grounds had been re-named Vauxhall Gardens, after the London pleasure park, and opened to the public. The kind of entertainment on offer can be gathered from the description in Bisset's *Poetic Survey and Magnificent Directory* of 1799:

> A rural spot where tradesmen oft repair
> For relaxation, and to breathe fresh air;
> The beauties of the place attractive prove
> To those who quiet and retirement love;
> There, freed from toils and labours of the day,
> Mechanics with their wives, or sweethearts, stray;
> Or rosy children, sportive, trip along
> To see rare Fireworks—or hear a song
> For oft in summer sweet powers
> Woos thousands to Vauxhall, to pass their hours.

It was urban Birmingham's escapist rural idyll, an antidote to the smoky town nearby. But not all occasions at Vauxhall were so peaceful. Balloon ascents in the 1820s, enormous firework shows and grand balls turned the place into a Midland equivalent of the Tivoli Gardens. Vauxhall was uniquely able to rise to the great occasion, as the following advertisement from August 1808 illustrates:

VAUXHALL GARDENS

The public are respectfully informed, the annual Celebration of his Royal Highness the Prince of Wales's Birth, will be To-morrow, (Tuesday), August 12, when will be

A GRAND GALA,

Comprising a Miscellaneous Concert, in which will be introduced several favourite Songs, Duets, &c. by Mrs Hatton...

Between the Acts of the Concert, a numerous Collection of

FIRE WORKS

In which, amongst a great Variety, will be a very superb new Piece, representing the Grand Star of Malta, and a

TEMPLE OF FIRE WORKS,

In the centre of which will be exhibited, a full-length Portrait of

ADMIRAL LORD NELSON,

The Gardens will be most richly illuminated, with Triumphal Arches, several appropriate Devices, and, for the last time, the Grand Naval Pillar. — Admittance One Shilling.

But all good things come to an end, and the creeping expansion of Aston and Birmingham, and particularly of the Ashted estate, undermined Vauxhall's rural pretensions. And the opening of Birmingham's first railway station at Vauxhall in 1837 only served to underline the closeness of the real world. In that year the grounds were described as 'once a favourite resort, but now deserted as unfashionable'.

The grounds were sold off to the Victoria Land Society in 1850. Even then Vauxhall Gardens saw themselves into oblivion in the grand manner, the first axe being taken to the trees immediately after a farewell dinner and ball on 16 September 1850. Earlier in the year, one Edward Farmer penned his eulogy sitting in one of the Vauxhall grottoes:

> There's scarce a heart that will not start,
> No matter what its rank or station,
> And heave a sigh when they destroy,
> This favourite place of recreation.
> If we look back on memory's track,
> What joyous scenes we can recall,
> Of happy hours in its gay bowers,
> And friends we met at Old Vauxhall.

But Birmingham's rural dream was not entirely lost with the felling of Vauxhall. The green mantle fell upon Aston Lower Grounds and Sutton Park, and, more recently, Cannon Hill Park has revived the traditions of Old Vauxhall with its annual combination of music and fireworks.

The success of such ventures as Vauxhall were made all the easier by the possibility of regular advertising. This became possible with the appearance of a regular newspaper in 1741. In that year Thomas Aris of London arrived in town to set up business as a printer and publisher. Aris was not the first to consider the need for a newspaper in the growing town; Thomas Warren, another printer, having ventured into the area in the 1730s. But, despite boasting Samuel Johnson as one of its contributors, Warren's *Birmingham Journal* was a short-lived affair.

The launch of *Aris's Birmingham Gazette* was marked by the kind of unpleasant circulation war not unknown in the newspaper world. In the space between announcement and publication (16 November 1741), Thomas Aris was beaten to it by Robert Walker, the publisher of the *Warwick and Staffordshire Journal*. At least, that was Aris's story. More likely, Walker had spotted an opportunity to expand his circulation at about the same time that Aris had moved into Birmingham. Aris need not have worried unduly; in two years his paper had taken over the rival and gained its intended monopoly. This gave him the opportunity to raise the price to 2d.

Aris's Gazette was a four-page weekly paper for the first century of its existence: government stamp duty (a halfpenny per copy) effectively precluded more regular publication. Aris's success was obtained by ruthlessly pursuing revenue through advertising. Local news was squeezed into a column on the third page. The rest of the paper was devoted to adverts for local events, such as that at Vauxhall quoted above, property sales and notices for patent medicines and the like, usually available on application at the Gazette offices. Foreign news was obtained from the London papers, which obtained theirs by subscription to European papers. Aris partly justified the price rise in 1743 by passing on the cost of meeting the London post at Daventry. The price of newspapers meant that most readers saw a copy in the coffee-house or pub. And by excluding any

21. The printer, John Baskerville (1706-75); a man of unorthodox views who came to an unorthodox end.
The printing business was continued after 1775 by his wife, Sarah.

obvious sign of editorial bias or political comment, Aris avoided alienating any of them.

If Thomas Aris was the printer with the most impact in Birmingham, he was not the most famous. A man called Baskerville could happily claim that title. John Baskerville came to Birmingham from Wolverley in Worcestershire, and set up as a writing-master in the Bull Ring in 1737. A promising, but ultimately low-key career in tombstone carving and japanning led him into the paper and printing business. The years of experimentation in lettering bore fruit in a series of publications which, as Macaulay wrote, 'went forth to astonish all the librarians of Europe'. An edition of *Virgil* in 1757 was followed by others of English and Latin classics, and in 1763 by a folio edition of the Cambridge Bible, heralded as the finest example of typography ever produced. Clearly the printer did not allow his ideologies (he was an atheist) to get in the way of his business deals! In the typeface that bears his name, Baskerville left a legacy still in use today.

In 1745 Baskerville leased an estate, which he called Easy Hill, on the western edge of town, upon which to build a house and workshops. The house stood near what is now Centenary Square, appropriately occupied by Baskerville House. What the estate looked like at the time of his death in 1775 can be gleaned from the sale notice:

> The out Offices consist of a large Kitchen, with Servant's Rooms over it, a Butler's and common Pantry, Brewhouse, two Pumps, one hard and the other soft Water, a four-stalled Stable, and Coach House, a good Garden, with Green-House, and Garden-House, spacious Warehouses and Workshops, suitable for the Mercantile Business, or any extensive Manufactory, together with about seven Acres of rich Pasture Land in high condition, Part of which is laid out in Shady Walks, adorned with Shrubberies, Fish Ponds, and Grotto; the whole in a Ring-Fence, great part of it enclosed by a Brick-Wall, and is, on Account of its elevated situation and near affinity to the Canal, a very desirable spot to Build upon.

The advert, understandably, does not mention that the purchaser of the estate would be buying the old printer as well, for Baskerville had insisted in his will that he be buried 'in a conical building in my own premises ... which I have lately raised higher and painted, and in a vault which I have prepared for it'. Baskerville's logic was consistent, if somewhat eccentric. Having disavowed religion for many years, he was not prepared to abandon his beliefs (or lack of them) by being buried in consecrated ground.

Baskerville's will, duly obeyed by his widow, was the beginning of one of the oddest sagas in Birmingham's history. Baskerville slept peacefully in his garden for 45 years, undisturbed by the destruction of his house in the 1791 riots. Then, in 1820, the extension of the canal involved cutting a wharf through the grounds and Baskerville's conical resting-place. Though the circumstances of his burial may have been unusual, there was nothing wrong with the work of the embalmers who had laid him to rest. The body, rudely awakened, was found to be in a remarkable state of preservation, with a sprig of laurel on his chest. So remarkable, in fact, that the great printer was put on display in a local warehouse. Here John Baskerville greeted his admirers with a smell that resembled decayed cheese. Disintegration was setting in, hastened by the fresh air that Baskerville thought he had seen the last of.

Complaints from neighbours led to his re-interment in a vault at Christ Church, the Anglican church at the top of New Street. The priests that Baskerville had rejected had got their way at last. But even then it was to be a troubled sleep. The demolition of Christ Church in 1898 meant that the energetic printer was on the move again, for one last journey to Warstone Lane Church of England cemetery. Whatever may have become of the printer's soul, his body had been remarkably active, and had gone forth to astonish quite a few antiquarians in his adopted town.

John Baskerville's conical tomb was an appropriate choice, for he sat at the top of a pyramid of literary activity in late 18th-century Birmingham. The rise of a literate readership led, not only to newspapers, but to libraries as well. In the days before munici-pal libraries, private and subscription libraries filled the gap. John Lowe and Joseph Crompton ran circulating libraries in the Bull Ring and Colmore Row respectively, and there were around ten in the town altogether. In 1779 the Birmingham Library was established on the model of similar institutions in Manchester and Liverpool by 19 subscribers, each agreeing to pay a subscription of 6s. a year. Two years later it moved into premises in the Swan Yard, where the librarian sat beside his fire and kept a watchful eye from 2.00 till 5.00 (Sundays excepted). In 1797 the old library moved into a purpose-built home in Union Street, on land that had once been Corbett's Bowling Green. The building was designed by William Hollins, with the following inscription above the entrance: 'Ad mercaturam bonarum artium profectus, et tibi et omnibus ditesces'. [Setting out to the market of the good arts, you will enrich both yourself and all others.]

Here the collection remained until, in 1899, the 70,000 books were removed to a new building in Margaret Street, where it remains as part of the Birmingham and Midland Institute.

There were others ways of acquiring a little learning too, for this was the era of the travelling scientist and showman. These performances, usually held in a local pub or hotel,

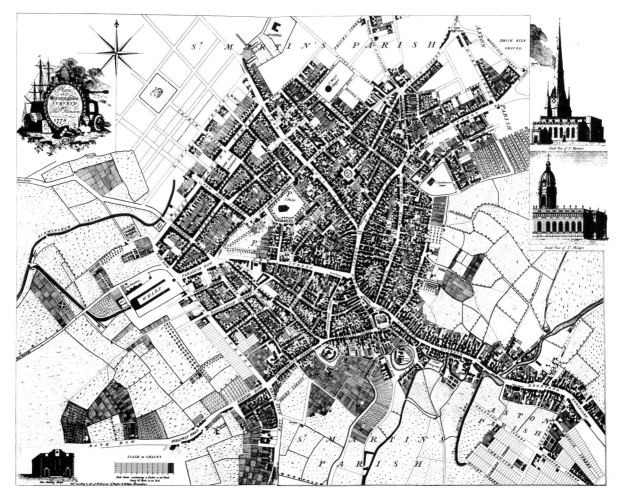

22. Bradford's 1751 map of the town. The development of Henry Bradford's estate (bottom right) has just begun.

ranged from a series of scientific lectures on Newtonian physics or electricity to sensation-alist flights of fancy, such as that by Boaz, who brought his 'Grand Thaumaturgick Exhibition of Philosophical, Mathematical, Sterganographical, Sympathetical, Sciateroconatical and Magical Operations' to town in 1780.

Few weeks went by without some such 'entertainment' visiting town, and 'definitely the last week of the exhibition' was always extended, before passing on to Wolverhampton or Coventry. In 1760 visitors to the *Seven Stars* in the Bull Ring could make the acquaint-ance of Mrs. Salmon's 'Royal Waxwork, representing the Royal Family of Great Britain richly dressed and in full proportion'. Paintings of famous battles were on display in New Street, as well as (in 1793) a working model of a guillotine. In the days before press photography and newsreel, they represented a unique opportunity for the average person to see what the King really looked like, or what was going on in France.

But the exhibitions were not always so educational. The public rooms of the town had their regular supply of fat men and wise pigs to lower the tone. In 1788, for example, under the headline 'The present age is allowed to be the Age of Wonders and Improvement in the Arts!', the *Gazette* ran an advert for a man who ate 'Pebbles, Flints, Tobacco Pipes or Mineral Excrescences':

> The wonderful Stone-Eater appears not to suffer the least Inconvenience from so ponderous and, to all other Persons in the World, so indigestible a Meal, which he repeats from Eleven till Twelve this Day at Noon, and also from Four in the Afternoon till Eight in the Evening, every Day in the Week, and positively no longer.

All this without an Arts Council grant!

Chapter Eight

Radicals and Rioting

Throughout the 1600s and 1700s dissenters of various hues had settled in Birmingham without ever swarming in. We have already charted the rise of a number of the Quaker families, and their successes in business and commerce. By 1790 there were Baptist churches in Cannon Street and Lombard Street; Congregationalist chapels in Carrs Lane and Oxford Street; Quakers in Bull Street; Methodists in Coleshill Street, Bradford Street and Cherry Street; Unitarians in Moor Street and Phillip Street. In addition there was a Jewish synagogue in the Froggery and a newly-opened Catholic church in Broad Street (designed to look like a factory so as not to attract attention). And in 1791, the year that awaits us, a new synagogue was in the course of construction in Severn Street, as well as a church for the Swedenborgians (the first of that sect in the country) in Newhall Street.

The town seemed to have attained an ideal cultural mix, and a shop-window for all religions. But shop-windows sometimes get broken, and the mix was not always so amicable. Charles Wesley, who once described Birmingham as 'a dry and uncomfortable place', saw his sermon at the opening of Moor Street chapel in 1764 disrupted by rioting. Worse trouble still followed the Jacobite Rising of 1715, when a mob attacked the Lower Meeting House in Digbeth. Dissenters were singled out for harrassment as presumed supporters of the Hanoverian cause. In Digbeth they satisfied themselves with burning the furniture and fittings, but on the next day did a more thorough job at the Upper or Old Meeting House in Phillip Street. The latter was gutted.

The Jacobite riots heralded a century of uneasy co-existence with occasional menaces. In addition to the attack on the Methodists in 1751, the Quaker meeting house had its windows broken eight years later for not sufficiently celebrating English victories in Canada. Anti-Catholic gatherings in 1780, in the wake of the Gordon Riots in London, narrowly avoided violence: perhaps because there was, as yet, no Catholic church in town to focus attention on.

23. The Old Meeting House dated from 1689. It stood on what was then Philip Street.

The Birmingham that erupted in violence in 1791 was the same place, but in very different political times. Since the events of that year are usually called the Priestley Riots (though the man from which they take their name was the chief sufferer from them), we should introduce the strong-minded minister of the New Meeting House.

Joseph Priestley had come to Birmingham in 1780 as a Unitarian minister, with half a dozen careers already behind him. He had been a teacher of Greek at Warrington Academy, and subsequently librarian to the Earl of Shelburne and tutor to the Earl's son. He had also served as a minister in Nantwich and Leeds, during which time he published his *History of Electricity*. As a scientist he was very much part of the establishment, a member of the Royal Society, the French Academy of Sciences and the Imperial Academy of Sciences at St Petersburg. As a theologian his reputation was rather less orthodox. He campaigned long and hard against the Corporation and Test Acts, which effectively barred dissenters from civil or military office.

Priestley was the kind of character that polarised opinions. To William Hutton's daughter, Catherine, he was 'mild, persuasive, and unaffected, as his sermons are full of sound reasoning and good sense'. To the hypercritical Mary Anne Galton he was 'a man of admirable simplicity, gentleness, and kindness of heart, united with great acuteness of intellect'. To his opponents he was a fanatic, a godless burner of bibles and a revolutionary. Within a few years of his arrival in Birmingham he had offended almost all of the established church, the more polemical of whom saw him as a new Guy Fawkes, intent on taking gunpowder to the establishment. The man who wrote books called *An History of the Corruptions of Christianity* or *The Importance and Extent of Free Enquiry* did not endear himself to traditionalists. Hutton suggested that to take on Priestley was the road to success for the Anglican priest.

One remark in particular marked him out for special treatment by the cartoonists and his opponents:

> We are, as it were, laying gunpowder, grain by grain, under the old building of error and superstition, which a single spark may hereafter inflame, so as to produce an instantaneous explosion; in consequence of which that edifice, the erection of which has been the work of ages, may be overturned in a moment, and so effectually as that the same foundation can never be built upon again.

Priestley employed the image despite the advice of his friend, Josiah Wedgwood, who recognised that it would only serve to arm his opponents. Priestley did not realise that the gunpowder he was laying down would explode under his own house.

The long smoking feud between Priestley and his supporters and the establishment (both civil and ecclesiastical) burst into flames in the summer of 1791. There can have been few occasions when a town has erupted for so purely political a cause, even if the after-effects were not quite so pure. The cause, however irrelevant it might have seemed, was the French Revolution.

There were many in England, Wordsworth, William Blake and Priestley among them, who saw the events of 1789 in France as a common cause of freedom throughout the world, and a spiritual breaking of chains. It was a revolution as yet unsullied by the ugly brutality that followed it: Louis XVI still lived, and France remained, in theory, a monarchy.

As the second anniversary of the Storming of the Bastille approached, an inflammatory hand-bill appeared in the bars of London and Birmingham:

Richard Brinsley Sheridan.   Dr. Priestley.   Sir Cecil Wray.   Charles James Fox.   J. Horne Tooke.   Dr. Theophilus Lindsey.

" A BIRMINGHAM TOAST, JULY 14, 1791."
From the original etching by JAMES GILLRAY: *Drawn on wood by G. H. Bernasconi.*

24.   James Gillray's cartoon of the Birmingham banquet shows Priestley toasting 'the King's head on a plate'. In fact, the Birmingham meeting was careful to express its loyalty to the king.

> My Countrymen—The second year of Gallic Liberty is nearly expired. At the commencement of the third, on the 14th of this month, it is devoutly to be wished that every enemy to civil and religious despotism would give his sanction to the majestic common cause by a public celebration of the anniversary.

The bill went on to suggest how the course of action undertaken in Paris might be appropriate to Great Britain, too:

> But is it possible to forget that our own Parliament is venal? your minister hypocritical? your clergy legal oppressors? the Reigning Family extravagant? the crown of a certain great personage becoming every day too weighty for the head that wears it? Too weighty for the people who gave it? Your taxes partial and excessive? Your Representation a cruel insult upon the Sacred Rights of Property, Religion, and Freedom?

As coded language goes, this did not take much breaking. Many dissenters distanced themselves from it, and indeed, it was suggested that the hand-bill had been a loyalist ploy to unite opinion against the radicals. But this was the atmosphere of mistrust and antagonism when the *Gazette* announced the meeting to be held in *Dadley's Hotel* in Temple

Row to celebrate Bastille Day: 'Any Friend to Freedom, disposed to join the intended temperate festivity, is desired to leave his name at the bar of the Hotel, where tickets may be had at Five Shillings each, including a bottle of wine; but no person will be admitted without one'.

Mischievously, the *Gazette* also announced that a list of those attending the dinner would also be published. For those opposed to the celebrations, it would constitute a hit-list, though no copy of such a document has survived.

Sometime between 6 July, when Priestley had asked Hutton to attend the dinner, and the 14th, the minister had decided that his presence there would only serve to inflame the atmosphere. Indeed, it was only after intense lobbying by the hotel's owner that the decision was made to go ahead with the celebration at all. An unpleasant outcome was anticipated, but not by everyone. Catharine Hutton recalled that her brother visited them at Bennett's Hill: '... and told us that a riot was expected on Thursday; but so little was I interested by the intelligence, that it left no impression on mind. The word *riot*, since so dreadful, conveyed no other idea than that of verbal abuse'.

While the Friends of Liberty were drinking their 18 toasts (the first of which was to King and Constitution) at *Dadley*'s, less well-ordered drinking was taking place at *Dee's Royal Hotel* in Temple Row. Their cry was 'Church and King for ever', though Hutton

25.   The assault on the Old Meeting House reduced it to rubble. Like Priestley's chapel it was a Unitarian place of worship. It was rebuilt on the same site five years later.

described them as 'people who would have sold their King for a jug of ale, and demolished the Church for a bottle of gin'. Around eight o'clock, long after the dinner at *Dadley*'s had broken up, a crowd of protesters gathered outside the hotel to break windows and lynch Priestley. From this point onwards, all hell was let loose. Having failed to find the minister at the hotel, the mob moved on to the two Unitarian meeting houses in Moor Street and Phillip Street. Priestley's New Meeting House was stripped and gutted; the Old Meeting was razed to the ground. From there they went on to call on a number of other non-conformist chapels in the town. But there was selectivity in the destruction: the mob was bribed to spare the new Swedenborgian church, and dissuaded from firing the Methodist building in King Street.

Having thus cleared away the unacceptable face of nonconformity in Birmingham, the focus of the violence then shifts out of town, to the houses of those perceived to be supporters of the French cause. Again, the first target was Joseph Priestley, and his house at Fair Hill.

Before Fair Hill is destroyed, let us spend a few minutes inside it. It stood in Sparkbrook, near to the turnpike gate on the Stratford Road, on land owned by Sampson Lloyd. Indeed, it was just a short walk from Lloyd's house called Farm. There was a drawing-room on the ground floor, together with a front and back parlour and kitchen. A staircase at the front led to the four bedrooms; one at the back takes us to the attic which Priestley converted into a library and study. In the attic too was accommodation for two maids and servant boy. Outside was a vegetable garden (Priestley became a vegetarian for health reasons), a brewhouse with laundry above, pigsty, coal and coke sheds and tool shed. Here also was the laboratory that the minister had built for his experiments.

Fair Hill was a Disneyland of science to visitors, particularly children. John Ryland, whose house at Easy Hill was soon to suffer the same fate as Priestley's, described the excitement of a visit to it. It was a world of scientific toys: the rain-gauge, the perambulator that measured distances, the magic lantern in the attic, and the air-gun: 'The mark which we most delighted in was the block upon which the Doctor's wig was dressed, which we placed on the wall of the coal-hole to shoot at'.

On the night of 14 July 1791, the house stood empty as the sound of voices on the Stratford Road grew louder. Dr. Priestley and his wife had escaped from Fair Hill about an hour before their uninvited guests arrived. It was late into the night when they began their assault on the house, breaking down the doors and throwing furniture and the doctor's library out into the garden. One witness reported that 'the highroads for full half a mile of the house were strewed with books'. Destroyed too was the laboratory, though Priestley's wine cellar was looted with more care, and many of the invaders felt themselves obliged to sleep off the effects in the garden.

It soon became clear that this was not to be a single night's trouble. The riot had begun to gain a momentum of its own, only part of which was devoted to retribution on the dissenters. In an ironic counterpoint to the events at the Bastille, the lock-up in Birmingham was broken open and a second day's disorder began. The next target was John Baskerville's former house at Easy Hill, and again the contents of the cellar attracted most attention. Unfortunately for a number of those enjoying an unexpected 'happy hour', the building was fired and the roof fell in before they were in a fit state to leave. As Hutton memorably put it, 'they were shepherded into eternity in a state of bestial drunkenness'.

26. Priestley's House, Fair Hill, looted on the night of 14 July 1791. Priestley was never to return to his house, or indeed to Birmingham, after that night.

It was at times like this that the forces of law and order in 18th-century England were shown to be wholly inadequate, when it came to orchestrated violence. Especially when it was rumoured that the magistrates and the establishment were tacitly in support of the loyalist backlash. Nevertheless, special constables were sworn in in St Philip's churchyard and set off (unsuccessfully) to defend Easy Hill.

Fair Hill and Easy Hill were down, but the full toll of casualties was only just beginning. The great families of Birmingham, who had risen so impressively in the previous half-century, were now running for their lives. The Huttons at Bennett's Hill in Washwood Heath, the Taylors at Bordesley, the Russells at Showell Green were all about to feel the full force of the mob. William Hutton was no dissenter but, as a Commissioner of the Court of Requests, he had made a fair few enemies in town.

One of the reasons that the Church and King Riots are so well documented and described is that the victims came exclusively from the 'chattering classes'. These were literate, educated, middle-class families. Two daughters were diarists; two fathers were writers and publishers; the rest were part of that close circle of dissenters that had grown so powerful in 18th-century Birmingham. They were also capable of fighting the lengthy claims for compensation that followed, with their exhaustive lists of properties and possessions stolen and destroyed. The narrative of William Russell's daughter is typical of the intimate and first-hand accounts that emerged from the four most traumatic days in her life:

> ... my father much urged my brother, sister, and me to leave, and recommended our going to a neighbour's, who lived in a retired spot about half a mile off. He wished himself to remain at the house as long as possible. Accordingly, we loaded ourselves with cold meat, pies, &c., and set off, intending to take up our quarters there till all was over, thinking we should be near to hear how things went, and profit by circumstances as they arose. As we passed across the fields we were alarmed by parties of men in their shirt sleeves, without hats, all half drunk; they were breaking the boughs from the trees and hedges, shouting, laughing, swearing, and singing in a manner that seemed hideous beyond expression. After much alarm and frequently hiding ourselves behind the hedges and trees, we at length arrived at the place of our destination.

The rioters' subsequent direction echoes the routes of migration of the wealthier Birmingham families. Different groups marched to Washwood Heath, Showell Green and Moseley, and Edgbaston. Edgbaston Hall, the home of William Withering, came within a whisker of destruction: investigation of Dr. Withering's wine cellar was interrupted by the arrival, after four days, of the military. And though a party of rioters was still active in the Kingswood area, the four days of anarchy were at an end.

The suspicion that the Riots could not have wreaked such havoc without the connivance of, or at least a nod from, the establishment, was only increased by the outcome of the trials of the rioters at the Warwick Assizes. Of the paltry 12 who were arrested, only four were found guilty, two of whom were subsequently pardoned. The remaining pair, Francis Field and John Green, were hung at Warwick on 8 September. William Hutton bitterly reported a wise-crack made some time after the trial. A gentleman hunting with Mr Corbett's foxhounds observed the dogs closing in for the kill and shouted, 'Nothing but a Birmingham jury can save him now!'.

At the Spring Assizes of 1792 the 15 claimants for damages found it equally hard going. Of the total claim of £35,000, only £27,000 was allowed, half of which was taken up by the cost of the trial. Still, it has to be said that this must represent an average return for an insurance claim even today.

National opinion was divided over the events that had made Birmingham the focus of media attention for many months. *The Times* reflected the view of many: it asserted the importance of law and order, but at the same time suggested that the victims had brought destruction upon their own heads. Nevertheless there was international sympathy for the victims, particularly Dr. Priestley. He was offered accommodation in France, but he eventually chose America. Certainly he had seen the last of Birmingham, and John Wilkinson, who had been instrumental in bringing the minister to that town, felt that emigration was the best policy: 'It is pretty evident to me that there are Bigots in this country who think it would be of service to what they call our Holy Religion, to have you destroyed by any means'. Priestley died in Northumberland, Pennsylvania in February 1804.

The events of July 1791 had many repercussions in the life of the town. Bearing in mind the long distance troops had to travel to deal with the trouble, military barracks were erected at Ashted. If armed intervention was to become a common part of Birmingham life, then at least the soldiers should have a permanent place of accommodation, instead of the billetting arrangements then in use. The building was completed in the summer of 1793 and soon proved its worth.

Political feelings continued to run high, exacerbated by the likelihood of war with France. In February 1793 an effigy of Tom Paine was hung and burnt by a crowd singing 'God Save the King'. There was also strong resistance to the rate being levied to pay for the damage caused by the Riots. In fact the Big Riot of '91 was followed by the Little Riot of October '93. Ugly gatherings in St Philip's churchyard to complain about the new rate were dispersed by troops from Ashted Barracks. Despite the arrest of 26 men, it was two days before law and order were finally restored.

This would not be the last time that anarchy reigned on the streets of Birmingham, but for the present we may turn to less gloomy subjects.

Chapter Nine

A Little Philosophical Laughter

The Church and King Riots interrupted something of a golden age in Birmingham. Not perhaps for those engaged in the rioting, but for those at the creative and intellectual end of the spectrum, things were humming. From the mid-1760s, a group of friends in the Midland towns of Birmingham, Lichfield, Derby and Stoke were engaged on what they called philosophy, and we would call geology, chemistry, engineering, educational theory and metallurgy. Simply put, they were inventing the modern world.

The Lunar Society, as they called themselves, was one of a number of scientific or philosophical societies formed in the industrialising towns of England. The slowness of the ancient English universities (of which there were still only two) to adapt their curricula to changing times left England without a professional research base. This, however, was not true of the Scottish universities, where educational reform had made considerable progress. It is not surprising that five members of the Lunar Society were graduates of Edinburgh, Glasgow or Aberdeen, though they all found it necessary to leave Scotland to further their careers.

But in England it was predominantly amateur experimenters who were pushing forward the barriers of scientific knowledge and experiment. Some, like Joseph Priestley, were pursuing their work purely for the intrinsic interest of it, and supported by covenants and gifts from his friends. Others, like James Keir, sought 'to make some discovery, by which he might increase his fortune'. Others still, like Matthew Boulton or Josiah Wedgwood, were already successful industrialists and looked to science to improve their manufacturing, or widen their product range. As James Watt said of Boulton shortly after his death:

> Mr Boulton ... possessed in a high degree the facility of rendering any new invention of his own or others useful to the publick by organizing and arranging the process by which it could be carried on ... His conception of the nature of any invention was quick and he was not less quick in perceiving the uses to which it might be applied and the profits which might accrue from it.

Watt was astute enough to recognise that this was the facility that underpinned his friendship with Matthew Boulton, and created the most dynamic business partnership of the Industrial Revolution. So important, in fact, that we will leave it to the next chapter to describe, and concentrate here on the other members of the Society and their Birmingham links.

First let me introduce them. Boulton, Watt and Murdock, the great trio from Handsworth, we will make better acquaintance of later. The sufferings of Joseph Priestley, his appearance and disappearance from Birmingham, have already been outlined. Erasmus

Darwin, the grandfather of Charles, was a Lichfield man and a scientist, who chose to write up many of his experiments in verse. William Small and William Withering were medical doctors, the latter replacing Small in the group after Small's death in 1775. James Keir was a chemist, whose work on synthetically produced alkali led to a hugely successful business in Tipton. The name of Josiah Wedgwood is familiar enough from the world-famous pottery that bears his name. Thomas Day, as far as his interests went, was on the edge of the Lunar Society, a radical thinker and educational theorist. Such interests were shared by Richard Lovell Edgeworth, but this did not prevent him turning out a series of innovative inventions. Samuel Galton junior was that most rare of creatures, a gunmaking Quaker, and a prosperous Birmingham businessman. John Whitehurst was principally a clock-maker, tied to the 'Lunaticks' by his interest in measurement and in geology.

This is not an exhaustive list, but enough for this brief introduction. Since the Society most frequently met at Matthew Boulton's house in Soho, all have a Birmingham connection. Those that actually lived in the town, or near to it, were Boulton, Watt, Murdock, Small, Withering, Galton and Priestley.

It is important to say at the outset that the Lunar Society probably never had the kind of formal, minuted gatherings that the name might imply. This was an informal circle of men with wide intellectual appetites, meeting occasionally to exchange ideas and demonstrate experiments. Membership, if such a term can be used, was by personal invitation, dependent upon contacts within the group. Given the distance some of the members had to ride to attend, and the difficulty of the roads, travel on or near a night of the full moon was easier, and hence the name 'Lunar'. If the title also implied magical practices, it was not a connection that they shied away from. They happily refer to themselves as 'Lunaticks' or 'conjurers', even if the tongue is playfully in the cheek. The letter from Erasmus Darwin to Boulton that introduced Richard Lovell Edgeworth to the circle exemplifies that fine line between science and magic, even though Darwin is cleverly parodying the contemporary bill-poster:

> I have got with me a mechanical Friend, Mr Edgeworth from Oxfordshire,—The greatest Conjuror I ever saw ... He has ye principles of Nature in his palm, & moulds them as He pleases. Can take away polarity or give it to the Needle by rubbing it thrice on ye palm of his Hand.
>
> And can see through two solid Oak Board without glasses! astonishing! diabolical!!! Pray tell Dr Small He must come to see these Miracles.

Darwin's letters, more than any others, show that mixture of camaraderie, intellectual excitement and fun that must have galvanised (to use an appropriate metaphor) the group. In April 1778 he wrote to Boulton:

> I am sorry the infernal Divinities, who visit mankind with diseases, & are therefore at perpetual war with doctors, should have prevented my seeing all you great men at Soho today—Lord! What inventions, what wit, what rhetoric, metaphysical, mechanical, & pyrotechnical will be on the wing, bandy'd like a shuttlecock from one to another of your troop of philosophers! While poor I, I by myself I, imprizon'd in a post chaise, am joggled, & jostled, & bump'd, & bruised along the King's high road, to make war upon a pox or a fever!

It is not surprising that many letters were addressed to 'Doctor Darwin on the road'!

It was only in 1775 that references in correspondence show that the circle we call the Lunar Society was up and running. But contacts between many of the chief protagonists had long been established. It was in 1765 that William Small went to meet Boulton in Birmingham with a letter of introduction from America's foremost philosopher and political thinker, Benjamin Franklin. Small had spent six years teaching at William & Mary College in Virginia, teaching amongst others Thomas Jefferson, later to be the country's second President. Small's (and Boulton's) contacts with America's leading thinkers were one of many lines of communication between the Lunar members and international thought.

On Boulton's advice, William Small established a medical practice in Birmingham. Sharing a house with John Ash, he was instrumental in the establishment of a general hospital in the town, and in the campaign to license the Theatre Royal. But his central role in the Lunar Society was even more vital. Many of the group's initial contacts were made through Small, as Edgeworth acknowledged in later life:

> By means of Mr Keir I became acquainted with Dr Small of Birmingham, a man esteemed by all who knew him, and by all who were admitted to his friendship beloved with no common enthusiasm. Dr Small formed a link which combined Mr Boulton, Mr Watt, Dr Darwin, Mr Wedgwood, Mr Day and myself together—men of very different character but all devoted to literature and science.

Small's premature death, at the age of 40, came close to breaking up the circle of friends before it had reached its full potential. But his replacement as Boulton's doctor and Ash's new house guest turned out to be a worthy successor in the Lunar Society, too. This was William Withering, a shy and sometimes irritable man, but a scientist of considerable achievements. Withering's interests lay principally in chemistry and metallurgy. But it was his work on botany, and particularly his treatise on the medical uses of the foxglove, for which he is best known.

27. Withering's monument in St Bartholomew's church, Edgbaston. His coffin was carried by six peasants employed at Edgbaston Hall.

There are two ways of dealing with the complex subject of the Lunar Society. One is through the personal contacts and relationships that drew and held the group together; the other is through their shared interests. Although these were men of irrepressible curiosity, ranging across the spectrum of science and the arts, certain subjects attracted especial interest and research. One was the issue of accurate measurement. This was John Whitehurst's link with the group. The Derby clock and instrument maker was in correspondence with Boulton from

1758, the beginning of a long and fruitful acquaintance. Whitehurst designed the first factory time-clocks, those tormenters of the late employee, which Boulton went on to manufacture and sell. In addition, he supplied both decorative clocks to Soho, and drew Boulton's attention to the Derbyshire mineral called blue john which the latter used in vase-making. Whitehurst was also to supply accurate weights and measures when Boulton devoted himself to the thorny topic of assaying precious metals. Often practical work led to more theoretical research: Whitehurst followed up his time-clocks with astronomical ones.

The ability to measure accurately furnace temperatures and metal expansion was of key importance to the industrialists in the group. Josiah Wedgwood, whose interests lay principally in subjects with direct implications for his business, corresponded and researched widely on pyrometry: what were the ideal temperatures for firing clays and glazes of different composition. James Watt too had specialised in instrument making while he still lived in Scotland, and continued to supply Small, Boulton and Darwin with measuring devices into the 1760s. Again necessity was the mother of invention: his surveying work on the Scottish canals necessitated accurate instruments, such as telescopes, micrometers and range-finders. Small continued to be concerned with telescopes and accurate microscopes ('because the present Microscopes deceive their users') right up to his death.

But it was Edgeworth that got to the Royal Society first with his 'perambulator or waywiser', an instrument that looked a giant pair of dividers and could be walked across the country, measuring distances. As he wrote in 1767:

> ... at the hazard of my Life, having then a violent sore throat, I came up to London on purpose and walked with the Perambulator in most exceedingly deep and dirty roads on a wet and cold day. The Tryal answer'd my expectations and satisfied the Committee, who were so good as to resolve unanimously that I deserved the Gold Medal of the Society.

But Edgeworth's trial was not quite at an end: 'Part of the Machine was lost by the Porter of the Society and I find by your Letter that my reward is deferr'd till I get another one made'.

Another subject that concentrated the minds of a number of the members was that of canals. Canals represented the most important break-through in transportation yet, and attracted the attention of any industrialist concerned about the carriage of his goods and the supply of his raw materials. It also represented a shrewd place to invest your surplus capital, and Boulton, Wedgwood, Darwin, Small, Keir, Day and Galton all held shares in the new canal companies. James Watt knew more about them than most: from 1767 to 1773, he had been employed in Scotland on a number of canal schemes. Again, business interests led to research, and Watt's work on improved pump-engines endeared him to many in the Society. Josiah Wedgwood, whose business suffered more than most from overland transportation, was a long campaigner for a canal link between the Trent and the Mersey. In 1766 he triumphantly turned the first sod for the cutting of the Grand Trunk Canal, to which Boulton too was a subscriber. Erasmus Darwin lent his hand with ideological support, and designs for a new kind of canal lock, using wheels and levers to lower the boat. Indeed, it was Darwin who introduced the Birmingham-based men to the subject of canals. In a letter to Boulton from 1766 he exhorted him: 'I desire you and Dr Small will take this Infection, as you have given me ye Infection of Steam-enginry: for it is well worthy your attention,

28. Joseph Priestley (1733-1804) spent 11 eventful years in Birmingham. His scientific research depended upon financial support from fellow Lunaticks.

who are Friends of Mankind, and open your ingenious hearts'.

Those Society members, whose researches and interests were driven by practical problems and their solutions, were admirably counterbalanced by a man like Priestley, who was essentially a careful observer of experiments. His closeness to men like Watt in Birmingham made it an ideal environment in which to compare notes, analyse outcomes and pass on results. His particular strength was in his observation of the reaction of metals to various solutions, and the analysis of the gases given off. Copper in a solution of sal ammoniac turned it blue: this was well known. Priestley examined the air above the liquid, and found that it became 'phlogisticated', that is, deprived of oxygen. In many cases Priestley began an analytical method that would gain in significance later. His work on nitrous oxide (which he called modified nitrous air) included exposing a mouse to it. Later work by Humphrey Davy led to the use of nitrous oxide, known as 'laughing gas', as an anaesthetic in dentistry.

Priestley's difficulty, and ours in fully appreciating his research, is the received concepts and vocabulary from which he started. He was himself aware of 'the force of prejudice, which, unknown to ourselves, biases not only our judgements, properly so called, but even the perceptions of our senses'. Nothing better shows this than the long survival of the concept of 'phlogiston' in his mind. To Priestley and his predecessors phlogiston was that substance released during burning and calcination, akin to light, heat and electricity. It would be some years after Priestley that its existence was finally disproved. He provided the experiments and the evidence, but was unable to make the final conceptual leap. To him the 'air' that was produced from heating mercury, in which a candle burned more brightly than in ordinary air, was air lacking phlogiston or 'dephlogisticated air'. To us it is oxygen. After various tests and experiments, he bit the bullet and breathed it himself:

> The feeling of it to my lungs was not sensibly different from that of common air; but I fancied that my breast felt peculiarly light and easy for some time afterwards. Who can tell but that, in time, this pure air may become a fashionable article in luxury. Hitherto only two mice and myself have had the privilege of breathing it.

During the 1780s at Fair Hill, Priestley was engaged on the separation and analysis of 'different kinds of inflammable air' (air that lacked phlogiston). He isolated inflammable air (hydrogen), combined fixed air (carbon monoxide), and sulphurated inflammable air (hydrogen sulphide), and was able to distinguish them by the different way they burned and by the variation in specific gravity. On the steep mountain of science, these were important foot-hills to climb, but his work on iron, combining it and burning it in different atmospheres, was also providing data that was highly relevant to the 18th-century industrialist.

Reading the letters and pamphlets of the Lunar members, it is often their nomenclature and vocabulary that distances them from us. When Darwin wrote to Boulton, 'As I was riding Home yesterday, I consid'd the Scheme of ye fiery Chariot', it is not easy to accept that here were practical considerations of the applicability of steam-power to transport. It would be another generation of French scientists who would convert the Lunar concepts into modern terminology. Indeed, James Keir was teased for his trendy adoption of the word 'gases', instead of 'airs', in his *Dictionary of Chemistry*. As Priestley said: 'I consider Mr Keir as a very able chymist, and useful writer, but I cannot help smiling at his new phraseology ...'.

Another alienating, though highly entertaining, factor was in their wilder flights of inventive imagination. Erasmus Darwin, in his *Botanic Garden*, written entirely in verse, saw no end to the achievements of steam-driven motion:

> Soon shall thy arm, Unconquer'd Steam! afar
> Drag the slow barge, or drive the rapid car;
> Or on wide-waving wings expanded bear
> The flying-chariot through the fields of air.

Darwin too made impressive, but ultimately fruitless, progress on a 'speaking-machine', the lips of which were driven by bellows. Edgeworth found the device extremely convincing, as he told the inventor in 1798: 'I placed one of your mouths in a room near some people in 1770, who actually thought I had a child with me, calling mama and papa'. And in 1798 the more sceptical Boulton drew up a contract (witnessed by Small and Keir) with him. But even here a shrewd business mind was at work:

> I promise to pay to Dr Darwin of Lichfield, one thousand pounds upon his delivering to me (within two years from date hereof) an instrument called an organ that is capable of pronouncing the Lord's Prayer, the Creed, the Ten Commandments in the vulgar tongue, and his ceding to me, and me only, the property of said invention with all the advantages thereunto appertaining.

Sadly, as with many of Dr. Darwin's ideas, he became distracted by another one before he had perfected the earlier.

But by no means did Darwin have the monopoly on crazy ideas. William Small, working on the assumption that ice would eventually cover the whole of Europe, came up with a 'project for producing perpetual summer' in 1773. This involved blowing up icebergs and floating them into the tropics to convert them into a temperate climate. Again Darwin was on hand to convert the idea into sympathetic poetry:

> While swarthy nations crowd the sultry coast,
> Drink the fresh breeze, and hail the floating Frost.

Perhaps the most striking example of the triumph of the theoretical over the practical was Edgeworth's decision to raise his son in strict accordance with Rousseau's educational principles, that is, in the surrender of discipline to 'natural' development. The boy grew up to be totally unmanageable and, more embarrassingly, Rousseau himself did not take to him.

Edgeworth's friend, Thomas Day, was simultaneously working on his own piece of social engineering. In his search for the perfect wife, Day had decided to train two girls that he took from a foundling-home. By educating them himself, far from the distractions of polite society, he would produce the perfect companion (and a spare). Having dropped one girl after an unsuccessful spell in France, he settled in Lichfield, clearly as far from polite society as he could get. But after all the attention he had lavished on his pupil, he still found the results disappointing. He scrapped the idea and apprenticed her to a milliner. So much for theory.

It seems churlish to leave this extraordinary group of men on such a defeatist note, and we will not, for the next chapter concerns Boulton, Watt and Murdock, the most successful partnership of the Lunar Society and of the Industrial Revolution.

Chapter Ten

The Golden Boys

Outside Birmingham's Register Office stands a sculptural conversation-piece. Three men in 18th-century dress appear to be discussing how to put up a deck-chair. Locally, the three gilded figures are known as the 'Golden Boys'. The piece was unveiled in 1956 and is the work of William Bloye, one of the city's most famous sculptors. It is Birmingham's tribute to three of its most influential names. But it is not the only place in Birmingham that the three men can be seen together. Facing each other across the chancel of Handsworth parish church, Matthew Boulton looks across to William Murdock. And in a small chapel near them sits James Watt. This is St Mary's church, but it has been dubbed with some justification 'the Westminster Abbey of the Industrial Revolution'.

Only one of the three was Birmingham-born, and we should begin with him. Matthew Boulton was born in 1728, the son of a toy manufacturer on Snow Hill. Unlike many of his future Lunar friends, Matthew did not receive a university education. A small private school in Deritend was his only formal education, after which he was quickly involved in his father's toy-making business. After the death of Matthew Boulton senior in 1759, his son took over.

Toy-making was one of Birmingham's most populous and influential trades, of which buckle and button-making were the largest single parts. In 1760 Boulton appeared before a House of Commons Committee to describe the process of buckle-making in the town. He estimated that over 8,000 were employed in the trade,

29.   Matthew Boulton (1728-1809), one of the pioneers of the Industrial Revolution. Josiah Wedgwood called him 'the principal manufacturer in England in metal'.

generating business worth £300,000, the majority of it for export. But there was far more to toys than buckles and buttons. A contemporary description of the products from *Sketchley's Directory* of 1767 show that it was capable of almost infinite variety:

> ... We shall here observe that these Artists are divided into several Branches as the Gold and Silver Toy Makers, who make Trinkets, Seals, Tweezer and Tooth Pick Cases, Smelling Bottles, Snuff Boxes, and Filegree Work, such as Toilets, Tea Chests, Inkstands &c &c. The Tortoiseshell Toy maker, makes a beautiful variety of the above and other Articles; as does also the Steel; who make Cork Screws, Buckles, Draw and other Boxes; Snuffers, Watch Chains, Stay Hooks, Sugar Knippers &c. and almost all these are likewise made in various metals.

Now there is ample evidence to show that Matthew Boulton was shrewd enough an operator to have made a considerable living in the toy line. Equally there is evidence that Boulton's business, particularly when he was expanding it (and he always was) was a high risk undertaking, and he sailed close to the rocks of bankruptcy on a number of occasions. But there's also no doubt that two marriages helped him along financially. Luke Robinson, an 'opulent mercer' of Lichfield had two daughters, Mary and Anne, each worth about £14,000, and Matthew married both of them. The first died just about the time that Matthew was inheriting his father's firm, after which (not without much agonising) he married the younger sister.

We can divide Boulton's career (he would have enjoyed the classical allusion) into three parts: his management of his father's business, his partnership with John Fothergill, and the partnership with James Watt. Roughly speaking, these coincide with three business premises: Snow Hill, the Soho Manufactory and Soho Foundry. But all three phases are characterised by the same Boulton industrial traits: expansion and diversification of products, increasing mechanisation and the creation of lucrative markets in Europe and among the rich.

When Boulton had appeared before the Commons Committee in 1760, he had stressed the importance of the European market to the Birmingham buckle trade. In 1761 he found in John Fothergill a partner with a wide experience of Europe and its markets, and one who was prepared to spend many months (as he did in 1766) travelling on the Continent and setting up trade links. But Boulton himself did much to improve contacts on a personal level, one gentleman entertaining others, as it were. In 1767 he wrote: '... each week brings forth new and unexpected engagements. I had Lords and Ladys to wait on yesterday. I have French men and Spaniards today, and the day after Germans, Russians, Norwegians ...'.

Boulton was astute to foster links that would subsequently spread his reputation and those of his wares beyond the first point of contact. Ambassadors in particular were entertained as a key link in a diplomatic chain reaction. He corresponded with Count Woronzow, the Russian ambassador, as well as English representatives in the courts of Europe, such as the ambassador to the Court of Naples, William Hamilton, or Sir Robert Keith, Envoy to the Court of Vienna. In one week in October 1772, he claimed to have entertained French, Danish, Sardinian and Dutch ambassadors.

From ambassadors it is but a small step upwards to the courts themselves. Visitors' books show Boulton conducting tours of his factory for Catherine the Great's favourite, Count Orloff, as well as Count Poniatowski, the King of Poland's nephew and many others. There were equally important contacts with the Hanoverian court at home. As early as 1759, the young Matthew and his brother presented an inlaid sword to the Prince of Wales, the future George III, and in 1770 Boulton visited the King and Queen himself. Forty years later, when the great manufacturer was in his final illness, George proposed to visit him 'in his sick chamber'.

Much of this would not have been possible had not Boulton moved markedly upward on the social scale. In 1761, about the same time that the partnership with Fothergill was formed, Boulton made the decision to relocate his business. The prerequisites of the new site were that it had to have a water mill, and remained close to Birmingham. He found it on Handsworth Heath, about a mile and a half from town. Local legend had it that the place was called 'Soho' after a hunting-cry often heard on the Heath. The current occupant, Edward Ruston, had already done some of the ground-work for him, diverting the Hockley Brook and forming a pool to power a mill for rolling steel, and building a house no more than 150 yards from the mill. Boulton took on Ruston's lease for £1,000 and began his improvements.

As a memorandum drawn up by Boulton explains, he found it necessary to rebuild the mill entirely to enable it to generate the necessary power for his great manufactory, which now began to take shape. The house too needed substantial work:

> ... & did accordingly expend a larg sum same year in finishing ye House within (which before was almost bare walls) & in makeing a new Kitchin Garden building planting above 2000 Firs & a great variety of Shrubs which in ye whole amounted to about 500 additional expence to ye House ...

As his subsequent partner, James Watt, put it, he turned 'a barren heath into a delight-ful garden'. It has to be said that this was achieved without much help from John Fothergill, who occupied the house before Boulton finally moved there. As Boulton irritably noted, the garden had 'not received ye assistance of one Load of Muck since F's residence'.

Improvements to Soho House and its land were to occupy Boulton for many a year. The house that stands there today is principally the result of Samuel Wyatt's reconstruction in 1789. This is a combination of Georgian classicism with whatever new technology could offer in the way of additional comforts: a central heating system, gas-lighting, and window frames made from a new alloy of copper, zinc and iron, and manufactured by James Keir at Tipton. Much has happened to the old place since Boulton left it for more heavenly rewards. A private school, a residential hotel and a police hostel are just three of its subsequent lives, together with (reputedly) the occasional spectral appearance by old Mrs. Boulton herself. Safe at last in the arms of the City Council, it is now a museum of the Industrial Revolution and of Handsworth, the centrepiece of which is room that witnessed the many meetings of the Lunar Society.

There is no doubt that entertaining nobility became a lot deal easier once Soho House was up and running. A steady stream (more steady than Hockley Brook) of visitors passed through it, as Boulton pointed out to Fothergill: '... his house at Soho for many years seemd like an Inn for the entertainment of Strangers'.

From this reputation stems the (slightly pretentious) Lunar nickname of the house: 'L'hotel de l'amitié sur Handsworth Heath'.

As for the manufactory itself, considerable time and expense went into creating arguably the most famous factory in the world. *Swinney's Birmingham Directory* describes it thus:

The building consists of four Squares, with Shops, Warehouses, &c., for a Thousand Workmen, who, in a great variety of Branches, excel in their several Departments; not only in the fabrication of Buttons, Buckles, Boxes, Trinkets, &c., in Gold, Silver, and a variety of Compositions; but in many other Arts, long predominant in France.

The latter included ormolu, or 'or moulu', a technique of gilding on brass with a mixture of ground gold and mercury which the French had monopolised until Boulton, not without a spot of industrial espionage, broke into the market. Ultimately though, ormolu was to be an artistic success, but a trading failure; the process did not lend itself to the techniques of mass-production in which Boulton and Fothergill specialised. Nevertheless, luxury items like this were an important means of spreading the fame of Soho across Europe.

But the Soho works was far more than a factory. The three-storey building included show-rooms, an important part of the visitor's itinerary, and accommodation for workers on the top floor. Since the works had been located on a green field site, this was the only practical way of ensuring a localised work-force. In a town that had specialised in small workshops, Soho dwarfed comparison, except with John Taylor's button-works, mentioned earlier. At its height the number of workers was close to a thousand. But it was not one

30.   Soho Manufactory on Handsworth Heath was completed in 1765. It was Birmingham's principal tourist attraction in the 18th century.

of those Satanic mills that characterised the cotton industry further north. Under one Soho roof existed a group of workshops, ploying the highly skilled industries common in Birmingham, but on a huge scale.

Matthew Boulton's break-through was to apply the techniques of mass-production to the artistic end of the market. In this he had close affinities with Wedgwood at Burslem. As he explained to the Earl of Warwick in 1770:

> It is from the extream cheapness that we are enabled to send them to every corner of Europe altho' in many places they have as good and as cheap Materials as we have, and have Labour Cent per Cent cheaper and yet nevertheless by the Super activity of our people and by the many mechanical contrivances, and extensive apparatus wich we are possess'd of, our men are enabled to do from twice to ten times the Work that can be done without the help of such Contrivances, and even Women and children to do more than Men can do without them ...

Even Erasmus Darwin, no stranger to mechanical contrivances, found the number of different tools 'prodigious': 'And the mechanic inventions for this purpose are superior in multitude, variety and simplicity to those of any manufactory in the known world'.

Boulton's conduct of labour relations was similarly ahead of its time. Workshop committees were established to control behaviour in the factory, with the authority to levy fines of one shilling for swearing and such like. The owner was also personally involved in the training and management of his work-force, as he explained in 1770:

> I have traind up many and am training up more young Country Lads, all of which that betray any genius are taught to draw, from which I derive many advantages that are not to be found in any manufacture that is or can be established in a great and Debauched Capital.

Perhaps most original of all was the establishment of the Soho Insurance Society. Each (male) employee made a contribution of between a halfpenny and fourpence per week, depending on income, into the 'treasure box' managed by six elders and a committee. The fund could then pay out sickness benefit if the contributor was unable to work. Funeral benefits of up to £5 were also payable, again dependent on income. But as the Rules of the Society make clear: '... if any one be found drinking at an ale house during the time he is on the box, he shall no longer be deemed worthy of pay ...'.

Despite the workshop committees, discipline at the Manufactory was not easy to enforce. St Monday, the tradition of absenteeism on the first day of the week, was still being observed, both at Soho and in Birmingham generally, until well into the Victorian era. Indeed, the Children's Employment Commission of 1862 found that at one factory in the town (not unrepresentative) almost a quarter of the work-force were absent on Mondays. Alcohol too made it difficult for Boulton to create the working conditions he wanted: 'Our forging shop wants a total reformation; it is worse than ever. Peploe has been drunk ever since his wife's death almost. Jim Taylor has been drunk for nine days past'.

With the concentration on highly skilled craftsmanship, it was important that Soho was well lit. The place was whitewashed regularly, improving both the light and hygiene, and became the first factory to be lit by gas. The first public display of the new lighting came in 1802 when the outside of the Manufactory was illuminated to celebrate the Peace of Amiens. In fact the last products to be made in the place were gas-fittings, until in 1863 the factory was demolished and replaced by a housing estate.

The size of Soho and the numbers of employees gave Boulton the flexibility he needed to expand his range of products and explore new avenues. In the early 1760s, for example, he took up the manufacture of articles of Sheffield plate, the only company outside the town that gave the process its name to do so. This involved the fusing of a thin veneer of silver onto a copper base, and was used for the manufacture of table-ware items, candelabra and trays. From this he moved on to silver plate, the same designs being applicable to both.

But there was a serious hindrance to the manufacture of solid silver in Birmingham, and it was a problem that Boulton met with characteristic energy. Objects of solid silver had to be assayed and hall-marked, and the despatch and return of items from the nearest Assay Office at Chester involved a round trip of 150 miles. Further away still were the offices at Bristol, York and London. This lengthy process not only delayed orders but also risked costly damage in transit, as well as theft. It was an issue not dissimilar to the battle being fought by the Birmingham gun-makers over the need for a local proof-house.

In 1771, after discovering that a set of candlesticks had returned from Chester in a damaged state, Boulton wrote with irritation: '... altho' I am very desirous of becoming a great Silversmith, yet I am determined never to take up that branch in the Large Way I intended unless powers can be obtained to have a Marketing Hall at Birmingham'.

Of course, Boulton and his Birmingham colleagues were not alone in complaining of this unnecessary impediment to free trade; the Sheffield silversmiths shared the same disadvantages. Accordingly, in February 1773, two petitions were presented to the Commons for bills to establish Assay Offices in Birmingham and Sheffield. There followed the familiar rounds of lobbying, and counter-lobbying by the London gold and silversmiths, pleading 'their shabby case', as Boulton partially described it. But success followed more quickly than it did with gunsmiths, and the bill received royal assent in March 1773. The story of how each town decided on their hall-marks has not yet been disproved. It is said that the *Crown and Anchor* in the Strand, a favourite resort for those engaged on Parliamentary business, suggested the two symbols: the anchor for Birmingham and the crown for Sheffield. The right to assay gold articles followed later.

Ironically, most of the other Assay Offices, including Chester, have now gone, but that in Birmingham still survives in Newhall Street. A Board of Guardians, only a proportion of whom may be drawn from the trade, supervises its activities. The present building opened in 1877, considerably grander than the earliest offices. Initially rooms were rented at the *King's Head Inn* in New Street, and the office was open for business on one day a week only. That first day must have been a busy one: Boulton and Fothergill alone sent 841 ounces of silver to be assayed.

At the time that the Assay Office opened its doors, and Boulton's silver poured in, Birmingham's principal manufacturer had reached his 55th year. The Manufactory at Soho was producing Sheffield and silver plate, ormolu ware, mechanical paintings, toys, medals, clocks and decorative ornaments, all done in the best possible taste and based on the best possible classical and renaissance models.

But these were still early days in an eventful life. North of the border, a man eight years his junior was having money troubles. The invention that could make his fortune was still on paper, the patent running out, and his backer in Kinneil was in financial difficulties. A promising career seemed to be running out of steam, as it were. But James Watt was about to meet Matthew Boulton, and life at Soho (and indeed the rest of the world) would never be quite the same again.

Chapter Eleven

Steam Power for the World

No aspect of Birmingham's history has received so much attention as the famous partnership of Matthew Boulton and James Watt. It is as much a chapter in the history of science and engineering as an episode in the development of Birmingham. We cannot go far without a word or two about the steam-engine that Watt inherited, improved and sold to the world.

As man went down the mines in search of coal or ore, he met the water table coming up. The difficulty of keeping a mine free of water in order to extract the minerals increased the deeper you went. The 'fire engine' that the Devonian, Thomas Newcomen, invented was designed to pump water out of the mine to allow mining to continue. Let us try to understand it. The trick was not so much the steam it produced as the atmosphere around, which, as we all remember, 'abhors a vacuum'. Now, if water is boiled and the steam is introduced into a cylinder and then condensed (by a jet of cold water), a vacuum is produced. Attach a piston to the top of the cylinder and atmospheric pressure sends it crashing down whenever the vacuum is created. Add a beam to the piston and as the one end is sucked downwards, the other end lifts up. Then a weight pulls it back down again. Alternate steaming and condensing keeps the piston and the beam pumping up and down.

This was Newcomen's 'atmospheric engine': simple, effective, but very costly on fuel. Once the next generation of engineers (men like John Smeaton) began to measure the amount of fuel necessary to create the steam to create the vacuum, it began to look less than efficient. In fact, most of the coal that the Newcomen engine was allowing to be mined was being used to power the Newcomen engine. Not an ideal arrangement. The problem lay in the condensing. No sooner was the water and cylinder heated to boiling point than it was cooled again by the cold water jet, and the heating had to start all over again. In addition, Dr. Joseph Black of Glasgow University had 'discovered' the problem of latent heat: that whenever water changes its state to ice or steam or back, a considerable amount of energy is lost. On both counts it seemed that the Newcomen engine might be improved.

Enter James Watt, a former pupil of Black's at Glasgow, and the separate condenser. Watt recognised (in May 1765, as he tells us) that if a separate chamber could be attached to the cylinder, and the steam was condensed here instead, then it would no longer be necessary to cool and re-heat the cylinder and piston on every stroke. Additionally the new chamber could return the condensed steam as warm water to the boiler, thus saving energy in the boiling process. It was this 'new method of lessening the consumption of steam and fuel in fire engines' that Watt patented in 1769. The patent was for 14 years.

31. The romantic, and entirely un-historical version, of Watt's discovery of steam-power. Watt claimed that the idea first came to him on Glasgow Green.

By the time Watt was drafting his patent he was receiving advice and encouragement from William Small and Matthew Boulton in Birmingham. The local connection was James Roebuck, a Birmingham doctor and friend of Boulton's, who was involved in iron manufacture near Stirling. Roebuck's iron-works needed coal, and his coal-mine at Bo'ness needed a better pumping engine. Watt, in return, needed cash. It was one thing to devise a theoretical model; quite another to procure the equipment to test it accurately.

It was on 7 February 1769 that Boulton made his first serious approach to Watt to set up a steam-engine partnership. Boulton used the fact of the Scotsman's recent parenthood to adopt a peculiarly appropriate metaphor: 'What led me to drop the hint I did to you was the possessing an idea that you wanted a midwife to ease you of your burthen, and to introduce your brat into the world'. Earlier in the same letter Boulton had written: '... my idea was to settle a manufactury near to my own by the side of the canal where I would erect all the conveniences necessary for the completion of engines, and from which manufactury we would serve all the world with engines of all sizes'.

Yet the midwife and the mother of inventions might not have come together but for a sad combination of circumstances. In 1773 Roebuck found himself in financial difficulties and no longer able to bear the costs of Watt's experiments. The latter had watched the first six years of his patent disappear without substantial progress. Reduced to canal survey work to support his family, Watt learnt in September that his wife had died in childbirth. The attractions of a new life, either in England or overseas, began to exert their traditional appeal on a wandering Scot. In November he wrote: 'I am heartsick of this country; I am indolent to excess, and, what alarms me most, I grow the longer the stupider ...'. On 17 May 1774 he set out for Birmingham. The engine he had been working on for Roebuck had been moved south and was waiting for him already.

The first problem to be faced, along with the continuation of tests on the engine from Bo'ness, was that of the patent. Unless this could be extended, it was unlikely that there was time for either of them to make their fortunes before it ran out. With Boulton's advice, who was an adept in the intricate art of parliamentary lobbying, Watt successfully negotiated a Private Act to extend the patent to the end of the century. The official partnership of Boulton and Watt was to run coterminous with the Act, beginning on 1 June 1775. For Boulton it was yet another partnership in his perennially expanding conglomerate.

Progress was swift. By early 1776 two of the new Watt engines had been sold and erected; one for a blast-furnace at Broseley, the other for Bloomfield Colliery near Tipton. Initially the new partnership was involved only in the design and supervision of the engines. The parts were made elsewhere and assembled on site, a premium being charged for the company based on the fuel saved by the new technique.

By the time the trade in 'reciprocating' engines was up and running, Watt had already turned his attention to a new issue: that of a 'rotative' engine to produce continuous circular motion. The reciprocating engine (moving up and down) had only very limited uses, mostly in pumping. The clamour for a rotating engine had long been growing louder. In 1781 Boulton wrote to his partner: '... the people in London, Manchester and Birmingham are steam mill mad ... I don't mean to hurry you but I think that in the course of a month or two we should determine to take out a patent for certain methods of producing rotative motion'.

Watt did not have far to look for an example. In 1779 a button-maker on Snow Hill called James Pickard had fitted a crank and fly-wheel to his Newcomen engine to drive a mill. The mill was initially employed to grind metals, but was later adapted as a flour mill.

Mention of Pickard's Mill affords us a temporary break from the rigours of cranks, flywheels and rotative motion, for in 1795 it became the centre of one of Birmingham's more notorious incidents. By the middle of that year the effects of war with France were having a devastating impact on the Birmingham economy. This, coupled with a severe winter and poor harvest the previous year, was producing a desperate situation. As the *Gazette* of 29 June recorded:

> The great scarcity of grain which is experienced throughout Europe (but in no country so little as our own), has considerably advanced its price, and of course neither the same quantity of flour, nor the same weight of bread, can be afforded for the like money, as in more abundant times.

This was the *Gazette*'s explanation; others suggested that some traders were using scarcity as an excuse to bump up their prices. Rumours that Pickard was hoarding grain and putting up his prices artificially were enough to provoke a reaction in the town. A mob, predominantly of women, made an assault on the mill, only to be driven off by a rapidly assembled troop of dragoons from the Barracks. This was but four years after the 1791

Riots and the forces of law and order were now better prepared for outbreaks of violence.

However, it was a sign of the mob's desperation that, unlike the events of '91, they did not melt away on the first appearance of the military. During a second attack on the mill the troops opened fire and two rioters (both men) were killed, both (according to the *Gazette*) shot by the same bullet. The Coroner returned a verdict of justifiable homicide. Two women and one man were sent to trial at Warwick as chief perpetrators of the violence.

But feelings that run this high are rarely dissipated by a volley of gun-fire. As the economic crisis continued, any baker suggesting an alternative diet of cake was likely to see his windows broken. In the late summer of 1800 more disturbances climaxed with another assault on Pickard's Mill. The redoubtable Mr. Pickard and his workers, unwilling to wait for military intervention this time, took the law and the rifles into their own hands. One rioter died in the incident.

It would seem that if the steam-engine that Pickard had adapted was successful, it was hardly having a beneficial effect on prices. Nevertheless, the invention was a step forward, even if (as is suggested) it only worked irregularly. The move towards rotative power, and the vastly increased range of uses that such an engine could incorporate, was underway.

Two years later Watt put his cards on the table and applied for a new patent. It specified 'Certain new methods of applying the vibrating or reciprocating motion of Steam or fire engines to produce a continued rotative or circular motion round an axis or centre, and thereby to give motion to the wheels of mills or other machines'. In fact, Watt itemised five different methods, most famous of which was that of two linked cogwheels, known as 'sun and planet' gear, and by the end of 1782 a sun-and-planet engine was in operation at Soho.

As with the early reciprocal engines, Boulton's business sense demanded that the new engine be used in a project that attracted maximum publicity. The site chosen could hardly have been more prominent: on the south bank of the Thames at Blackfriars Bridge was Albion Mills, the largest flour mill in the country. Here, between 1786 and 1789 two engines were erected and, after qite literal teething problems, they worked successfully. Boulton estimated that for each bushel of coal consumed, 11 bushels of wheat were ground, though he felt that these figures could be improved upon. In addition, the engines could be used for hoisting wheat and flour to and from the barges in the river below. The new factory became one of the wonders of London, and by June 1790 the sales of flour from the Mill amounted to £6,900.

But the story was to end badly. At about the time that James Pickard's mill in Snow Hill felt the fury of the mob, Albion Mills were destroyed by fire. The suggestion that it was arson was probably not unfounded, though it was never proved. Certainly these were dangerous days for millers, even though the smaller operators in London were equally pleased to see their mighty rival reduced to ashes.

1791 had not been a good year. Not only had Boulton watched the end of the Albion Mills project and many of his friends driven from town by the Birmingham Riots, he had also faced his first serious industrial dispute at Soho.

But what of the third member of that conversation-piece on Broad Street? William Murdock had left his native Scotland for Birmingham in 1777, and was chiefly employed in the supervision of engine erection in Cornwall. Here was a county, with its tin and copper mines, crying out for reciprocating engines. Boulton in turn needed an increasing supply of copper for his Soho Mint. Such was Boulton and Watt's investment in the area that Murdock spent many years resident there, 'flying from mine to mine'. But Murdock was also aware, probably before his employers, of the potential impact of the rotative engine, not only for mill work, but as a form of transport, too.

Early in the 1780s (the exact dates are disputed) Murdock built a tiny model of his steam-carriage. It is reputed to have run around Murdock's living room in Redruth in 1784. Other stories tell of a larger scale-model that zig-zagged along the lanes of Redruth and frightened the local pastor who 'took it to be the Evil One'. Quite why Murdock decided not to patent his invention is uncertain, but it does appear that Watt felt threatened by his employee's creativity and Boulton did not encourage his work either. Had they done so, the advances made by Stephenson's Rocket in 1829 might well have been made 30 years earlier.

As it was, William Murdock has

32. William Murdock (1754-1839), pioneer of gas-lighting and steam-driven transport. His revolutionary compressed-air doorbell was adopted by Sir Walter Scott for Abbotsford.

to be content with just the one mould-breaking invention: gas-lighting. By around 1795 Murdock was experimenting on coal-gas down in Redruth, using a retort and copper and iron tubes. By passing the gas through water he was able to clean it of impurities. But it was after his return to Soho in 1798 that the experiments became public. As Murdock himself describes, he:

> constructed an apparatus upon a large scale, which during many successive nights was applied to the lighting of their principal building, and various new methods were practised, of washing and purifying the gas. These experiments were continued with some interruptions, until the peace of 1802, when a public display of this light was made by me in the illumination of Mr. Boulton's manufactory at Soho, upon that occasion.

It has been estimated that by 1800 Boulton and Watt had erected around 450 steam-engines. Initially, as has been said, the company were involved little in the manufacturing process. In stages Boulton was to change all this. First (in 1781) he erected a two-storey engine-shop to manufacture some of the smaller engine parts. By the mid-1790s this was employing about 50 men. Then, in 1795, land was purchased a mile away from the manufactory to build the engines themselves. With the patent rapidly expiring, it was essential for the company to move into manufacturing proper, since Watt's engine drawings would soon not be worth the paper they were designed upon. In fact it was yet another new company that controlled the foundry: Boulton, Watt and Sons, for another Matthew Boulton and another James Watt were ready to carry on their fathers' work.

The foundry opened in 1796 with a celebratory dinner for the workmen. One of the guests noted that everything from cutlery and mustard pots to tablecloths and drinking cups were kept as 'souvenirs'. Within three years the new factory, sited on the Birmingham Canal, had turned out 43 engines.

Matthew Boulton, meanwhile, had moved on to another project. Access to an unlimited supply of rotary engines permitted him to move into the minting business, where the new steam-operated presses could produce coins of much higher quality than currently available. Initially the presses did contract work for companies like the East India Co. and foreign governments, medallions and trade tokens. In 1797 he broke into the home market, helping out the over-burdened Royal Mint with issues of pennies and two-penny pieces. Later, having perfected the minting equipment, he was able to sell it abroad.

By the end of the century, the old partners seemed to be drifting apart to their own individual projects. James Watt, the earlier mid-life crises forgotten, began to settle into a comfortable semi-retirement. He had married again, and moved to a 'moderate' house at Harper's Hill in the Jewellery Quarter. A snapshot of the Watts' life in 1790 is provided by Mary Anne Galton, a frequent visitor:

> ... there Mr. and Mrs. Watt resided with a very simple establishment of two maids and a man-servant, all brought up under their own eye, and trained by Mrs. Watt in the thrifty and far-seeing habits of the most enlightened Scotch housewifery; besides which they had two little pug-dogs, which were likewise taught by Mrs. Watt never to cross the unsullied flags of the hall without wiping their feet on the mats, placed at every door of entrance ... The mental fatigue of Mr. Watt at this period was often so great, that I have heard he required from nine to eleven hours' sleep to recruit his powers, and his evenings were uniformly spent in some light amusing reading.

But by this date the family were already planning a move up the social ladder to the 'handsome mansion' called Heathfield in Handsworth. This was to be Watt's 'Soho House', designed by the same architect, Samuel Wyatt, who had transformed Boulton's residence. And like his partner, Watt began to buy up surrounding land to create the small country estate of woods and kitchen garden and orchard to live out the life of a gentleman. The addition of a workshop-garret and forge showed that retirement was not the only thing on his mind.

James Watt is necessarily remembered for the advances he made in the design of steam-engines, but another invention had an enormous impact on commercial life both at Soho and elsewhere. This was his press-copier, which he patented in 1780 and marketed under the company name James Watt & Co. The method was similar to that of transfer printing, and a reverse copy of a document could be transferred onto thin paper. By turning the copy over the document could be read through the paper. James Keir, a fellow member of the Lunar Society and business associate, was able to offer advice on the composition of the ink. The process revolutionised office work at Soho in the essential and time-consuming copying of correspondence and engine drawings. Thousands of these copies are preserved in the Boulton and Watt Archive in Birmingham Central Library (Archives Division).

The successful development of this invention was not Watt's last word on the business of copying. Towards the end of his life or, as he described it, 'the production of a young artist entering upon his eightieth year', Watt spent considerable time on the creation of a sculpture copying machine. A rapidly revolving cutting tool was connected by a series of bars to a feeler that advanced slowly over the sculpture, usually a bust, to be copied. The device is recalled in a monument to Watt erected in the street named after him outside the Queen Elizabeth II Law Courts. The piece, one of the city's more popular public artworks, is nicknamed 'the Wattilisk'.

The machine was still in place and in progress in Watt's garret when the inventor died at Heathfield in 1819. Sadly for Birmingham's heritage, the house at Heathfield was demolished in 1927, though the garret has been reconstructed in the Science Museum in South Kensington. The same year also saw the demolition of William Murdock's house on Sycamore Hill in Handsworth. Here Murdock had moved in 1817, installing gas-lighting, central heating and a doorbell that ran on air pressure.

The decline of the Boulton and Watt companies was long and slow. After the retirement of the two senior partners, the firm seemed to lose its instinctive ability to run with a good idea. Crucially they missed the opportunity to corner the market in gas street-lighting, though they continued to lead the world in engines for steam-boats. The first orders were for two Clyde steamers in 1813, and over the next 12 years the firm produced engines for around fifty vessels. In 1857-8 the Foundry manufactured the screw engines for the *Great Eastern*, the largest steam-ship of its day.

Of Matthew Boulton's great manufactory, there is little left to tell. It was closed after the death of James Watt Junior in 1848 and the buildings knocked down a few years later. The foundry continued to operate until 1896, when it was occupied by W. & T. Avery Ltd. This was, however, no precipitous decline for a famous site: Avery's rose to become the world's largest manufacturers of weighing machines, but they had little further use for steam-engines. All that now remains of Boulton's original site is the row of workers cottages, called Foundry Row. William Murdock lived for six years at no. 13, before moving to Sycamore House.

So ends the tale of Boulton, Watt and Murdock, three men who above all others put Birmingham on the international map. Murdock was buried beside his former employers in Handsworth Church in 1839, 20 years after Watt and 30 after Boulton. As for the town itself, it was just beginning to get up a full head of steam.

Chapter Twelve

Cleansing, Paving, Lighting

It does not seem long since John Leland was riding down what he considered the one street of the town. But it was 250 years ago, and Birmingham was growing apace. In 1785-6 a new survey of the place was undertaken, by which it was calculated that the town contained 53,735 persons, living in 9,773 dwelling-houses (exclusive of Deritend and the Foreign). There were 173 streets, a considerable proportion of which were new. One of the new streets that would not have been included was Moseley Street, being in the hamlet of Deritend. Here on the town's rural fringe there opened in 1787 the *Apollo Hotel*, bowling-green and gardens sweeping down to the bank of the river Rea and 'peculiarly adapted for Public and Musical Entertainment'. As the advert in the *Gazette* announced, 'The Place is in an improving state and increasing neighbourhood'.

But in spite of its increasing size, Birmingham shared with many other towns problems of a lack of control and government. The mixture of medieval corporations, manorial courts, parish vestries and public meetings that decided policy was hardly the way to run a local government. The town had become a complex machine of conflicting demands and interests, and needed a little professionalism in oiling the parts. The problems were the lighting and planning of streets, pollution of the streets and the air, rising crime and bad housing. The solution, as many towns saw it, was a local Act of Parliament, empowering a group of officials to meet and decide policy. They were known as Improvement or Street Commissioners.

For almost a hundred years, from 1769 to 1851, it was the Street Commissioners who ran the town of Birmingham, until their role was usurped by the new town council. In fact, they were no less amateurs than the authorities they succeeded (50 were chosen from the citizens according to a property qualification), but by virtue of a series of parliamentary bills their powers were far greater.

It was in April 1769 that 'A Bill for Laying Open and Widening certain Ways and Passages within the Town of Birmingham; and for Cleansing and Lighting the Streets, Lanes, Ways, and Passages there; and for Removing and preventing Nuisances and Obstructions therein' received Royal Assent. We might almost call it the Drainpipe Bill, for it included the specification that:

> ... all Spouts and Gutters belonging to, and conveying Water from, the Tops of Houses, &c., shall, within nine Calender Months, after the Passing of the Act, be removed, and the water conveyed by Pipes down by the Sides or Fronts of such Houses, &c., to be done at the Expence of the Landlords.

33.   Looking south from the tower of St Philip's, the 1850s skyline is a mixture of church spires and chimneys. Beside the Town Hall stands the circular building known as the Panorama, used for the display of huge, panoramic paintings.

There had been little opposition to the bill in the Commons, but a considerable amount in the town. An opinion poll, perhaps the first to be carried out in Birmingham, revealed figures of almost six to one against the bill, though the nature of the question posed cast some doubts on the reliability of the verdict. Roughly speaking, the question had been: Is anything worth a new rate of eight pence in the pound? And the instinctive answer, of course, was no. Many property owners (including William Hutton) stood to have their independence infringed by new regulations, not to mention the demolition of buildings that the Commissioners found obstructive. One complainant found a moral aspect in the street-lighting proposals: it was, he argued, 'for the Conveniency of lighting the Affluent or Extravagant Home from Taverns and Ale-houses in dark Nights'.

Up till the 19th century Birmingham's growth had been one of piecemeal private development and in-filling. The Colmore Estate, Old Square and the area around St Philip's had essentially been built on unoccupied land. The Street Commissioners were the first to concern themselves with redevelopment, distant ancestors of Herbert Manzoni and the Highbury Initiatives. Birmingham's redevelopment, still in progress, began at this time.

Once the bill had become law the Commissioners acted with remarkable energy, laying the foundations upon which the great Victorian city of Birmingham was to be built. Three buildings in particular were a lasting testimony to their redevelopment of the town, all from the 1830s, when they were most active. One, the Market Hall, has now disappeared. The other two, Curzon Street station and the Town Hall, remain. Together these three encapsulate the Commissioners' chief areas of activity: markets, railways and civic buildings.

Changing the town's marketing habits took a lifetime; after all, these were traditions that had grown up over centuries. As we have already seen, the Birmingham markets occupied most of the lower streets of the town, from Corn Cheaping (also known as the Bull Ring) through to High Street, New Street and Dale End. Each patch was devoted to a different kind of product, but the growing importance of the town as a trading centre had left these traditional sites overcrowded and insanitary. The chief problem was that the area around St Martin's was too crowded with buildings to allow the free movement of traffic on market days. Hutton describes the chaos that was 18th-century market day in Birmingham:

> For the want of a convenient place where the sellers may be collected into one point, they are scattered into various parts of the town. Corn is sold by sample, in the Bull Ring; butchers' stalls occupy Spiceal Street; one would think a narrow street was preferred, that no customer should be suffered to pass by. Flowers, shrubs, &c., at the end of Philip Street and Moor Street; beds of earthenware lie in the middle of the foot ways; and a double range of insignificant stalls, in the front of the shambles, choak up the passage: the beast market is kept in Dale End: that for pigs, sheep and horses in New Street: cheese issues from one of our principal inns: fruit, fowls and butter are sold at the Old Cross: nay it is difficult to mention a place where they are not. We may observe that if a man hath an article to sell which another wants to buy, they quickly find each other out.

It was after the passing of the 1769 Act that the cattle market had moved to Dale End. This was probably designed to be a purely temporary measure, while the Commissioners busied themselves about clearing the Bull Ring site for a more integrated market.

The one still point in the Bull Ring, the constant that allows us to imagine the shape of the place that the Commisioners came, saw and conquered, is St Martin's church. But the 18th-century St Martin's was surrounded by a crowd, almost a circle, of mostly wooden buildings: the row of butchers' stalls called the Shambles and an arc of buildings to the north of the church, of which the best known was the Upper Roundabout House. The legal battle to demolish the latter was a protracted one, but once it had been won, or lost, the concept of an open market-place was at last possible. All the more possible when, in the early 19th century, Richard Pratchet and friends raised £12,000 as a loan to the Commissioners to purchase the land once occupied by the manorial lord. The moat in the eye of historians was more of a log in the eyes of the Commissioners, and Birmingham's link with its medieval past was about to be severed. The change was emphasised by the Board's purchase of the market rights of the lord of the manor in 1806.

The site was cleared, the moat filled in, and the general market opened for business in 1806. This was followed, on 29 May 1817, by the New Beast Market (also known as Smithfield), and a penalty of £20 for anyone attempting to sell cattle, sheep or hay in any other part of the town. Butchers' stalls occupied the site of the Roundabout House in 1785, and a fruit market opened in Worcester Street in 1792. Again, anyone 'throwing down' or 'piling up' fruit in any other place would be fined.

Not all this activity was happily received by the inhabitants, but the force of change seemed to be irresistible. To one writer of epigrams, the sale and subsequent demolition

of the venerable Old Cross in August 1784 seemed to sum up the modern age into which
the town was moving:

> Conscience's court by auction goes,
> Bidders though few, the hammer does
> The business in a trice;
> At sixty pounds the blow is struck,
> Ten more knocks down the bell and clock;
> Commissioners—no price.

But the site of the Old Cross was not long to remain unoccupied, for it was to be the
site of Birmingham's first public statue. And curiously for a town just about as far from
the sea as you can get, the monument was to salute Britain's greatest naval hero.

Horatio Nelson, hero of Copenhagen, the Nile and Trafalgar, had the satisfaction of
achieving cult status during his lifetime. At a time when affection for the monarchy was
in decline, Nelson substituted admirably. The people of Birmingham, not a town of sea-
farers but one that was involved economically and industrially in the war effort, had
enormous respect for the man, both alive and dead. In the middle of a national tour, Nelson
visited the town on 29 August 1802 and was greeted with the kind of adulation now
reserved for pop stars. The party consisted of a curious ménage of Lord and Lady Nelson,
their son, and Sir William and Lady Hamilton, and they stayed at *Style's Hotel*. The night
must have been a disturbed one, if for no other reason than the crowds outside clamouring
for a sight of the hero at the hotel window. The visit consisted of a trip to the theatre and
a guided tour of the principal manufactories of the town, including Soho, Eginton's stained
glass works, Clay's japanning factory and Phipson's pin manufactory. This, in fact, was
a fairly standard itinerary, made unusual by the vast numbers that drew Nelson's carriage
through the streets.

A grand lunch, some songs by Lady Hamilton, a visit to the Blue Coat School, and
he was gone. But the occasion lingered long in the memory, and the news of his death at
Trafalgar, three short years later, touched a nerve that the tough old industrial town did not
know it had. The circumstances of his death, soon to achieve mythical status, led to a
mixture of pride and grief that sought a more permanent memorial to the man and his
memory. Birmingham was not alone in this: places as far apart as Liverpool, Glasgow,
Norwich and London also began to consider how to make their feelings manifest.

A public meeting was held on 23 November 1805, just a month after the battle, 'to
take into consideration some plan for erecting a Monument, Statue or Pillar, to the memory
of the late gallant hero'. A public subscription was announced and was universally subscribed to, from private donations to collections in schools, factories and pubs: well over
£2,000 was raised. The question of the nature of the monument was less universally agreed
and was the subject of a battle no less intense than Trafalgar itself. One school of thought
campaigned for a statue of Nelson; another argued that the monument should have some
utilitarian value. Birmingham came close to having a column on top of a post office or
chemist's to commemorate their famous visitor. The latter had appeal because of the
absence of a tradition of statuary in the town. One issue that did not spark a disagreement
was the site of the memorial: everyone agreed that the Old Cross had marked the spiritual
centre of Birmingham, and it was there that the naval pillar, statue or whatever it was to
be should stand.

On 13 June 1806 it was finally decided that a statue it should be, and that William Westmacott, who was also commissioned to make Liverpool's monument, should design it. It was the same Westmacott who was hired by Alfred Bunn in 1819 to redesign the interior of the Theatre Royal. This was a work not destined to survive as long as the Nelson monument: it went up in flames in the following year. The work was unveiled on the Jubilee Day of George III in 1809, and was the first statue of Nelson to be erected, as well as Birmingham's first public statue. Whether because of its position in the centre of the market-place, or because of the public nature of its erection, Nelson's statue has always retained its place in the affection of the Birmingham people. One individual, an auctioneer from High Street called Joseph Farror, bequeathed sixpence a week in perpetuity for the cleaning of the statue and its base. If Lord Nelson had cast his good eye upon the events taking place around his feet, then he would be much entertained. The statue was the focus for Daffodil Day, an annual commemoration of Benjamin Disraeli, and if there were not daffodils around the statue, then the Bull Ring flower-sellers used it to display their wares instead. Alternatively the quack doctors of the Victorian market made their claims for a universal panacea from there, as has many a generation of preacher and soap-box orator.

More recent times have not been so kind to the old sailor. During the air-raid years of the Second World War he disappeared inside a large protective crate, and the redevelopment of the Bull Ring in the late '50s saw him moved from the Old Cross site to a position on Moor Street. His final resting-place in the redeveloped Bull Ring of the '90s was also a subject of some controversy. Birmingham's tradition of treating its statues like chess pieces is a long one.

Nelson was not the only piece of art-work to appear in the cleared space that had become the Bull Ring. Richard Pratchet, the town's high bailiff, whose fund-raising had

34.   The Bull Ring in 1812 showing both Nelson's statue and, in front of the church, Pratchet's Egyptian Folly. The tower of St John's church can be seen on Deritend.

substantially assisted the Street Commissioners in their grand scheme, fixed upon the old water pump as an object worth redeveloping. This forgotten curiosity that had stood behind the Shambles was now in a prominent position after the latter's demolition. Pratchet commissioned William Hollins, a local architect, to redesign it. Hollins, arguably Birmingham's first creative artist, inspected the site and decided that the ideal architectural style to stand between the gothic church he called a basilica and the proposed neo-classical monument to Nelson should be an Egyptian pyramid. Nelson's fame as hero of the Nile was probably the initial inspiration; Hollins' fertile imagination did the rest.

Consequently the old village pump in the Bull Ring became the Egyptian conduit in the forum, not without local scepticism. The artist wrote a spirited defence of his imaginative leap in the *Gazette* in January 1808:

> I have ornamented it with a representation of the Papyrus, grouped in form of quarter columns at each angle, with Grecian Honeysuckles, and with an Urn at the top, which last may be considered as a symbol of our departed Hero's ashes; as proper append-ages, the Lion's Head is significant of that Hero's strength and prowess in battle ... as disgorging the water, it is a symbol of the element, for the Egyptians believed water to be the strength, and principal of all things.

A few days later, the *Birmingham Commercial Herald* published an aggrieved reply by the pump itself, poking fun at Hollins' pretensions and suggesting that 'much learning had made him mad':

> That, although your Petitioner is somewhat stricken in years, he disdains the imputa-tion of having become a Driveller, which it is evident the said clothier has attempted to cast upon him, by having affixed to him a slobbering bib as part of his apparel.

Given the depth of local philistinism, it seems hardly surprising that artists were unwilling to risk their necks on the block of popular taste. The experiment in public art ground swiftly to a halt, and it would be many years before another statue graced the streets of Birmingham. In September 1852 a German visitor, J. G. Kohl, expressed his amazement that in a city of 200,000 living specimens of humanity, there should be only one statue among them: 'Birmingham and Leeds appear to me, among all the large towns of England, to be the two most destitute of taste, ornament, and enjoyment'.

There was another consequence of the removal the Old Cross; small though it was, its disappearance left the town without a venue for public meetings. The Street Commis-sioners themselves had never used it, preferring to rent rooms in Spiceal Street and Dale End. What took its place, in Moor Street, was a complex of buildings, consisting of courtroom, prison and public offices, the foundation stone being laid on 18 September 1805. It opened for business in October 1807, a year after the completion of the prison. For the first time in the town's history the institutions of the law, the poor law and local government were gathered into one place.

The Public Offices cost almost £11,000 and were designed by the same William Hollins whose Egyptian flight of fancy had caused such amusement in the Bull Ring. Sadly Hollins was again to face criticism for the unnecessary use of classical ornament for so utilitarian a building. Nevertheless, it was a considerable improvement on its predecessors, but still proved inadequate to a town of 85,000 people in times of large public meetings. When Birmingham was the venue for the mass rallies that preceded the passing of the Reform Bill in 1830-2, the town had recourse to John Beardsworth's Repository on

35. The Public Office in Moor Street, completed in 1807, was often condemned as too ornate for a public building. It contained courtrooms and a prison. In September 1842, surprisingly, there was not a single prisoner in confinement.

Cheapside, or to the open space of Newhall Hill. The Repository, a local landmark topped by a gigantic white horse, was the venue for horse sales and contained a large open space surrounded by a gallery.

The year that the Public Offices opened can be seen to mark, as well as any, the end of the first phase of the Commissioners' work. There was much still to do. The markets were still in a transitional stage and road improvements had only just begun. And the Public Offices were only the first of a generation of large public buildings needed to reflect Birmingham's growing status and reputation. But there were other major changes taking place in the town for which the Commissioners were not responsible, though they might ease their introduction. A transport revolution, hard on the heels of the industrial one, was underway.

Chapter Thirteen

A Transport Revolution

Towns appear and grow through the accidentals of geography: a river here, a coalfield there. In many ways the medieval towns and villages were shackled to their geological past, their function in the economy determined by position and surroundings. Even Birmingham, whose energetic pursuit of trade and industry had allowed it to rise above its geographical restrictions, knew its limits: the nearest navigable river lay at Bewdley, some thirty miles away. But by the 18th century, there were ways of re-drawing the map, whereby contour lines and soil types no longer took precedence.

By the early 1700s the roads and trackways leading into the town were feeling the strain. Eighty pack-horses a day were struggling in with fruit and vegetables from Evesham (the road was not good enough for carts), and in 1726 it was said that the road to Wolverhampton was 'dangerous and almost impassable by reason of the great number of carriages constantly employed in carrying of iron, goods, and coal'. Many roads had become 'hollow ways', worn down by constant use of an unprotected surface. Since the care of the highways fell upon the parish, no amount of rate levying was able to do much more than keep them open.

The advent of the turnpike, a kind of privatised road network, transformed this situation. Key arterial roads, funded by tolls and administered by trusts, opened up a new era in land transportation. The roads to the Black Country, and south and west towards Bromsgrove or Halesowen were progressively turnpiked as the century advanced. There would be delays as horses and coaches passed through a series of turnpike gates, but the additional revenue undoubtedly improved travelling conditions. Expenditure, however, was often as uneven as the road itself. The Bristol Road, which was turnpiked in 1726, suffered badly from the intense traffic in salt, iron and coal. In 1772 a sum of £5,000 was spent on the first five miles leading out of Birmingham, but improvements dwindled away further out, as did the road.

The turnpike on Deritend was established in 1788, mainly to fund the rebuilding of the bridge, and to improve flood prevention in the area. The toll was twopence for a four-wheeled carriage and one halfpenny for a horse. This act was extended in 1822 to pay for the widening of the lower part of Digbeth, as well as the repair of two other bridges on Cheapside and Bradford Street. When the road was finally disturnpiked, only eight of the original 95 trustees were still alive. The Bristol Road was disturnpiked as late as 1872, but in most cases it was during the first half of the 19th century that the gates were removed. The gate in Deritend was removed in 1828, and that at Five Ways in 1841.

36. The *Stork Hotel* in Old Square was a popular destination for the carriage trade. There was extensive stabling in the rear and inside 'an excellent billiard table' to amuse the delayed traveller. The photograph dates from *c*.1870.

It was the route to London that benefited least from the changes. In 1765 the cost of carrying goods from London to Birmingham was around 10s. per ton. Hutton's journey to the capital in 1784 took over 19 hours, but even this was something of an improvement on the two and a half days it would have taken him half a century before. By the 1770s *Aris's Gazette* was full of advertisements for new coach routes and services, each claiming to be faster or more 'friction free' than the others. Fifty-two services were travelling to London and 16 to Bristol, carrying around half a dozen people each.

Coach services were a highly entrepreneurial adventure. Nicholas Rothwell of Warwick, whose Birmingham to London service was launched in 1731, also dealt in private carriage hire and hearses. His advert stated that the journey to London (if God permit) began at the *Swan Inn*, and took in Warwick, Banbury and Aylesbury en route, at a cost of 21s. per person. As the century progressed increasing competition led to some extraordinary vehicles being seen on the roads of England. The writer, Thomas de Quincey, spotted one coach that could easily have sprung from his drug-crazed imagination: '... the beast from Birmingham, our green-and-gold friend from false, fleeting, perjured Brummagem, had as much writing and painting on its sprawling flanks as would have puzzled a decipherer from the tombs of Luxor'.

But travel by road was vulnerable, not only to the condition of the highway, but also to intervention by the inappropriately named 'gentlemen of the road'. But for every robber equipped with a horse and legendary status, there were many more footpads, operating within walking distance of their homes, in the darkness on the edge of town. The roads around Sutton Coldfield were particularly prone to this kind of criminal activity. Again the *Gazette* dutifully printed accounts of daring robberies and perilous escapes, counter-balancing the confident adverts of the coach proprietors. In May 1742 the Birmingham to London stage-coach was held up near Banbury by an infamous highwayman named Sansbury. The newspaper reported with undisguised glee that Sansbury unprofessionally allowed his success and the alcohol on board to go to his head. He was arrested in a nearby cornfield, sleeping off the effects.

By the middle of the century there was at last an alternative to the roads, and it was one that the Birmingham industrialists grasped with both hands. At the *Swan Inn* on 4 June 1767, James Brindley outlined the results of his survey for the cutting of a navigable canal between Birmingham and the Black Country coalfields. Canals would be unlikely to increase the speed of transportation, but the

BIRMINGHAM STAGE-COACH,

In Two *Days* and a half; begins May the 24th, 1731.

SETS out from the *Swan-Inn* in *Birmingham*, every *Monday* at six a Clock in the Morning, through *Warwick*, *Banbury* and *Alesbury*, to the *Red Lion Inn* in *Aldersgate street*, *London*, every *Wednesday* Morning: And returns from the said *Red Lion Inn* every *Thursday* Morning at five a Clock the same Way to the *Swan-Inn* in *Birmingham* every *Saturday*, at 21 Shillings each Passenger, and 18 Shillings from *Warwick*, who has liberty to carry 14 Pounds in Weight, and all above to *pay One Penny a Pound*.

Perform'd (if God permit)

By Nicholas Rothwell.

The Weekly Waggon sets out every *Tuesday* from the *Nagg's-Head* in *Birmingham*, to the Red Lion Inn aforesaid, every *Saturday*, and returns from the said Inn every *Monday*, to the *Nagg's-Head* in *Birmingham* every *Thursday*.

Note. By the said Nicholas Rothwell at Warwick, all Persons may be furnished with a 'By Coach, Chariot, Chaise, or Hearse, with a Mourning Coach and able Horses, to any Part of Great Britain, at reasonable Rates: And also Saddle Horses to be had.

37. Rothwell's coach called at the *Swan Inn* in New Street, the town's premier hotel and coaching house. In the same street stood the *Hen and Chickens*, from which the 'flying coach' service was launched in 1742.

ability to carry heavy goods far outweighed this drawback. The cost of the canal to Wolverhampton reached six figures, paid for by the sale of shares of £140 each. Within 20 years of opening, these shares would have more than doubled, and by 1792 had passed £1,000.

The local act authorising the project was passed on 24 February 1768, and the first stretch, from Wednesbury to Paradise Street, opened on 6 November in the following year. The first wharf for coal was at Newhall Street, the main wharf at Easy Row being completed a year later. Soon after (in 1772), the stretch linking the B.C.N. to the Staffordshire and Worcestershire at Aldersley Junction would also be completed. Not everything had gone according to plan: the decision to climb the hill at Smethwick, rather than tunnel through it, was one that the company would come to regret. The 12 locks were not only time-consuming, they were highly wasteful of water, the canal company's most precious liquid asset.

Ironically, B.C.N.'s loss of water in the Smethwick locks has been our gain. The company ordered a steam-engine from Boulton and Watt to pump water back up the 31 feet to the top lock. By March 1778 it was at work, running at 11 strokes a minute and consuming 64 lbs of coal by the hour. James Watt himself supervised tests after its installation: it was, after all, only a short walk from Soho. The Smethwick engine, as it was called, remained in operation until 1891, when it was moved to Ocker Hill, and then (in 1959) to the Birmingham Science Museum. Though not quite Watt's first working engine, it was one of the first, and the only example of his first type of steam-engine to survive.

Nevertheless, whatever the long-term disadvantages of Brindley's cut, the arrival of the first barges of Black Country coal was a moment to savour, both for the proprietors and all those who stood to benefit from cheaper fuel. Birmingham's resident poet, John Freeth, recorded the excitement in the unlikely titled 'Inland Navigation: An Ode':

> What mortals so happy as Birmingham Boys?
> What people so flushed with the sweetest of joys?
> All hearts fraught with mirth at the Wharf shall appear,
> Their aspects proclaim it the Jubilee year,
> And be full as gay in their frolicksome pranks,
> As they who were dancing on Avon's green banks.
> There never in war was for victory won,
> A cause that deserved such respect from the Town;
> Then revel in gladness, let harmony flow,
> From the district of Bordesley to Paradise-Row;
> For true feeling joy on each breast must be wrought,
> When Coals under Five-pence per hundred are brought.

To Freeth, that small stretch of newly-cut canal opened up new vistas of trade and enterprise. Today Wednesbury; tomorrow the world:

> Birmingham, for arts renowned
> O'er the globe shall foremost stand:
> Nor its vast increase be found
> To be equall'd in the land.
> If the will of fancy ranges
> From the Tagus to the Ganges,
> Or from Lapland Cliffs extend
> To the Patagonian Strand,
>
> For mechanic skill and pow'r,
> In what kingdom, on what shore,
> Lies the place that can supply,
> The world with such variety?

The new canal company established offices at the bottom of Paradise Street, roughly where Alpha Tower now stands. Behind its double arch, the coal wharves lay, twin pronged

38. The B.C.N. Canal Offices in Paradise Street were demolished in 1912. Here was the gateway to a network that boasted 'more canals than Venice'.

like a tuning fork. These too have now gone, lying beneath the Central Television studios. Indeed much of the wharfage at this unloading end of the voyage from the Black Country has followed it into oblivion. Gone too, if it was ever there, is the 'old red-brick house, with very white steps and very red bricks, and a plate on the door, bearing in fat Roman capitals the words "Mr. Winkle"'. Here stood the house of the wealthy wharfinger, paid a visit by Mr. Pickwick and friends in Charles Dickens' novel.

The arrival of the canal transformed this western quarter of the town, with the opportunity of transporting raw materials cheaply. The brass industry in particular took advantage of the new situation. Birmingham had made a reputation for the manufacture of brassware early in the 18th century, but the brass-works in Coleshill Street were an exception to the rule. Most brassworkers worked directly from sheets of the metal, imported from Bristol, rather than buying the raw materials. By 1781 the increasing cost of copper (£20 a ton), and the opportunities presented by the Birmingham Canal, led the Birmingham Metal Company to establish works off Broad Street to make the brass itself.

The new company already had a ready market in the town: the makers of brass fittings for machinery, including the steam-engine, toymakers, coffin furniture manufacturers and many others were only too willing to buy their brass locally. By Victorian times, Birmingham was the centre of the brass trade, with over 200 manufacturers and over 400 works by 1865. A Spanish visitor remarked on the extraordinary prevalence of green hair in the town, a sure sign of the brassworker. Today the Brasshouse (converted into a pub) remains in Broad Street as a testimony to Birmingham's single most important industry. Any green hair now seen in its vicinity is purely cosmetic.

By 1793, the year that marked the high-point of canal speculation across the country, one hundred boats a day were plying their trade on the Birmingham Canal. A series of acts had authorised new canals through the town: John Smeaton's Birmingham and Fazeley (1783), the Worcester and Birmingham (1791) and the Warwick and Birmingham (1793), to name but three. The Birmingham and Fazeley joined the Warwick Canal at Digbeth, while the Worcester and Birmingham met the Stratford Canal at Kings Norton. The 13 locks at Farmer's Bridge linked the Birmingham Canal to the Birmingham and Fazeley at Aston Junction. In 1839 it was said that 'nearly 70 Steam Engines, and about 124 Wharfs and Works are already seated on the Banks of the Canals, between Farmer's Bridge and Aston'.

A network of interlocking canals had been established, though relations between the various controlling companies were seldom amicable. The seven-foot bar between the Birmingham and the Worcester and Birmingham Canals at Gas Street Basin is surviving testimony to the bitter rivalries that intermittently punctuated the development. A lock was only cut through it in 1815.

More important than the branches themselves was the access that they provided to the river systems and ports. Autherley Junction provided a link, via the Staffordshire and Worcestershire, to the Severn and Bristol. Fazeley was a link in the watery chain that led to the ports of Liverpool and Hull, and the junction between the Warwick and Oxford Canals at Napton provided a route to London. However you re-arranged the geography or changed the mode of transport, Birmingham remained at the centre.

The connections that this network provided were far-reaching. The Warwick and Birmingham Canal, for example, connected the Digbeth Branch to Sri Lanka. This was the route taken by the weekly shipment of 3,000 chests of tea to the Bordesley Street depot of Ty-Phoo, each barge carrying between 250 and 400 chests. The company re-located here in 1923. From the wharf the huge assignment was broken down and packaged into the familiar ¼ lb and ½ lb packets. The trade continued until the German bombing raid of 10 April 1941 when an incendiary destroyed the whole complex.

By the 1820s, however, it was clear that the main arterial route to Wolverhampton was in trouble. It was a problem familiar to the motorway designers of this century: traffic had far exceeded the capacity of the system to handle it. A pamphlet of 1825 (admittedly produced by a railway company) alleged that in the years 1820-4 the canal had been closed for maintenance or because of ice on an average of 30 days per year. The engineer Thomas Telford was commissioned to survey the route, and his analysis was devastating:

> I found adjacent to this great and flourishing town a canal little better than a crooked ditch, with scarcely the appearance of a haling-path, the horses frequently sliding and staggering in the water, the haling-lines sweeping the gravel into the canal, and the entanglement at the meeting of boats incessant; while at the locks at each end of the short summit crowds of boatmen were always quarrelling, or offering premiums for a preference of passage, and the mineowners, injured by the delay, were loud in their just complaints.

Telford's solution was for a new reservoir at Rotton Park, and a radical re-cutting of the canal, across the circuitous Brindley loops and through the Smethwick hill. The latter

39. Old Worcester Wharf in 1913, the stretch of canal below Gas Street Basin. The Birmingham and Worcester Canal was completed in 1815, linking the town with the river Severn.

was undertaken in 1829 and was, at its deepest, 71 feet. Above it towered the largest canal bridge in the world, with a span of 150 feet. Telford's new canal had taken two miles and three hours off the route to Wednesbury.

The decision to streamline the cut to Wolverhampton was probably influenced by another new factor: the advent of the railway. But let us first take stock of the impact of the canals upon the geography and economy of Birmingham. It is a familiar boast that Birmingham has more miles of canal than Venice, a claim now difficult to substantiate because of the filling in of so many wharves and branches within the city. There were, after all, about 550 private branches and basins within Birmingham Canal Navigations (which includes the Black Country). Discounting these, there are roughly 33 miles of canal, comprising around 3.1 per cent of all navigable waterways in the country.

The tonnage of goods transported on B.C.N. rose steadily until the end of the last century, when it reached 8½ million tonnes per annum, almost 20 per cent of the national total. A daily total of 31½ million gallons of water was recycled from the bottom of the system to the top. But the advent of road transport tolled the knell for all this activity, and the canals of Birmingham were left (metaphorically, at least) high and dry. Leisure use, however, has done what industry could no longer: it kept them open. And by an accident of planning, the proximity of the canals to the prestige developments of the International Convention Centre, National Indoor Arena, and the night-life on Broad Street has focused attention on this hidden amenity in the city centre. Even James Brindley has been given a new lease of life: his face peers down into his canal from high on the wall of the I.C.C.'s energy centre, while the office, shopping and leisure development opposite is named Brindley Place in his honour.

Alternatives to the canal were long in gestation. As early as 1768, William Small had written to James Watt that he hoped soon to travel 'in a fiery chariot of your invention'. The application of steam power to rotative motion was a puzzle that captured the minds of many of the members of the Lunar Society, and their contemporaries, too. One member, Richard Lovell Edgeworth, was already considering the possibility of a steam-car that ran on rails. Only William Murdock went as far as producing a demonstration model. But Murdock's working model was never built upon, and the concept of a steam-driven car, or even balloon, was allowed to go cool.

By the 1830s, however, a new generation of inventors turned once more to the problem. Strange machines were seen chugging along, or more often toppling over, on the streets of Paris, America, and Britain. In Birmingham, Dr. William Church, an American inventor who settled in the town around 1822, created a huge three-wheeled steam-car and ran it successfully to Coventry and over the Lickeys in 1833. But his concept of a Birmingham to London steam-coach fell victim to the poor quality of the roads and its own low speeds.

More successful, though equally doomed, was the steam-car designed by the Heaton Brothers. In the summer of 1833 it did the run to Wolverhampton twice in one day, carrying 30 passengers, and followed it up with a round trip to Coventry. But its promising career fell down on a clause in the manifesto. Shares had been issued on the promise that the car would average eight miles an hour during the trials. Falling marginally short of this, the contract was torn up and the experiment abandoned.

But steam-driven transport was now firmly on the agenda. The only question was what it would run on. As early as 1824 a group of Birmingham businessmen were already considering a rail link between Liverpool, London and Birmingham. This was a little premature, given that no trains were yet running, but it was clear that the financial muscle to pioneer railways was there. Within 15 years it would be steaming into Birmingham, and another new age was beginning.

Chapter Fourteen

The Railway Age

In the same year that Victoria was crowned queen, three railway companies and a vast army of navvies were closing in on Birmingham. If the scenario sounds rather like a war, this was probably not far from the case, although it was a war that ended more in mergers than bloodshed.

Birmingham's strategic and industrial importance naturally encouraged links with the other main commercial centres of the kingdom: London, Liverpool, Manchester and Derby. After parliamentary approval was granted to the London and Birmingham Railway in 1833, and to the Grand Junction Railway in the same year, the race was on in earnest. Indeed, so swift was the progress that the G.J.R. from Liverpool arrived too early for a railway station. The intended terminus in Curzon Street and the viaduct approaching it were still being completed. All this without the threat of a People's Charter!

It was on 9 July 1837 that an experimental posse of six coaches and 36 passengers made the journey from Liverpool to the company's temporary terminus at Vauxhall, the station taking its name from the nearby pleasure park. On the following day a return trip was planned:

> ... the whole town was in a state of great commotion and excitement, owing to the public opening ... At seven o'clock precisely, the bell rang, and the opening train, drawn by the Wildfire engine, commenced moving. The train consisted of eight carriages, all of the first class ... It started slowly, but upon emerging from the yard, speedily burst off at a rapid pace ... the immense multitude as far as the eye could reach, gave expression to their admiration by loud and long continued huzzas, and the waving of hats and handkerchiefs.

Birmingham's first railway station has, not surprisingly, disappeared. By 1839 the line into the intended terminus in Curzon Street had been finished, and Vauxhall was abandoned as a passenger station. Duddeston station, on the line to Walsall, now stands on the site.

Once the service was in full operation, it would take the first-class train four and three-quarter hours to cover the 97 miles to Liverpool at a single fare of one guinea. The second-class 'stopper' added another half hour to the journey, but would cost only 14 shillings. Taking your dog would cost three shillings. A total of six trains ran daily. In 1839 the Grand Junction route to Liverpool grossed profits of £348,000, four-fifths of which came from passenger fares.

Like the Grand Junction, the London and Birmingham Railway was aiming at a terminus in Curzon Street. The geography of Birmingham made it less costly to approach

40. The Curzon Street portico was Birmingham's equivalent of the Euston arch. Unlike the latter it has survived. It is the oldest railway terminus in the world still in its original location and is a Grade 1 listed building.

the town along the river valleys to the north-east, creating that extraordinary congestion of lines in the area now known as Heartlands. That the London line was not completed until a year later is hardly surprising. Enormous technical and geological difficulties were faced by the engineers, George and Robert Stephenson, and (more directly) by the navvies working on it. Perhaps 20,000 men were engaged on the line, 10 of whom were killed in the Watford tunnel. Its success was as much a triumph of the will as anything, for early calculations had cast grave doubts on the economics of the thing.

As if to salute the enterprise, but more probably to impress the customers, magnificent triumphal entrances to the line were constructed at Euston and Curzon Street. The London entrance has been demolished, but the Curzon Street portico, designed by Philip Hardwick, remains as a monument to a grand conception. Here were offices, the directors' board room and a refreshment room. The wings on either side through which passengers passed have now gone, as the portico itself almost did in the 1970s. The building has now been restored for office use, though one feels that some historical role still awaits it in the future.

However questionable the undertaking might have looked (and £5½ million was a brave investment), the London route was an immediate success, recouping £700,000 in its first year. The journey time to the capital was halved overnight.

The Grand Junction Railway and the London and Birmingham Railway had arrived, but the big railway adventure was only just beginning. In February 1842 the Birmingham and Derby Junction Railway opened its station in Lawley Street, close to the Curzon Street termini but around 40 feet below in the valley. A year earlier the Birmingham and Gloucester Railway had also arrived in Curzon Street, abandoning its previous terminus at Camp Hill.

Four railway companies were now operating from or near Curzon Street, together creating the out-of-town inter-city station (or rather, stations) that Birmingham has been promised (or threatened with) in recent years. The idea may now have its attractions, but in the 1840s the situation was far from ideal. Curzon Street was a mile, or one shilling in cab fares, away from the town centre, by a very indirect route. This may have been preferable for the railway engineers, but it was hardly convenient for their customers. There were two solutions to this anomaly: one was to create a more direct road to the stations; the other was to redirect the trains to a more central site.

Even with the steadying hand of the Street Commissioners, Birmingham planning was anarchic enough to pursue both ideas simultaneously. While the road that was called Albert Street was being cut between Park Street and Moor Street, the railway companies were planning to desert Curzon Street for the town centre. Such a move would have been inconceivable in the early days: the cost of buying up property and land to place a station in the centre of Birmingham was beyond the means of the individual companies, saddled as they were with the initial development costs. But the confidence born of steady profits, and a series of mergers, allowed them to turn their attention to the concept of 'Birmingham Central'. In 1844 Birmingham and Derby merged with Birmingham and Gloucester to form the Midland Counties Railway. Then in 1846 the G.J.R. and the London and Birmingham formed the L.N.W.R. (London and North Western Railway).

In fact, the costs of a line into the centre of Birmingham were not as high as those that prohibited such a connection in many towns. Such was the geography of the place that a tunnel could be cut under the sandstone ridge on which the town centre stood. At the lowest point on the ridge lay an area of damp ground known as the Froggary, where Birmingham housing was at its worst and poorest. It was not the only site considered: there were rival claims for a station on Snow Hill. But for the new town council it was an opportunity to kill two birds with one stone. The area around King Street and Peck Lane was the most dangerous in town, with a permanent police presence. Given that the Grammar School backed onto it, this was an added source of worry. (Ironically, when the station was operational, the streets around it became a favourite haunt of prostitutes instead, meeting travellers off the trains to offer them 'a good time'.) The councillors voted 16-6 in favour of the New Street site, and an Act of Parliament was obtained on 3 August 1846. The Act stipulated that the new station would be for passenger use only, and that a public footpath through it should be kept open at all times.

As the central station grew, several old landmarks disappeared: the town's first synagogue in the Froggary, as well as the first theatre in King Street that had been converted into a Methodist chapel among them. Also destined to fall was the famous old public house in Peck Lane called the *Minerva Tavern*. Also known as 'Joe Lyndon's', this was the drinking den of the Birmingham conservatives, and an alternative to the radical crowd at *Freeth's Tavern*. It was probably here that the notorious 'Church and King' Riots were plotted. Here too in 1825 *The Birmingham Journal* was planned and launched, a conservative reaction to what the circle saw as an attack on them in *The Times*. The paper was published every Saturday 'at twelve o'clock precisely' from Spiceal Street, but remained in Tory hands for only seven years. Its sale in 1832 saw it change to Birmingham's most radical newspaper.

All this history had now gone, but there were compensations in the magnificent new railway station that was being created. The traveller, George Borrow, said of it: 'That station alone is enough to make one proud of being a modern Englishman'. The chief glory was its roof, said to have been the largest iron and glass roof in the world, with a single span of 212 feet. Into its construction (by Messrs. Fox, Henderson & Co.) went 120,000 feet of glass, weighing 150 tons, and 100,000 feet of corrugated-iron sheeting. Beneath it lay a forest of Doric pillars, each weighing over five tons. A contemporary description, however, added tellingly: '... we fear that but few of the many thousands who are yearly under this wonderful roof pause for even a few moments to notice and admire the skill and taste which have been employed in its construction'.

By the end of the century it had become, as it is today, one of the busiest stations in the country. An observer in 1896 recommended the best time to see it:

> But New Street Station, congested and bewildering to its utmost ... must be seen when the great multitude is surging to the Onion Fair, or the Cattle Show, or on some night when the great muscular crowd from the Black Country invades the city intent on the delights of the pantomime.

By the middle of this century, Victorian splendour had been replaced by post-Victorian grubbiness: it was damp and cold with poor lighting and a leaking roof. And the leaking roof was not improved by the dropping of bombs through it during the Second World War. Throughout the period 1964-71 New Street station was entirely re-built, with a shopping centre above it to preserve the public right of way.

The tunnels into the station that saved so much money on acquiring property are now perceived as a mixed blessing. Stephenson's tunnel to the north-west, the entrance of which can be seen behind the National Indoor Arena, caused much concern to the engineers and architects of the International Convention Centre. The tunnel, 11 metres below, cuts across the corner of the complex close to Symphony Hall; not an ideal companion for an 'acoustically perfect' concert hall. A series of measures, including the laying of new sleepers on rubber and the capping of the foundation piles with large rubber bearings, served to reduce vibrations to an almost imperceptible minimum.

One problem cannot be obviated: the tunnel is the busiest stretch of railway line in the country and congestion is intense. But such is New Street's constricted site that B.R.'s only long-term solution is either a return to the original out-of-town station of the 1830s or the diversification of termini, perhaps using Snow Hill.

But let us return to the history book. New Street station formally opened on 1 June 1854, though it had been in use for a couple of years already. Through it passed the trains of the L.N.W.R. and Midland companies, together with the Stour Valley (high level) line to Wolverhampton. But the argument over the comparative merits of New Street and Snow Hill was not quite over. In fact the real war was just about to begin.

Enter two more companies to muddy the clearing waters: the Birmingham and Oxford Railway and the Birmingham, Wolverhampton and Dudley Railway. Since these two were soon merged (in 1848) into the Great Western, let us just call them the G.W.R. What distinguished the G.W.R. from its rivals was its incompatibility in terms of rail width. At seven feet, its gauge was much wider than the 4 ft 8½ in. of the other lines. The battle

41.   The *Queen's Hotel*, next to New Street station, opened in 1854. Its telegraphic address was 'Besthotel Birmingham' and it had a great local reputation for afternoon tea.

was not dissimilar to that between incompatible video or satellite systems of recent years, and Parliament's decision to ban the wide-gauge was one based on market and monopoly, more than on merit.

The G.W.R. station in Birmingham was at Snow Hill. Although a tunnel now connects it with Moor Street, this was originally a deep cutting that was subsequently built over. The result was one of Birmingham's grand shopping malls, known as the Great Western Arcade. But a combination of rivalry and effective parliamentary lobbying by the L.N.W.R. led to a series of hurdles being placed in front of the late arrival. Chief among them was the insistence that the track included both narrow and broad gauge, and that a link be provided to the L.N.W.R. at Curzon Street. The result was the Duddeston Viaduct, an architectural masterpiece of 1,100 yards that went nowhere. By the time it was built, New Street station was finished and the proposed connection was irrelevant.

Despite the obstacles, the G.W.R. successfully established its Birmingham station at Snow Hill in 1852, and opened its low-level line to Wolverhampton two years later. At the time Snow Hill hardly matched the grandeur of its New Street neighbour: it was little more than a wooden shed. Indeed the large station and hotel remembered with affection by so many Brummies only reached its final form in 1912, and only lasted for half a century afterwards.

As a key link between Birkenhead and Paddington, Snow Hill was far from being a poor relation to its L.M.S. cousin. In 1964, for example, 130,000 passenger trains used the station, only 45,000 fewer than New Street. Passenger statistics are similarly impressive:

7½ million, as opposed to over 10 million at New Street. Yet five years later it was gone, even though the crumbling edifice survived into the '70s. Since then Snow Hill has been the focus for many pipe-dreams and planners' fantasies. A central bus station was planned there, together with an indoor sports stadium, when Birmingham made its first bid for sporting attention as host for the Commonwealth Games. As early as 1972, Snow Hill was the planned centrepiece of a rapid transit network linking Birmingham and the Black Country. Such an idea remains at the centre of the region's transport plans for the 21st century. In an area as congested as the West Midlands transit routes cannot afford to be ignored: Snow Hill has now re-opened as a commuter terminus, reconnected with the tunnel to Moor Street. And the old Birmingham, Wolverhampton and Dudley line behind it waits expectantly for a new role.

Of course, the inter-city routes through Birmingham are only half the railway story. The commuter lines, such as those to Harborne and Kings Heath, were key elements in the expansion of Birmingham into the suburban hinterland. Places like Moseley and Balsall Heath might have long remained rural villages but for the ribbons of Victorian terraces that followed the rail links. Such population movements were hardly ever accidental. Railway companies bought up swathes of land to built their railways, and then sold off the residue to speculative builders. Such an arrangement assisted both the housing sector and the railways themselves in providing the new lines with their first customers. At the end of the last century, residents of Brighton Road in Balsall Heath might have seen a regular procession of commuter services taking the half-hour trip from Kings Norton into the city centre, while 20 trains ran from Harborne into town.

Such suburban lines had important recreational roles as well. Day-trippers from the city packed the trains to Sutton Park, with additional services laid on at bank holidays, particularly Whit and Easter. The station at Bournville, as well as providing an important link in Cadbury's distribution chain, was also the starting-point for the workers' excursions to the seaside. The G.W.R., in the expansionist times before the First World War, was quick to recognise in its advertising the attractions of 'Birmingham and its Beautiful Borderlands'. The Birmingham and North Warwickshire line was promoted as offering the opportunity of exploring 'leafy Warwickshire', 'Shakespeare's Country' or 'the green fields of Shirley'. Better still, an *Up to Date Property Register* encouraged the urban employee to live there instead, and commute into the city.

It was hardly likely that an industry that relied so heavily on metal-work would not have its effect on Birmingham employment, too. It began with the supply of screws to Brunel for the fastening of rails to sleepers, but expanded to take in the whole panoply of rolling-stock and railway equipment. Much of this industry was concentrated in Saltley, an inevitable consequence of all the lines that converged on that area. By the 1880s the Metropolitan Carriage and Wagon Co. (later Metro Cammell) employed around 1,200 at its Saltley works, a stone's throw from Brown Marshall's and Co. that employed a similar number. By 1949 over 9,000 were employed in rolling-stock manufacture, much of it for export. Metro Cammell was as an international exporter as any, supplying rolling-stock to companies as far afield as Tasmania and China. Many foreign travellers, such as Helen Caddick of West Bromwich, found themselves reminded of home as they sat in an Indian railway carriage made in Saltley.

But there were few parts of the industry that did not buy from Birmingham manu-facturers. Joseph Wright's made engine parts; Chance Bros. supplied the red and green

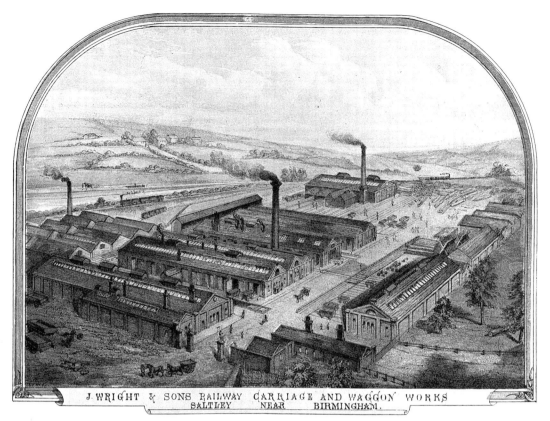

J. WRIGHT & SONS RAILWAY CARRIAGE AND WAGGON WORKS
SALTLEY   NEAR   BIRMINGHAM.

42.   Joseph Wright's works concentrated on making engine parts. It was later incorporated into the Metro Cammell works that occupied the site. This view dates from 1859.

glass for signals, while Bassano and Fisher of Liverpool Street moved from carriage springs to making a wide range of fixtures and fittings for railway stations and lines.

Whether we talk of railways or canals, Birmingham's geography and industrial growth had placed it at the centre. By 1831 there was a population of 110,914 and it was rising fast. Whether you call it migration, immigration or new settlement, a lot of people were arriving in town to try out that rumour about 'getting rich by nightfall'.

Chapter Fifteen

New Settlers

One of the better Brummagem broadsheets of the 19th century is entitled 'How to Get a Living, or, The Rigs of Birmingham'. Better than any historian could manage, the anonymous balladeer gives an impression of street life in the busy town that was beginning to draw in migrants from across the country, and indeed across the world.

> There's some a drinking, some a storming,
> Some a going about informing,
> Some a going telling lies sir,
> Some a bawling mutton pies sir ...
>
> There's some a singing, some a wrangling,
> And some a washing, some a mangling,
> There's some a cobbling up old shoes sir,
> And some crying the whole week's news sir ...
>
> There's cherries, plums, and lily-white muscles,
> India rubber, stays and bustles,
> Boas, fine new-fashioned hats sir
> Pickled eels and stinking sprats sir;
> Brass rings and watches made of gold sir,
> New red herrings seven years old sir,
> And if the palaces you pop in sir,
> There's a lot of old women drinking gin sir.

Between 1841 and 1851 the population of Birmingham rose by 22 per cent, as the prospects of employment in the town rose, and the long trek to the Midlands was preferable to conditions at home. Jobs might be on the borderline of poverty, but at least they lasted through the year, and the city offered a range of possibilities far beyond that of the country. And many had travelled much further than rural Worcestershire to try their luck. Jews and Italians, as well as other migrants from the British Isles, began to give the town a multi-cultural feel, long before the term was invented. By 1800 a Jewish community was already well established; Jewish names appear in the earliest Birmingham rates books and the first trade directory of 1767 lists 'Michael and Barnet Freidberg, glasscutters of Dudley Street' and 'Mayer Opnaim, merchant of Snow Hill' amongst others. The new arrivals were from Eastern Europe, predominantly Poland, Prussia and Germany, and they found a toehold on Birmingham life in the Froggary, a damp and depressed street off Peck Lane.

Life was not easy. Many began their trading careers as hawkers, emerging from the Froggary with 'portable shops" to hawk around the Bull Ring. The move into more reputable trades came later. The anti-noncomformist backlash of the 1790s hit the Jews too, with occasional attacks on their synagogue. The first synagogue in the Froggary was rebuilt in 1791 and a second erected in Severn Street in 1809. The latter was broken into and pillaged four years later, but funds could only be found for its repair in 1827. It was never easy for such groups to integrate themselves fully into English life: until the repeal of the Test and Corporation Acts in 1827 non-Anglicans were barred from public office.

By the 1850s, with a population approaching a thousand, a new synagogue could be built on Singers Hill. This building, by Yeoville Thomason, was opened in 1856 and still stands. By now many trades in the town had their Jewish element. In 1852 there were 16 Jewish pawnbrokers, as well as tailors and jewellers. One Jew in particular made his impact on the jewellery trade. Jacob Jacobs came to Birmingham from Sheffield in 1852 and was instrumental in setting up the industry's first trade association, the Birmingham Jewellers and Silversmiths Association, as well as leading a deputation to persuade the Princess of Wales to wear jewellery in 1887.

Although some wealthier members of the community were able to move into the more affluent suburbs of Handsworth and Edgbaston by the 1870s, some streets in the centre of town retained a strong Jewish influence. Hurst Street had a synagogue, a Hebrew school and a boarding-house for Jewish market traders; it had the added attraction of a

43.   Staff of the Electric Theatre in Station Street in 1911. The cinema industry was one which benefited considerably from the influx of Europeans into the city. Seated on the left is the Belgian, Felix Allard. The cinema was owned by Joseph Cohen who, like Oscar Deutsch, was a Jew.

number of music halls to a community much involved in the stage, both as performers and patrons. But the Hebrew community was to suffer more than most from the advent of the railways in the centre of town. New Street station was built over the Froggary and two Hebrew cemeteries in Granville Street and Betholom Row (off Bath Row) were rendered unusable by the cutting of railway lines through or near them. The bodies from Granville Street were transferred to the new Hebrew cemetery at Witton; Betholom Row (which opened in 1823) remained in use for non-Birmingham Jews and indeed part of the burial ground still survives.

The need for a school that gave Jewish children a rudimentary education in the 'three Rs', as well as in the Hebrew language and religion, led to the foundation of a Hebrew National School in 1840, replaced by another in Hurst Street three years later. Initially there were around seventy pupils, the girls being taught separately on Sundays and Wednesdays. By 1904 the number had passed 600, but the percentage of families sending their children for a distinctively Hebrew education was falling. Birmingham retains a thriving Jewish community, particularly in Moseley, but one that is now scattered across the city.

A similar diaspora has befallen the Italian community that once occupied a small number of streets (but principally Bartholomew Street) off Digbeth. By 1914 they numbered about seven hundred, mostly originating from the villages around Rome. Many were street traders in the Victorian period, giving Birmingham its first real taste of ice-cream. For this the Digbeth location was perfect: broken eggs came from the egg market in Moor

44.   Cannon Street in 1892. Camillo Biglio operated from here as a confectioner in 1878 before opening perhaps the first Italian restaurant in Birmingham.

Street and ice from Fazeley Street. Less reputable was the trade in street urchins. A well-heeled *padrone* bought children for a few liras in Italy and transported them back to Birmingham. Here they graduated from exhibiting Madonnas to playing the hurdy-gurdy, accompanied by mice and monkeys. All profits, of course, to their employer.

Compared to the tiny Italian community and the small Jewish one, the Irish element in Victorian Birmingham was considerable. As early as 1828 there were around five thousand in the town, though many of these were seasonal workers, drifting away to more rural climes when the summer months came. By 1861 the figure was nearer 11,500, as the potato famine drove many across the Irish Sea. Irish migration followed a familiar pattern; people from one part of the country following families and neighbours to the same destination on the mainland. Most of the Birmingham Irish hailed from Connaught, particularly Roscommon or Galway. Their destination within Birmingham was equally specific; the majority ended up in Green's Village, the Inkleys, London 'Prentice Street or Park Street. Here they experienced the worst that Birmingham had to offer, made worse still by the necessity of taking in lodgers or the wider family network in order to pay the rent: '... several families frequently occupy each room from the cellar to the garret, the whole presents an appearance of filth, neglect, confusion, discomfort and insalubrity ...'.

Most of the first wave of settlers found work as poorly paid unskilled labourers (in 1851, 35 per cent gave their profession as labourers), a profession that included children, too. The difficulties felt by a rural society trying to adapt to the worst kind of urban existence were legion (and not limited to the Irish either). Language (many of the earliest migrants were Gaelic speakers), religion and cultural and family ties drove the Irish into close-knit and inward-looking ghettoes, with the accompanying problems of disease, over-crowding and insanitary conditions. A period of recession, such as that of 1855, increased their vulnerability. In that year 3,000 orders of admission to the workhouse were made by the Guardians, but most preferred to seek out-relief or starve than submit to the workhouse regime.

The growth of Catholicism in Birmingham reflected that of the Irish population. In the early 19th century only St Peter's in Broad Street (1786) and St Chad's (1808) served the Catholic community. A number of other churches and chapels appeared as the Catholic community grew. John Henry Newman, who converted to Catholicism in 1845, moved his family of Oratorians to a former gin distillery in Alcester Street in 1849, ministering to the poor and living on salt beef and cod. Three years later they moved to Hagley Road where the order still remains. The presence of Newman, one of the country's leading Catholic thinkers and writers, gave the Oratory an international reputation; its literary and artistic importance are perhaps not as well appreciated. Gerard Manley Hopkins was there as a novice priest in 1867, while the novelist J. R. R. Tolkien stayed for some months in 1904 after the death of his mother at the Oratory retreat at Rednal. The composer, Edward Elgar, was also a resident while working on his musical setting of Newman's *Dream of Gerontius*. Newman became a cardinal in 1879, 11 years before his death. But although his rooms at the Oratory are exactly as Newman left them, the church (completed in 1909) was rebuilt as a memorial to him.

Birmingham's importance in the revival of Catholicism in the 19th century was reflected in the reconstruction of St Chad's in 1839-41 by Augustus Pugin. It became Birmingham's Catholic cathedral and the first in post-Reformation England. Indeed, it would be another 64 years (in 1905) before Birmingham became the centre of an Anglican diocese.

45.   A contemporary illustration of the Murphy Riots in Park Street in 1867. Reading of the Riot Act by the mayor did not prevent a serious breakdown in law and order.

The relatively peaceful cohabitation between Catholic and Protestant, Irish and English, was shattered by the events of June 1867. In that month William Murphy, a convert from Catholicism, arrived in the town as a member of the Protestant Evangelical Mission. Barred from the Town Hall, Murphy set up his 'mission' in a wooden building in Carrs Lane, a location that had the advantage of being close to the Irish Catholics against whom his rhetoric was directed. While Murphy railed at Catholic doctrine ('no mass for no money') and Catholic priests ('murderers, cannibals, pickpockets and liars'), an ugly cocktail was being mixed outside. Anti-Catholic mobs, Irish roughs, impartial looters and confused police battled for control of the streets. Park Street in particular was looted, defended and garrisoned, and on the evening of 17 June the Mayor read the Riot Act both there and in the Bull Ring. Ultimately though, the Murphy Riots were as much a descent into random lawlessness (as had happened in 1791) as any serious breakdown in relations between the two communities. Birmingham remained Murphy's base up to his death in 1872 (he is buried at Key Hill), without ever again witnessing the major confrontations of 1867.

The Irish found themselves crammed into the worst of the Birmingham slums, back streets into which even the police would only venture in numbers. And though the

Improvement Scheme began to clear away some of the worst housing, some of the worst neighbourhoods remained intact. A satirical verse in the Town Crier of 1882 ran:

> Where are the peaceful Inkleys fair?
> Where I did roost at night,
> And murder and manslaughter were
> Among its pleasant sights.

During the 1870s especially, gang warfare, often divided along ethnic lines, made such streets even more hazardous. Rows between neighbours were usually settled out in the street with whatever weapons came to hand, and police involvement was resented. Many such affrays were drink-related, ending in cuts, bruises and regular appearances at Moor Street Police Court. But habits were too ingrained to be reformed by courtroom scenes that often degenerated into farce. Whether the guilty were Irish or English, they were not to be cowed by the presence of a magistrate. The more interest the Birmingham authorities took in the slums, particularly the campaign against drunkenness, the greater the danger of a head on collision.

The Navigation Street Riot of March 1875 marked the high (or low) point of street violence. On this occasion a constable was killed and the 12 arrests that were made resulted in one man being hung and a number of others (members of the notorious Chiving Gang) facing a lifetime of penal servitude. The fate of Jeremiah Corkery was celebrated in one of the last street broadsheets of that declining genre:

> The sentence it was passed Corkery's die was cast,
> On the scaffold, Oh what an awful fate.
> Alas! he is no more, his friends they suffer sore,
> Take warning before it is too late.

The verse was almost as awful as the consequences.

Given the importance of the issue of Home Rule to the politics of Chamberlain's Birmingham, it is surprising that the struggle for Irish independence has only rarely had a major impact on the town. Although rumours of Fenianism in Birmingham persisted through the 1860s, it was only in 1882 that the police had a major incident to investigate. In March an Irish-American, George Whitehead, was arrested for having explosives in his house in Ledsam Street. His claim that he was using nitro-glycerine for hanging wallpaper did not stick. The I.R.A. campaign of 1939-40 resulted in a number of arrests and expulsions, but not before bombs were exploded in city centre stores, Snow Hill station and the Paramount cinema in New Street. But Birmingham did not have the major casualties that other cities, such as Coventry, experienced. That was all to change in 1974, as we shall see later.

Any suspicion over Irish neutrality in the early 1940s were forgotten when the Republic became an important recruiting ground for the depleted council workforce. Many Irish women came over to work on the buses or in the hospitals, and by the early '50s around one-third of transport workers in the city were Irish. Jobs were relatively easy to find, accommodation was another matter; most found themselves inevitably in the crowded inner zone of Balsall Heath, Sparkbrook and Small Heath; areas that have retained a large Irish population. The old traditions of double-letting a bed once more re-appeared and many young men and women found themselves paying £2 a week for a room that they shared with five or six others. The problems of accommodation and integration faced by this new generation of migrants were acknowledged with the setting up of an Irish Community Centre in Digbeth in 1968.

The influx of Irish people in the '40s and '50s was reflected in the 1991 census figures. Of the 38,000 born in Ireland (North and South), almost two-thirds were in the 30-65 age bracket. But statistics alone cannot begin to describe a community that may contain fifth generation migrants, but who still wear a shamrock with pride on St Patrick's Day.

The patterns of migration in the 20th century are considerably more complex than those of the nineteenth. Chinese workers arrived during the First World War to work in the factories, many of whom remained to form a small but distinctive community in the city. The first Chinese restaurant in Birmingham, the Tong Kung, opened at Holloway Head in 1956. Groups of Vietnamese and East Africans arrived as a result of political or economic difficulties in their homelands. A mosque for Yemenis had opened in Balsall Heath in 1943. Of settlement from the Caribbean and the Indian Sub-Continent we will have more to say in a later chapter. Principally this was a post-war phenomenon, but even as early as 1944 a mosque had been established in Speedwell Road, Edgbaston, to serve Muslims arriving from India.

Chapter Sixteen

King Tom and the Democrats

As William Murdock later told the Royal Society, the first public demonstration of gas-lighting was the illumination of the Soho House and manufactory in 1802. Curiously, he must have omitted to draw the attention of the reporter from the *Gazette* to the fact, for the latter omitted to mention it. Nevertheless the celebrations at Soho to mark the Peace of Amiens were a spectacular sigh of relief from a town that had seen enough of French wars:

> The house was adorned on the summit of the roof by a magnificent star, composed of variegated lamps, and the centre window was embellished by a beautiful transparency, in glass, of a female figure, in the attitude of offering a thanksgiving for the return of peace. The manufactory was illuminated throughout its spacious with upwards of 2,600 coloured lamps, disposed into the forms of G.R., with the word "Peace", above which was placed the crown, with a star of exquisite brilliancy. In the centre of the front, a transparency represented a dove, the emblem of peace, descending on the globe; on the left wing, another represented the Caduceus of Mercury between two Cornucopias; and on the right, a beehive decorated with flowers.

All this plus fireworks, free beer and three Montgolfier balloons!

There was some excuse for a celebration: the previous 10 years had been as bad as any period in living memory. Birmingham's reliance on foreign markets, particularly France and America, had left her vulnerable to the economic collapse caused by war. The diary of Julius Hardy, a buttonmaker, gives us an eyewitness account of the precipitous slump and its effect on the town's traders. At the end of April 1793 he is forced to make half of his workers redundant. On 1 May he writes: 'What a deadful contrast does the nation exhibit now, when compared with our situation in the latter end of last year. In so short a space as a few months, from great prosperity we are plunged into general misery and wretchedness'. Hardy goes on to catalogue the recent bankruptcies: Joseph Boyce, a Deritend brassfounder; John Lowe, a bookseller in High Street; John Brooke, an attorney 'who owes more than twenty thousand pounds'. Brooke's fall 'by drawing bills without a property at hand to cover them' pulled down others who had endorsed them. So tightly interconnected were the businesses and bankers of Birmingham that a recession could topple them like a row of dominoes. On 5 May, Hardy reports another failure:

> Early this morning, three men walking near the rivulet which rises towards Bromsgrove Lickey and comes down to Deritend Bridge, some little above a place called Vaughton's Hole, found on the bank by the waterside a coat and hat, with letter under it: which they not being able to read, took up along with his cloathes to Mr. Carless' house at Mosseley [*sic*], thinking by appearance they were his, with intention to enquire. Soon

as they arrived some said they were, others they were not; but suspecting it might be so they returned to the place, where by that time a number of people had assembled, and in the meantime had got out of the water the drowned corpse of Mr. Carless, late a draper in High Street. It is generally believed he committed this rash act sometime in the preceding afternoon ... He had for some years past been in the Banking business, issued five guinea notes, and had experienced many losses; so that finding himself, it might be, greatly embarrassed, he sought relief from his grief and trouble in this terrible way.

The buttonmaker's apprehensions as to the consequences of the recession were common to many. Who would pay the poor levies? And without them, how would the poor eat? His ultimate fear was one that would haunt the conscience of the nation for the next 40 years: 'Well it would be, did but our statesmen and governors consider these things sufficiently. I fear, if the pressures of want and lack of work continues long, lest the common people should rise upon their rulers, and so occasion dreadful tumults in the land'.

House-building and land speculation were also hit by the recession, nowhere more spectacularly than in the Crescent. Here, on land that was once part of Baskerville's estate, a local speculator planned an elegant terrace of 23 Georgian houses on the edge of town. The estate agent's blurb read: 'There is not the least possibility of any future buildings ever excluding the inhabitants from a most agreeable prospect of the country'. Indeed, one potential purchaser had to convince his wife that a house there was not 'so far in the country'. This was 1788; seven years and 12 houses later, Birmingham's version of Bath was in trouble. And when the green shoots of recovery sprouted, industry too was moving into Cambridge Street, offering an agreeable prospect of factory chimneys. The Crescent was never completed, though some of the houses hung around for centuries. The last to be occupied was no. 18 which gave its name to the Crescent Theatre, which moved out in 1964.

As the small industries slumped, many in the town found themselves once more vulnerable to the vicissitudes of hard winters and bad harvests (the two coincided in 1794-5) as in the old pre-industrial days. The poor law system, which relied on the delicate balance between haves and have-nots, was thrown into chaos and the workhouse creaked at the seams.

Birmingham's once lauded social coherence appeared to be in disarray, and Hardy's fears seemed to be coming true. Twice Pickard's flour mill was attacked and again in May 1800 rioting broke out, aimed at the town's principal millers and bakers, assumed to be fixing bread prices artificially high. Troops were called out to quell the outbreak, even though the principal protagonists were women. Among those called into action were the Loyal Birmingham Volunteers, a kind of voluntary home-guard or 'Dad's Army'. Despite their patriotic intent to stand up to Napoleon, they had seen little excitement other than chasing the odd bull-baiter. This must have been a welcome chance of real action. In July 1795 the *Gazette* helpfully advised that families could save money by eating wholemeal bread, a suggestion two centuries ahead of its time! Another helpful comment appeared in December 1799: '... hawthorn berries, which are this winter in uncommon abundance, have been found very fattening for pigs. It will be a great saving of grain to farmers, and relief to the indigent, to employ poor children to collect the berries at 6d. a strike'.

The wave of charitable work that accompanied the disturbances was not entirely altruistic, for it was the benefactors that stood to lose most from the breakdown in law and order. Nevertheless a number of initiatives sought to plug the gap between poor relief and starvation. In December 1793 a liberal subscription was formed 'for the purpose of supplying the labouring poor with bread, and potatoes, during the depth of winter'. A note in the *Gazette* suggested that this was more an investment than a charity: 'May an Honourable Conclusion of the present War soon restore, in all their Plenitude, the Arts of Peace, and the grateful Mechanic will then repay with Industry the Protection extended to him in the hour of Sickness and of Want'.

The first cook-shop, selling meat soup at a penny a quart, opened in Peck Lane in 1797, and was followed by a string of charity soup-shops, providing their nourishing mixture of beef, vegetables, rice and peas. Another institution, set up by Owen Owens in the 1790s, sought to rid its subscribers of the fear of 'burial at the expense of the parish'. The Society for the Decent Burial of Men, Women, and Children gave its subscribers a respectable interment at the cost of one penny per week, as well as supplying clothing for the bereaved. By 1795 there were almost 2,400 subscribers, and in 1800 it was joined by a similar General Providential Society 'for the Relief of the Indigent Sick and the Assistance of Old Age'.

The peace celebrated to such effect in 1802 was to last less than a year. In 1803 the war with Napoleon was renewed, and so it continued until the latter finally met his Waterloo. Peace there may finally have been, but prosperity did not accompany it. A gun-making town such as Birmingham did not always appreciate peace as an unmixed blessing. Indeed, it turned out that the decline in government demand that followed the peace produced a worse slump than that produced by the war. Investment did not return as it should have done, prices dropped, and a deflationary spiral was underway. In 1816, the tumbling price of pig-iron once more brought the rioters onto the streets of the town.

Back in 1793, Julius Hardy saw that it was as much the fragility of the economy as the war that was the problem. The government was willing to let the Bank of England, a private company, dictate economic policy. When the latter was unwilling to reflate, the knock-on effect passed through the London bankers and on to the provinces and, unless currency was freely passing through the country, the effect was stagnation. The button-maker's private thoughts were soon to be given public voice by a young Birmingham banker. His name was Thomas Attwood.

The man who was later to be called 'the very first economist of the Age', 'King Tom' and 'the most

46. Thomas Attwood (1783-1856), one of Birmingham's first two Members of Parliament. His final Birmingham home was The Grove in Harborne.

47. Attwood & Spooner's Bank at the bottom of New Street opened in 1791. Its demise in the 1850s was marked by acrimony and considerable debts. It was taken over by the Birmingham Joint Stock Bank.

important man in England' was a partner in one of Birmingham's largest banking establishments. Attwoods and Spooner, founded in 1791, stood next to the *Hen and Chickens Hotel* on New Street. It should be said that the 18th-century bank was not concerned with private savings; its profits lay in the issuing of bank-notes and lending to businesses, and the only guarantee of safety was the property and savings of its owners, themselves usually businessmen. As the British economy bumped along on the bottom, Attwood watched the decline and fall of local industries, taking the bank's loans with them. An economic strategy was steadily developing in his mind, but in 1812, at the age of 29, he found himself, perhaps a little prematurely, embarked on 40 years of campaigning. His appearance in the limelight followed from his appointment as the town's high bailiff. Not a necessarily important post, but in the absence of any kind of representative democracy, a prominent one.

The main thrust of Attwood's campaigning was to shake the government out of what he saw as indifference to provincial England. Two issues, having a devastating effect on Birmingham's trade, seemed to epitomise that indifference. The first issue, and the one that marked the beginning of Attwood's political career, was known as the Orders-in-Council. Enacted in 1807, the Orders banned all trade with territory held by the French. Crucially this affected Anglo-American relations and, after retaliatory action by the Americans, Birmingham's lucrative trade with the U.S. was on the rocks. But the second issue was already making negotiation even more complicated: the East India Company's monopoly of trade with the Far East. Here was a familiar problem: a London-based company monopolising a trade to the exclusion of all others. The same thing had happened over guns and coins (and would happen again over exhibition centres). Put the two together and it seemed to show that the British government was prepared to block provincial trade to the west and to the east. A campaign was launched to re-write the East India Company's charter and to revoke the Orders-in-Council.

Birmingham was not alone in the campaign, but its voice (and Attwood's) was prominent. In 1812 the Orders-in-Council were revoked and in the following year the lid was lifted off trade with the East. After the 1812 success, Attwood's coach was carried into town: it was to be the first of many such acclamations.

Birmingham empowered its high bailiff because it had no other voice. A population of 85,000, it had less parliamentary representation than deserted villages in Wiltshire; that is, none at all. Then again, neither had Manchester nor Wolverhampton. What the events of 1812-3 had made clear was that the urban centres of provincial England had a powerful voice, but no representation in Westminster. Surely these two could be put together as well.

Thomas Attwood, not by nature a popularist, recognised that only by industrial representation in the Commons would the government be shaken out of its torpor and persuaded to take a more interventionist role in the economy of the country. He characterised the Commons as a seat of 'ignorance, imbecility and indifference'. Later, with first-hand experience of the place, he revised his estimate downwards. Oxbridge scholars, he said, controlled the House, lacing their speeches with literary allusions divorced from reality. They were more interested in going to Ascot than listening to the voice of commerce and manufacturing (by which he meant principally himself). With words such as these, the movement for reform had begun.

The focus for the many meetings that eventually led to reform was Newhall Hill, now a run-down street that runs up to the Jewellery Quarter, but then a piece of open land to the left of St Paul's Square, where for a few months some fairground entrepreneur set up the 'Russian Mountains', a giant helter-skelter that ran from the cliff-top on Graham Street down the valley and up again. The comedian, James Dobbs, who incidentally had once demonstrated his new reaping machine on a field of artificial corn on the stage of the Theatre Royal, lamented the passing of the old hill (and much of the rest of the town) in 1828:

> But what's more melancholy still
> For poor old Brummagem,
> They've taken away all Newhall-hill
> Poor old Brummagem!
>
> At Easter time, girls fair and brown,
> Used to come rolly-polly down,
> And show'd their legs to half the town;
> Oh! the good old sights of Brummagem.

Both the tradition and the girls had bitten the dust. In its pre-development days, however, the hill formed a natural amphitheatre, large enough to contain the thousands that would gather there for the mass rallies.

The initial campaigns were organised under the auspices of the Hampden Club and its chairman, George Edmonds. Edmonds stands out as one of the great characters of 19th-century Birmingham. The son of a Baptist minister, he ran a school, published a newspaper (for which seditious organ he was imprisoned), and campaigned tirelessly for reform and universal franchise. He was also the creator of an artificial language, a generation before Esperanto. His universal langue, despite some early enthusiasm for it in Spain, failed to obtain the universality he wished and he died, no longer in his right mind, in Birmingham workhouse.

The first Newhall Hill meeting in January 1817 was led by Edmonds, and demanded 'such a reform in the Commons House of Parliament as will restore frequent elections and general suffrage'. A petition attracted 21,000 signatures. More meetings took place in July and August of 1819. But the first wave of dissent was destined to fall. The arrest of political subversives and pamphleteers, together with press hostility and the bloody events at Peterloo, squeezed the movement dry. As yet the campaign did not have a broad enough base to turn the tide.

It was 1829 when the tide finally began to turn, and again it coincided with a period of economic stagnation. Moves to transfer the Parliamentary seat of East Retford (a rotten borough that had lost its franchise because of corruption) to Birmingham had initially been defeated, but the combination of political reform, plus the economic changes advocated by Attwood, had become a manifesto that could once more be taken on to the streets. In January 1830 a new organisation known as the Birmingham Political Union (B.P.U.) announced its presence. The leaders of the Union were a mixture of prominent industrialists and businessmen, together with the shop owners and small businessmen that played such an important part in Birmingham life. The former group included Thomas Attwood, Joshua Scholefield and George Frederick Muntz. The latter had James 'Goose' Evans, a japanner, who had once fainted at a union meeting; Joseph 'Pigmy' Ernes, a button-maker, and Thomas Parsons, a metal dealer. In its leadership at least the union could justify its claim to be 'a General Political Union between the Lower and the Middle Classes'.

Political campaigning, unlike wars, is not confined to the summer months. If the B.P.U. was to draw the large audiences necessary to express the breadth of its appeal, a warmer venue was needed as well as Newhall Hill. With the Public Office excluded because of its size, the union was grateful of the offer by John Beardsworth, a sympathiser and owner of the biggest indoor hall in town. This was Beardsworth's Repository on Cheapside, a massive horse-market, once the home of the horse called 'Birmingham' that won the St Leger.

Like any political campaign, if the movement was to widen its appeal it was essential to mix mass rallies with a little refined public relations. On 11 October 1830 a sit-down banquet for 3,700 people at the Repository captured the imagination, at least of those lucky enough to be inside. 3,500 lbs of meat, 11,000 pints of beer, fanfares, toasts and speeches graced the evening. The speakers expressed solidarity with the cause (though not necessarily the methods) of the French Revolution. 'Revolution' was the word that dare not speak its name, but it lurked behind the avowals of patriotism and liberty, spreading fear through the corridors of Westminster. The success of the B.P.U. and of Attwood in particular was so to mobilise public opinion that the threat need not be explicitly spoken.

By the end of 1830 the events in Birmingham and elsewhere were having their effect. In London the Lord Mayor's Parade was abandoned for fear of violence, if not assassination, and Wellington's Tory government resigned. The new prime minister was Lord Grey, elected on a mandate of 'redress of grievance before it is too late'. Grey presented the first Reform Bill to the House; it was by no means 'democracy at a stroke' but it was too radical for many and it fell. A second bill followed.

THE "BRUMMAGEM" MOUNTEBANK.

A Sketch from the TOWN HALL. — The *East*-end of the Church in the distance.

48.   A cartoon of 1836 in the wake of the Reform meeting in the Town Hall 'which would overawe the House of Lords and perhaps the throne itself'. Attwood teaches George Muntz to dance.

By now the B.P.U. had 9,000 members and was already advocating a more radical overhaul of the democratic process than was on offer in either of the two bills: disenfranchisement of rotten boroughs, representation for the large towns, suffrage for all tax-payers and secret ballots. It was virtually the same agenda on which the Chartists would campaign a few years later. As the Whig government inched forward, there were fears that a compromise between radical and gradual Reform was slipping out of reach.

Chapter Seventeen

The Far Side of Newhall Hill

By the middle of September 1831, the second Reform Bill had successfully passed through the Commons. But the natural conservatism and vested interests of the Lords still presented a formidable hurdle. There was still a feeling that the campaign needed a last 'big push' to convince the Lords. Once more Newhall Hill was to be the focus of national attention. At 10.00 a.m. on 3 October, church bells summoned the faithful to a rally larger than any Birmingham had seen. It was the day of the second reading of the bill in the Lords. It is now impossible to be certain how many attended: as with mass rallies today the claims of the organisers and those opposed to the cause differ enormously. The union itself claimed 100,000. The numbers were swelled by delegations from the Staffordshire Unions and the Black Country colliers and ironworkers. (There was an irony here that most of those present would never become enfranchised anyway: full suffrage was another hundred years away.) Three hours later, as the crowds dispersed, the meeting was pronounced a huge success. Back in the capital, things were not quite so successful: the second reading was lost by 41 votes.

The Birmingham church bells that had called the reformers to the Hill were now rung in mourning, but for whom they were tolling was another question. Certainly the very survival of the Lords was at stake if the second chamber killed off the third Reform Bill. But as the new bill inched from reading to reading, the Reform issue was toppling prime ministers like nine-pins. Grey fell and was replaced by Wellington; he in turn failed to form a government. The Union leaders called for another rally on the Hill on 7 May 1832.

This was to be the 'big one', the one commemorated by the painting *The Gathering of the Unions*. Graham Street Chapel stands on the cliff-top in the distance; below the union flags and banners fly. They came from the Black Country, Coventry and Warwick, from Droitwich and Redditch and beyond, in numbers estimated (though not reliably) to be 200,000. They sang the Union hymn:

> Shall honest labour toil in vain
> While plunder fattens on the land!
> Still shall a tyrant faction's reign
> People and King at once command?
> No! it may not, shall not be,
> For we must, we will be free.

The banners were for Attwood, King and Country, a combination of causes that at last seemed possible.

49. The famous view of the 1832 gathering on Newhall Hill. Attwood's coach is almost lost in the crowds at the centre of the picture.

We have, I think, spent enough time on Newhall Hill to cut the story short. The third Reform Bill passed through its remaining stages and became law in June 1832. Attwood's return to Birmingham was a triumphal procession, and the town's resourceful manufacturers made a killing on commemorative mugs, medals and even garters with 'King Tom's' head upon them. The election of the president and vice-president (Joshua Scholefield) of the Political Union to the Commons as Birmingham's first M.P.s was a formality. These two men were the ancestors of those many that have represented the city since, a list that includes: John Bright, George Dixon, the Chamberlains, Roy Jenkins, Dennis Howell, Roy Hattersley and others.

Attwood was to hold his seat from December 1832 until his resignation through ill-health in December 1839; Scholefield till his death in July 1844. The latter's son, William, continued the Scholefield tradition until 1867. All were Liberals: it would be many years before Birmingham elected a Conservative member. For Attwood the events of 1832 were the top of fortune's wheel. His many attempts to get economic reform onto the Commons agenda met with indifference and failure. His dire warnings of the dangers of an expansionist Russia equally fell on deaf ears, though it did endear him to the Poles. Polish visitors were a common sight at his house in Harborne.

The unveiling of a new statue of Attwood (in January 1993) has revived interest in one of Birmingham's national figures. He is now the only one to be commemorated with two statues; the earlier monument was erected in 1859 in 'the most conspicuous position in town' at the New Street entrance to the L.N.W.R. station. It later followed the traditional migration of Birmingham statues out of town to Calthorpe Park, and thence to the site of his former house in Sparkbrook. This residence, together with those in the Crescent and the Grove in Harborne, has disappeared. Attwood himself once talked of being buried on

Newhall Hill to be close to the 'faithful buttons and buckles' of Birmingham who had raised him to such pre-eminence. In fact he lies in Hanley churchyard. So much for pathos.

Anyone who has gone through the mincer of school history will know that the 1830s were the most complicated period of English history. How did reform become Chartism? When did Whig become Liberal (or vice versa)? Who passed which Bill when? The only consolation is that the towns of England were going through a period of similar confusion, as the Conservatives re-grouped and the Liberals splintered in various directions.

One moment of certainty first. The passing of the Municipal Corporations Act in 1835 allowed towns like Birmingham to apply for a Municipal Charter. Even here the advantages were far from universally recognised; in fact, as with the Street Commissioners Act, the town seemed to be divided down the middle. So limited would be the powers of the new Corporation that its usefulness, given the presence of Street Commissioners, was questionable. The new Corporation would extend far beyond the Commissioners' patch to cover the area of the whole parliamentary borough, including Edgbaston, Bordesley, Duddeston and Nechells. There were old loyalties there to be trampled upon. And there was always the thorny old question of the need for increased rates to pay for it.

Nevertheless, a charter was granted and received by the High Bailiff on 1 November 1838. The new council was to consist of a mayor, 16 aldermen and 48 councillors representing the 13 wards. On 5 November the Charter was read to the people of Birmingham in the Town Hall. The first elections took place on Boxing Day of that year, with the Liberals securing most of the seats. This was hardly surprising: Conservatives were still on the whole opposed to the Charter, and in the registering of burgesses (local electors) there were distinct signs of discrimination against their supporters. Indeed the early council elections show a remarkable apathy on the part of the electors. In the 1844 election in Ladywood Ward, for example, only three of the 226 burgesses bothered to vote. Worse still, in the 1842 election in St Mary's ward one solitary elector turned out. If this was democracy in action, it was not very impressive, though it did simplify the counting. Indeed, in the same elections only one in five of those entitled to vote did so. Add to this

50.   Samuel Lines' painting of the town from the tower of St Philip's. Colmore Row is on the right, leading to the spire of Christ Church, New Street. It dates from 1821.

the fact that of the total population of 182,922, about one in three was a burgess, then you have a system with teething troubles. Franchise did not extend to any householder under £10, and of course it was limited to men.

The turn-out for the first elections in 1838 had been a little more encouraging. The returns for Edgbaston ward, for example, were as follows:

Charles Sturge	180	R. T. Cadbury	109
Clement Scholefield	179	S. Haines	100
H. Van Wart	169	J. Fereday	98

Those on the left were Liberal; those on the right Tories. Among the familiar families here represented, the name Van Wart might make us pause. Henry Van Wart was an American, born at Tarrytown on the Hudson in 1783. He became a naturalised British citizen and set up as a merchant in the Jewellery Quarter. More famous still was his brother-in-law and sometime house-guest, Washington Irving. It was at the Van Warts' residence on Camden Hill that Irving composed the famous children's story, *Rip Van Winkle*, in 1818. Indeed, Irving drew much inspiration from his visits to Birmingham: his Bracebridge Hall has its origins in the Jacobean mansion known as Aston Hall.

On 27 December the Council met for the first time and chose William Scholefield as its first mayor. Again a line was established that would later include a host of Chamberlains, Cadburys and many of Birmingham's prominent politicians. These were the events that the people of Birmingham celebrated in such memorable style in July 1838, filling Aston Hall grounds with 11,000 spectators and almost as many participants. The fire-breathing dragons, nicknamed Egbert and Ogbert, were not desperately historical, but their trial run in Cambridge Street before the show was an historical event in itself.

Birmingham was now able to display its own coat of arms, and a committee was formed to decide between the five submitted designs. They were a curious mixture of the ancient and modern. One showed a lion passant, together with a muscular man holding the lictor's axe, sharing the stage with a locomotive engine. There were quiescent lambs, caps of liberty and serpents on pillars. The mottoes too varied between 'Emporium of the World', 'Peace, Law and Order' and 'Unity, Liberty, Prosperity'. Birmingham was almost lumbered with the easily misinterpreted motto 'Fortitudo et Rectum'. In the end the choice fell upon the fourth design which centred upon the old coat of arms of the Birmingham family, along with the motto 'Forward'.

However, it is necessary for a grant of arms to be made by the College of Arms. In their eagerness (to be charitable) to use the new seal, the Council forgot to make an application, so for 30 years the arms were used illegally. Had the opponents of the Charter got hold of this morsel, there would have been enough red faces in the Council to fill a gymnasium. To add insult to injury, the arms of the de Berminghams were also wrongly copied. By 1867, when the errors were discovered, three different coats of arms were being displayed in the town. The medallist, Joseph Moore was commissioned to make hasty modifications.

The revised coat of arms was still not the one in use today. When Birmingham became a city in 1889, yet another modification was made. The de Bermingham arms remained, but were now accompanied by two supporters (almost a full house at Birmingham City), representing art and industry. The arms were altered again in the 1930s, and in 1976 to incorporate parts of the Sutton coat of arms. As the city continues to ponder

51. One of the many incorrect versions of the borough arms. The supporting figures were added in 1889, but the shield shows squares instead of lozenges.

on the adoption of an appropriate logo, it is reassuring to know that the issue goes back over 150 years.

Compared to what followed, the problem of the coat of arms was a minor hiccup. Almost immediately upon its creation, the new council faced a major, not to say terminal, crisis. But for the reasons behind it we must turn away to the wider field of national politics.

To many the Reform Bill of 1832 was only the first rung on a long ladder of political reform. As we have already seen, the Birmingham Political Union had already committed itself to a wider campaign for household suffrage, salaried members of Parliament, the abolition of a property qualification, ballots and triennial elections. With one exception (the length of a government's term of office) these were the five points of the 'People's Charter', presented to Parliament by Thomas Attwood in June 1839 with a petition of 1,286,000 signatures.

Chartism was an evolving movement, as the ground shifted after the Reform Bill period, but in many ways the first real demonstration of its appeal came in the mass rally at Holloway Head on 6 August 1838. The meeting attracted perhaps 100,000, with delegates from across the country, and once more Thomas Attwood was the chief spokesman. The campaign was wider than the five points of the Charter, for it took in the newly reformed Poor Law, the Corn Laws as well as the government's economic policy.

Once more Birmingham became the focus for a national movement, for the Convention found the town a less threatening location for its meetings than London.

The mass meetings of the B.P.U. had passed off without trouble, but not so the Chartist ones, and in the summer of 1839 Birmingham had its worst outbreak of civil disorder since 1791. Much blame was heaped upon the the Chartist leaders, and indeed it appears that a radical strain had developed that alienated former Unionists like George Edmonds. But there were other causes too, not least the government's attempts to nip the movement in the bud by the imprisonment of 'agitators' such as Fussell and Brown. The movement had the use of Lawrence Street chapel for meetings (it would subsequently be taken over by the Owenite Socialists), but the focus for most activity was the Bull Ring and, on 4 July 1839, violence erupted there.

With the town council unable to enforce a ban on meetings, the mayor sought the assistance of central government. Using the newly-opened railway line, a unit of Metropolitan

Police, numbering around sixty, was despatched to the Midlands. They arrived to find the Bull Ring already full of demonstrators. The story is taken up by an eye-witness, James Jaffray:

> The police fought their way to the standard bearers and demolished the flags, whilst others knocked down all who opposed them. For a moment they partially cleared the Bull Ring, but the people rallied; some tore down shutters of the shops in the neighbourhood; others smashed them in pieces and supplied the crowd with bludgeons; others again picked up heavy stones, and thus armed they returned to the charge. The police, who were by this time scattered, were surrounded and most of them overpowered ... and had it not been for the arrival of the military the entire of them would have fallen a sacrifice to the fury of the people.

Those of the London police who were not already on their way to the General Hospital re-grouped and began an exploration of one or two of the more notorious Bull Ring pubs, including the *Market Hall Tavern* and the *Grand Turk*, where agitators were thought to be lurking. With the Bull Ring occupied by men in uniform, the demonstrators turned their attention to Holloway Head. The railings of the nearby St Thomas's church provided the more confrontational of them with the most primitive of weaponry.

For the next 10 days tension remained high, though disturbances were limited. The Convention could now add injury to the long list of political grievances they felt. The secretary, Lovett, published a catalogue of the new outrages. The Birmingham people's right to meet in the Bull Ring had been violated by an unconstitutional force from London, and that instigated by the very men who had once shared the Chartist cause. Lovett rapidly found himself under arrest, though he was later released on bail.

On 15 July trouble once more erupted around the Bull Ring and a number of shops were looted and destroyed, and the contents of an upholsterer's shop were used to make rudimentary torches. By 10.00 a.m. it seemed that the whole market-place was on fire. When the fire-engines arrived (and that profession was still very much in its infancy), the *Nelson Hotel* was ablaze. In all 11 businesses from butcher and baker to candlestick-maker were looted: 'The confusion and alarm of the night were terrible. Many of the inhabitants in the Bull Ring and neighbourhood fled with their families, account books, and such portion of their valuable property as could be easily conveyed away'.

It seemed that the twilight world of Birmingham that lay in the streets around the Bull Ring had emerged to devastating effect. There were numerous arrests, including many young boys, and the new prison in Moor Street was packed. Of those arrested four were transported and 11 sent to jail. The full cost of the rioting amounted to £20,000. In the Lords the Duke of Wellington declared that 'he had been in many towns taken by storm, but never had such outrages occurred in them as had been committed in Birmingham'.

The Chartist riots could not have come at a worse time for the new Town Council. Not only did they seem to suggest that the body was not in control of Birmingham, the brush that tarred the agitators might also be waved at a number of councillors who, if not exactly sympathisers, had long been fellow travellers. Just as the council was petitioning Parliament for the power to establish a police force (already granted to most municipalities), all hell was let loose on the streets of Birmingham. It was all most unfortunate, except to the town's conservatives, who had always claimed that the Charter of Incorporation was flawed anyway, if not actually illegal.

At the second reading of the Police Bill, Sir Robert Peel made a strong attack on the Birmingham Council as unfit to control its own police force, and proposed instead a force of around 300 under the control of a government appointed commissioner. In August 1839 this very different Police Bill came into effect for a period of three years, and the council was in the curious position of levying a rate for a police force that was not under its control.

Worse still was to follow. Just as the new council had been stripped of its overcoat, it was in danger of losing its trousers as well. During the arguments over the Police Bill, severe doubts had been cast over the validity of the Charter. Certainly there were technical errors in the way the Charter had been drafted and enacted, but really the arguments were ideological. Conservatives in Manchester and Bolton too had succeeded in suspending their municipal charters. To them local government was in the hands of radicals (nay, quasi-revolutionaries), not fit to levy rates on a people that were not fully convinced of the need for them. This, of course, was not an argument that was restricted to the 1840s.

For three years the Corporation was effectively powerless. Stripped of a police force, unable to levy rates and with a suspect Charter, all that it could do was hold meetings and send the occasional loyal greeting to the Royals (as they did to Queen Victoria in 1840). Even the Quarter Sessions had to be suspended.

It was not until 1842, when the Police Act came to the end of its term, that the Charter was finally confirmed, and the Corporation allowed to police its own borough and erect a borough gaol. In many ways 1942 would have been a more appropriate date to celebrate Incorporation than 1938, though by then the city had other things on its mind. At last, in 1842, the Corporation of Birmingham had authority over the borough, except for those powers still in the hands of the Street Commissioners, the Overseers of the Poor of Birmingham and Aston, the Surveyors of Deritend and Edgbaston, the Commissioners of Duddeston and Nechells ...

Chapter Eighteen

The Musical Town

No one could have been more surprised (had he still been alive) than Sir Robert Peel, when the grateful townspeople of Birmingham erected a statue to him in 1855. The man who had done more than most to put a spoke in the wheel of local government, was the Prime Minister that finally accepted the validity of the Charter of Incorporation in 1842, and Birmingham was happy to express its gratitude, at least posthumously. The statue that gazed purposefully down New Street had cost 2,000 guineas and was the work of Peter Hollins, who had succeeded his father, William, as 'sculptor-in-chief' for the town. Such artistic niceties were lost on the lorry driver who demolished it in November 1926. Its current location, outside the Police Training College on Pershore Road is appropriate and presumably a lot safer!

This was only the second public statue to be erected in the town, after the statue of Nelson in the Bull Ring. Given the mixed reaction to the 'Egyptian Conduit', this was hardly surprising. But sculpture aside, Birmingham had already come of age as an artistic centre to match its growing industrial status and, in music in particular, it had broken into the European circuit.

The story of the Triennial Music Festivals is one of those many faceted tales that includes music, social clubs, charity and churches, and it is not easy to know which thread to follow. Let's go clubbing.

The late 18th century had been marked by the rise of amateur debating societies and philosophical clubs among the middle classes. The Birmingham Robin Hood Free

52. Peel's statue moving to its new home on the Pershore Road. It was cast by the firm of Elkington & Mason and was the first statue to be electro-plated.

Debating Society, for example, met at the *Red Lion* in the Bull Ring during the 1770s. Entry cost sixpence, but women were admitted free. A similar society used Mrs. Ashton's Coffee Room in the Cherry Orchard, that rapidly disappearing piece of land from which the modern Cherry Street takes its name.

Another group that met in the Cherry Orchard, or rather in a bar nearby, was the 'Musical and Amicable Society', whose core was the choirs of St Philip's and St Bartholomew's chapel. The latter had been built in 1749 on Masshouse Lane to serve the expanding eastern side of the town, on land given by the ironmaster, John Jennens. The society mixed rehearsals and drinking, not an uncommon combination with church choirs! As their banner proclaimed:

> May the Catch and the Glass go about and about
> And another succeed to the Bottle that's out.

From one of this circle, James Kempson, came the proposal in 1766 to hold a charity concert for 'the aged and distressed housekeepers' near St Bartholomew's, which was held on Christmas Day of that year. The idea of linking musical concert to charity was not an original one, but it was new to Birmingham. This was to become an annual event right up to Victorian times. But another charitable project was also forcing itself upon the attention of the music-makers.

In November 1766, the local physician, Dr. John Ash, published in the *Gazette* a proposal to build 'A General Hospital for the Relief of the Sick and Lame'. With the population of the town rising and its health in consequent decline, the need for such an establishment was pressing. Only the infirmary attached to the Workhouse fulfilled this need, and that was restricted to parishioners of St Martin's and St Philip's. Ash's call for subscriptions brought an immediate response, from landowners like the Holtes and Goughs, industrialists like Boulton and Taylor and a number of clubs and societies. The site of the new hospital was to be Summer Lane, and the initial estimates of costs suggested £3,000. Work on a 100-bed ward began, and slowly ground to a halt. By 1767 those with money had found another place to invest their hard-earned savings, and the shell of the new building was being used as a football ground. And had it not been for the funds raised from musical events, it might well have remained so.

It was in September 1768 that the first three-day musical festival was held to raise funds for the hospital. The format was one that would be followed for many years: sacred music, including Handel's *Messiah*, was performed in St Philip's (by a choir conducted by James Kempson), while secular concerts were held at the theatre in King Street. So confident was the organising committee of a good turn-out that a special one-way system was devised to prevent a carriage-jam in King Street: 'Ladies and Gentlemen are desired to order their Servants to drive their Carriages down Peck-Lane and up King-Street, as they go to and from the Playhouse: the Streets will be lighted from the Playhouse to the Ball room'. The optimism was not to be dashed: receipts of £800 gave a net profit of almost £300. The 18th-century equivalent of Live Aid was under way.

The concerts of 1768 were intended as a one-off boost to the Hospital's funds, but 10 years later, with the Summer Lane building still languishing, another festival was penciled in for September. Here the receipts were to be split between the hospital and St Paul's Church. The latter had been commenced in 1776 to relieve congestion in the desperately overcrowded St Martin's. As with the hospital, land was not a problem (Charles Colmore

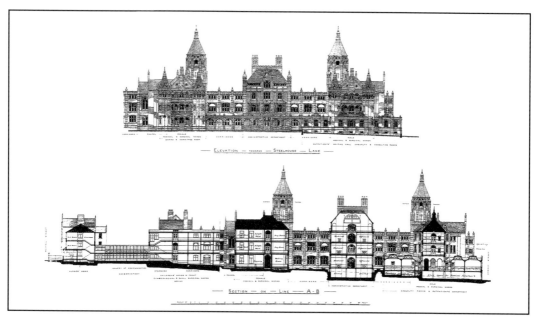

53. Designs for the new General Hospital in Steelhouse Lane. It was opened by Princess Christian of Schleswig Holstein in 1897 and is the largest of the city's many terracotta buildings.

had donated it), it was the spiralling cost of building the church that delayed its completion, and generous donors pretended to be out when the time came to put hands in pockets.

Once more music came to the rescue, and the festival held in 1778 was to be the first in a line of triennial festivals that continued right up to the First World War. Within a year, the General Hospital had been completed and opened on 20 September 1769. There were 40 beds (something of a climb-down on the original proposals), 10 patients, four physicians (including Ash and William Withering) and four nurses. There was even a barber to shave the patients, as there was at the workhouse. From such small beginnings the multi-million pound industry that is the Birmingham Health Authorities arose. The General was later expanded with two wings and additional beds until, in 1897, it transferred to a new building in Steelhouse Lane. We will return to Birmingham's hospitals later.

By the 1820s the Music Festivals were bringing in receipts of around £10,000, a third of which was directed to the hospital. The missing two thirds were the result of the increasing cost of attracting 'star' performers to the event. Probably the finest *diva* of her day, Angelica Catalani, appeared in the festivals of 1811-23, and was 'big box-office', as they say. Equally the festivals directed by Joseph Moore (1802-49) were characterised by an increasing variety of performers and music.

By the middle of Moore's term of office, the success of the event was putting considerable strain on the venues. Although the Theatre Royal provided a larger auditorium for secular concerts (and for the end of festival ball), St Philip's was struggling to cope with the day-time concerts. Once the doors to the church were opened, concert-goers abandoned their decorum and scrummaged ruthlessly for seats. As a local paper described the rush in 1823: 'Although at the first rush some little derangement took place in the female costume and some caps were scattered amid the crowd, still we did not hear of any serious accidents.' Nor was mayhem restricted to the audience. So intent were the people of Birmingham to get a clear view of the great and the good arriving at the concert that they removed a few hundred feet of railings from the churchyard. (Actually these railings had always been something of a bone of contention among the townspeople. The Street Commissioners had attempted to get the whole of St Philip's fenced off, much to the annoyance of those who used it as a running track.) But the Iniskillen Dragoons were on hand to maintain some semblance of order.

It was not long after the 1823 Festival that pressure began to grow, both from the Festival Committee and from the ratepayers, to find a more convenient location for the event. The idea was taken up by the Street Commissioners for the building of a 'town hall' to seat 3,000. At first the intention was to build it in Bennett's Hill, near to the Public News Room, but by 1829 the Commissioners' eyes were focused clearly on Paradise Street. Not only could the location of the Birmingham's greatest building have been different, the architect could have been as well. The Commissioners looked long and hard at the design supplied by Charles Barry, the architect of the Houses of Parliament, as well as the rebuilt Grammar School on New Street.

Instead, the choice fell upon Messrs. Hansom and Welch, two young and ambitious architects. Like Barry's, Hansom's design was a classical one, based on a temple in Rome. But so ambitious were the architects that their tender for the contract greatly under-estimated (by about £8,000) the cost of construction. With Hansom made bankrupt as a result, another architect, Charles Edge, stepped into his shoes to complete the work. These delays, together with the internal modifications necessary to accommodate the magnificent organ, meant that the building was not finally finished until 1849. The organ cost £3,000 and was commissioned from a London firm by Joseph Moore, after a fact-finding tour of the European organ-makers. Legend has it that when, in more recent times, Michael Jackson and his brothers performed at the Town Hall, they were proudly informed by the manager that the organ had been played by Mendelssohn. 'Who?' came the reply.

It is probably not realised that the Town Hall is not built of stone but of brick, which was then faced with Anglesey marble. At the time when it was built (long before the Council House or Post Office) it dwarfed its surroundings, and set a standard of municipal splendour in the area that later architects found hard to match. Certainly when the council set about commissioning the Council House in the 1870s, the successful design had to harmonise with its dominant neighbour.

Building the Town Hall had not only been a disaster for the original architects. During construction, the breaking of a pulley led to the deaths of two workmen. Their monument, consisting of the base of one of the surplus Town Hall columns, stands in St Philip's churchyard.

Despite not being finished, the Town Hall played host to the 1834 Festival. The first piece played, on the morning of 7 October, was the appropriately rousing Coronation Anthem, *Zadok the Priest*. One of the soloists at that first concert was the 16-year-old Clara Novello, another of the great Italian *divas* to grace the Festivals.

A full account of the Birmingham Musical Festivals would almost amount to a history of 19th-century music. Some of the composers that wrote for or appeared at the Festivals are less known today, though securing them was a significant coup at the time. Men like Neukomm, Gounod and Arthur Sullivan (more famous for his collaboration with Gilbert) were highly influential classical composers of their day. Others such as Mendelssohn, Dvorak

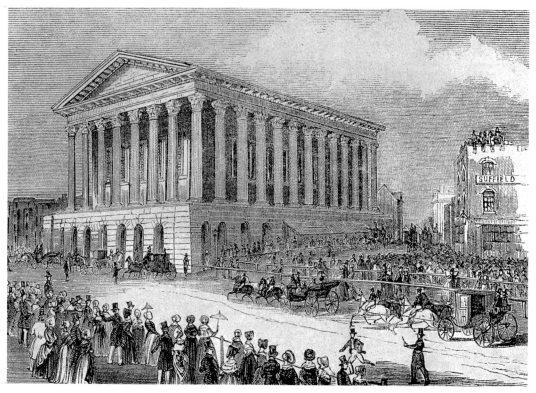

54. The Town Hall during a festival. The architects, Hansom and Welch, beat Rickman and Barry in the architectural competition. The design was based on the temple of Castor and Pollux in Rome.

and Elgar have maintained their popularity. We should also mention one or two of the stars in the seats too. Cardinal Newman attended the rehearsals for Gounod's *Redemption*, and the novelist, George Eliot, annoyed her neighbours by sobbing during the 1840 Festival. She is not the only great novelist to have appeared in the Town Hall; a few years later Charles Dickens would be giving the first public reading of *A Christmas Carol*. This was on 27 December 1853, and repeated three days later with reduced seat prices (at Dickens' request) to allow the working people of Birmingham the opportunity to attend. These readings too were fund-raising events to set up what became the Birmingham and Midland Institute in Paradise Street and now in Margaret Street. They were one of the great novelist's many visits to Birmingham: in 1848 he appeared in two plays at the Theatre Royal.

The first performance of Mendelssohn's *Elijah* in 1846, a work specifically written for the Festival, was the culmination of a nine years' link with Birmingham. His Piano Concerto in D Minor was also composed for the 1837 Festival. Sadly his death in 1847 spelled the end of the friendship, though the presence of the manuscript of his great oratorio in the Central Library maintains Birmingham's link with the composer.

Elgar's connections with the city were strong anyway, for he was a Midlander and Professor of Music at the University. Indeed, the premiere of his *Dream of Gerontius* in 1900 did more to shake the friendship than build upon it, so under-rehearsed and full of errors was the first performance.

Triumphant though the Triennial Festivals became, they were not without their critics. As early as 1829 the Quaker, Joseph Sturge, had criticised the use of divine oratorios for such mercenary reasons as fund-raising. Much later, Sir Arthur Sullivan compared Birmingham's musical life to a boa-constrictor that gorged itself every three years and fasted in between. This was a little unfair as we shall see.

More justifiable complaints were voiced by some of the performers. The choir and orchestra had traditionally drawn its members from far and wide: Birmingham was hardly big enough in the early 19th century to provide the 330-odd needed to fill choir and orchestra. In 1834, for example, Birmingham was home to a little over half of the choir, the rest being drawn from as far afield as Liverpool and Canterbury. Having arrived in Birmingham, the performers were forced to pay the inflated price of board and lodgings that prevailed during the Festival. If that was not enough, in the pre-railway days many found themselves reduced to walking home and sleeping rough on the road to London. As the *Musical Times* facetiously commented in 1837: '... it would seem that among the benefits conferred by the Festival to the General Hospital, there is a chance of its occasionally supplying it with a few patients'.

The First World War spelt the end of many institutions in Britain, and the Musical Festival was one of them. Sullivan's criticism of the Festival with the implied neglect of music in the years between events was a key argument in the decision not to revive it after the War. As a vehicle for star performers and new works it was finished, though the Festival Chorus still survives today.

Another musical institution that came to an end during the War casts doubt on Sullivan's assessment of Birmingham culture. Harrison's Popular Concerts (after the founder, Percy Harrison) were a series of concerts in the Town Hall begun in 1853. Here again was an endless list of star names, from sopranos like Adelina Patti and Clara Butt and pianists such as Paderewski, Clara Schumann and Percy Grainger, to conductors such as Elgar, Charles Halle and Henry Wood.

Not all the alternatives were on so grand a scale. Max Mossel, who taught violin at the Midland Institute School of Music, organised a long series of chamber concerts in the Grand Hotel from 1825 to 1898. Nor was Herr Mossel's violin playing always restricted to such grand surroundings. In 1899 he played in one of the 'Court and Alley Concerts', arranged to bring the beauties of classical music to Birmingham's less salubrious quarters. A male voice choir and several soloists performed in Court No.1, Dartmouth Street, scrubbed clean by the expectant residents (probably in more than one sense of the word). The *Weekly Post* described the occasion thus:

> The throbbing notes of a simple melody penetrated case-hardened poverty-stricken bosoms; the liquid tones that fell from the quivering strings had in them something that could raise the dwellers of Court No.1 above their squalid selves, and for a moment when the strains had ceased there was a hush, which is the greatest tribute to an artist's power.

One of the influential features of the Triennial Festivals had been the internationally known conductors that presided over them. Men like Michael Costa (conductor 1849-82), Hans Richter (1885-1909) and Henry Wood (1912). The mantle thrown down after their demise has since fallen upon the shoulders of the City of Birmingham Symphony Orchestra. The first concert (as the City of Birmingham Orchestra) was conducted by Elgar in 1920.

Subsequent conductors have included Adrian Boult and, more recently, Simon Rattle. The orchestra is one of only two (the other is in Chicago) to be funded by the local authority. Such an arrangement has not been without its drawbacks: Boult was for many years promised a new concert hall which never materialised. Rattle has been more successful, and Symphony Hall, a part of the International Convention Centre, is perhaps the greatest gift that any city could give its musical standard-bearer. Costing around £60 million, with revolutionary acoustics (ironically based on classical concert-hall design), it now stands at the centre of Birmingham's post-war musical revival. Symphony Hall has now taken its place on the circuit of international artists and orchestras, though its size (a little over 2,000 seats) has meant that large-scale opera productions have found it necessary to use the vast arenas of the N.E.C. and N.I.A.

The base established by the C.B.S.O. has been built upon in more recent times. A resident ballet company at the Hippodrome is the result of a change of names and homes for the Sadler's Wells Company, now the Birmingham Royal Ballet. In 1992 Birmingham's designation as 'City of Music' was a testimony to a place that had re-discovered its musical centrality. Particularly important was the decision to use professional success to galvanise amateur performance and participation, and to emphasise the multi-cultural nature of Birmingham's continuing musical heritage.

55. Birmingham's acclaimed Symphony Hall in the International Convention Centre. Doors on either side of the organ lead to a huge reverberation chamber, often used to enhance the sound choral works.

But there is another tradition out there that has remained relatively untouched by the grand classical tradition of the Music Festivals. Such are the cultural divisions (reflected, I have to confess, in this book) that the richness of popular culture, from ballads to music hall, and pop song to rap and bhangra, have to be concentrated in the next chapter.

Chapter Nineteen

From Ballads to Bhangra:
Birmingham's Popular Culture

Let us take a Saturday night walk in the Birmingham of 1871:

> Out on the streets again, where the usual features of Saturday night in Birmingham are noticeable. The bald, old professional beggar, who stands immoveable with his abject head uncovered and his gin-sodden face turned down. The man and his wife who sing alternative verses of a doggerel ballad on the theme of the day. Strolling along High Street we are pretty sure to come upon two blind men who play a concertina between them, and shuffle at a snail's pace along the gutter.

By the 1870s, the street ballad had a long history. At the top of the market were men like John Freeth, whose *Convivial Songster* was published in 1780, putting into verse and song his satirical comments on the times. As proprietor of the Coffee House named after him for 48 years (until his death in 1808), he provided one-man entertainment for his customers:

> Who when good news is brought to town,
> Immediately to work sits down,
> And business fairly to go through,
> Writes songs, finds tunes, and sings them too.

At the other end of the scale were the street-balladeers, buying a bundle of sheets from a printer, and selling them at one halfpenny each, with musical accompaniment. Best-sellers here were the tales of appalling murders, followed inevitably by hanging, laced with moral advice and condemnation. Similarly popular were the political songs and back-street romances, usually ending in the loss of a maidenhead or electoral office. Some were not unique to Birmingham, but re-printed by a local entrepreneur. Others, like *The Rigs of Birmingham*, would have had a local appeal.

Let us continue with our walk:

> Saturday is a good night at the theatres, and Mr Manager Simpson and Mr Manager Rogers know exactly what their patrons require. They want a couple of good, stirring dramas for their sixpences. Plenty of sensation scenes and 'hair-breadth 'scapes'. Theatrical managers must bow to the voice of the 'gods'.

By this date the Theatre Royal on New Street was no longer the only theatre in town. In 1856 the Birmingham Music Hall had opened in Broad Street, and by the 1870s, after a few changes of name and owner, it was safely installed as The Prince of Wales Theatre.

The Prince of Wales mixed a little Shakespeare with a lot of burlesque and melodrama, but its speciality in the 1860s and again in the 1930s was the pantomime. Indeed the pantomime was one of the great Victorian institutions. Local magazines such as *The Owl*, *The Dart* and *The Town Crier* covered them in obsessive detail, and held ballots among their readers for the best show and the best actress. During her heyday, the competition was invariably won by a local girl—Vesta Tilley. Scripts, entirely in verse, were published separately, and plots often involved a local scene. *Bo-Peep* at the Prince of Wales in 1865 contained both the Bull Ring and Aston Hall. What they all had in common was the final 'transformation scene', a series of special effects that sent their audiences home dazed and happy.

The pantomime was not a Victorian invention, for it had long been a summer tradition at the Theatre Royal. But it was only when the theatres began to remain open during the winter months (after 1820), that the traditional Boxing Night premiere took hold. It was in the 1930s, under Emile Littler, that the P.O.W.'s pantomime reached its zenith, a spectacular run that came to an end with a direct hit from a German incendiary on the night of 9-10 April 1941. As the manager put it when he saw the damage: 'That's it then!'. The final vestiges of the house that had welcomed Henry Irving, Ellen Terry and Beerbohm Tree were removed in 1987 for preparatory work for the International Convention Centre that now occupies the site.

But as the 19th century progressed, Birmingham's night-life was becoming increasingly competitive. In 1846 Henry Holder, the proprietor of the *Rodney Inn* in Coleshill Street, opened the building next to it as a concert hall. After Holder it continued life as the Birmingham Concert Hall, and later as the Gaiety. The variety show mixed romantic songs, comedy and feats of gymnastics. Similar fare, though appropriately a little more down-market, could be had at the London Museum and Concert Hall in the Bull Ring, known locally as 'The Mucker', which opened in 1863. The latter might offer accidents as well as the gymnastics, as a correspondent complained to the *Morning News* in 1872. A child of eight had fallen from the trapeze three times before the audience insisted on a premature end to the show.

Both the London Museum and the Gaiety followed a familiar pattern by converting to cinemas early in this century. The museum became the Bull Ring cinema, with a reputation for gory melodramas that gave it another nickname: the 'Blood Tub'. Amazingly, given the almost continuous redevelopment that has gone on around it, the building is still there, tucked behind the *Royal George* public house on Park Street.

The Victorian proprietors were never failing in their search for the unusual gimmick to attract their customers. The Steam Clock Music Hall on Morville Street took its name from a steam-driven time-piece on the façade, and Curzon Hall on Suffolk Street (roughly where the Holiday Inn now stands) was the first building in Birmingham to be lit by electricity. An entrepreneur called Fred Maccabe installed it at the hall entrance to advertise his show in September 1878.

Curzon Hall (1865) was the most all-purpose of all the Birmingham venues, except possibly for Bingley Hall. Used in its early days for the Birmingham Dog Show, the oldest event of its kind, it continued to offer a mixture of circuses, minstrel shows, boxing and concerts. Hamilton's Excursions, which used animated canvases to transport the audience to far-off places, was a popular alternative to the Christmas pantomime. Even as the century ended this versatile hall was not through half of its uses. From 1899 Walter Jeffs,

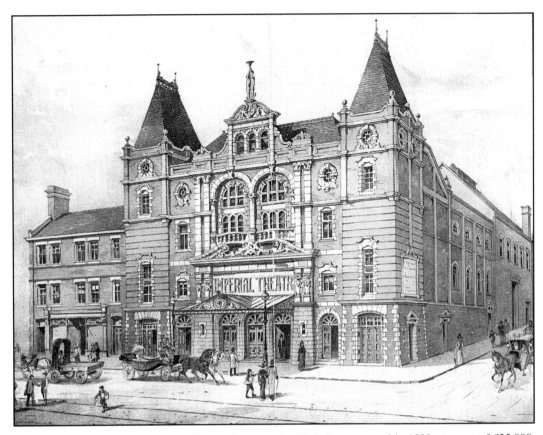

56.   The Imperial, later the Palace, Theatre, in Bordesley High Street opened in 1899 at a cost of £25,000. It converted to a cinema in 1929. During the Second World War it was requisitioned by the Ministry of Food as a food store.

the pioneer of Birmingham cinema, showed Edison's animated pictures there, and during the First World War it served as a recruitment office.

Most spectacular of all the Birmingham music halls was the Empire in Smallbrook Street, which began life in 1853 as Day's Crystal Palace. Appropriately it contained a huge mirror from the Great Exhibition at the Crystal Palace, but even that was upstaged by the magnificence of the gold, pink and green interior, the paintings on the ceiling and the ornate classical architecture. Sadly the Empire too was to fall victim to war-time bombings, but remains famous as one of the country's great music halls and (in 1910) as the theatre that staged Charlie Chaplin.

It is clear from the newspapers of the time that concert-going in Victorian Birmingham was rarely the restrained and refined activity it has become today. The London Museum was frequently invaded by the local hooligans known as the 'Peeky Blinders', for whom the corner of Park Street was a regular meeting place. Suitably loaded with beer from the pubs and fruit from the market, they could reduce any performance to a brawl and any performer to a still life with fruit. Indeed a barman was killed during a brawl in 1890. Even the Theatre Royal could have more drama in the 'gods' than on the stage. The (legal) practice of reducing seat prices after the interval, and the (illegal) one of hoarding them inside, meant that the gallery was often invaded by roughs, tumbling spectacularly over the the heads of the audience to reach their unallocated places. Again the practice produced its fatalities, when the roll failed to stop at the front rail.

Of the range of theatres and music halls that Victorian Birmingham offered, three are still with us today. The Hippodrome on Hurst Street began life as a circus in 1899. Its original name, the Tower of Varieties, suggested a link with Blackpool, but its distinctive Middle-Eastern tower showed little resemblance to the Eiffel Tower of the seaside resort. The tower survived until 1963, though there had been many changes of owner and decor in between. The stage that welcomed Marie Lloyd and George Robey has long since gone; the Hippodrome (a name adopted in 1903, but not continually used) is now central to Birmingham's cultural renaissance, with considerable financial commitment from the city. As home to the Birmingham Royal Ballet (formerly Sadler's Wells) and second home to the Welsh National Opera, it remains a key element in the city's high culture and to the regeneration of the Hurst Street area as an entertainment quarter. Very little is new in town-planning: this area had been earmarked as 'theatre-land' as early as the 1950s. Sadler's Wells switch to Birmingham was a highly risky enterprise in the cultural battle between London and the Provinces and required extensive alterations and extensions to the Hippodrome stage and rehearsal rooms. Its ultimate success would depend upon the city's ability to be a regional centre of the arts.

The Alexandra Theatre began in 1901 as the Lyceum. Rarely has the place strayed beyond its role as a theatre, offering plays of a generally popular appeal. After the disappearance of the Prince of Wales, this has been Birmingham's principal pantomime venue, particularly after the closure of the Theatre Royal in 1956. The 1992-3 production of *Aladdin* with Britt Ekland and Danny La Rue was, financially, the most successful production in British pantomime history.

The Repertory Theatre stands somewhat apart from this tradition. Unlike the many theatres that have changed their names, the Rep. has kept its name and changed its theatre. For

57. The city's first regular picture shows took place at Curzon Hall, in Suffolk Street in 1899. The building was later reconstructed as the West End cinema, finally closing in 1967.

the first 20 years of its existence (1913-34), the driving force of the company was Sir Barry Jackson, whose commitment to high, sometimes minority, drama drove the company along a financial knife-edge. Its home (from 1913) was in Station Street, the first purpose-built repertory theatre in England. Indeed the company, though not the first, is now the oldest surviving repertory in the UK. A list of the actors who trained there is itself testimony to the Rep's influence on the course of British drama: Laurence Olivier, Peggy Ashcroft, Edith Evans and Noel Coward, to name but a few. Shaw's *Back to Methuselah* was premiered there, and in 1969 it brought Richard Chamberlain, the idolised hero of *Dr. Kildare*, out of the operating theatre and into the repertory theatre to play Hamlet. The young star of the screen turned down a cowboy movie at Hollywood to pick up £46 a week in Station Street.

Shortly afterwards, the Rep. moved to its new home in what is now Centenary Square, the building by Graham Winteringham being opened in 1971. This marked the end of long and intense negotiations between the Council and A.T.V. over sites and funding, the original intention being to open a theatre at the new Television Centre on Suffolk Street. The new Rep is ideally placed to take advantage of the regeneration of the Broad Street area, surrounding the I.C.C. While the work on the Convention Centre was in progress, the Rep staged the first three productions of Kenneth Branagh's Renaissance Company and the directorial debuts of Derek Jacobi and Judi Dench.

In 1901 a night on the town could take in a choice of eight theatres, together with the Theatre Royal in Aston and the Carlton in Saltley. But already there was one item on the bill that spelt the end of the golden age of theatre. Curzon Hall was advertising two daily shows of Eddison's animated photography, concentrating on footage from the Boer War, accompanied by the Edgbaston Military Band. (Three thousand spectators a night astonished!)

Aston's Theatre Royal shows in microcosm the pattern of 20th-century entertainment. Its 32 years as a theatre ended in 1925, when it closed, to be re-born two years later as the Astoria cinema. But the large screen's reign was to be even shorter. In 1955 it was converted into television studios for A.T.V. Another 15 years later and the building was demolished, to be replaced by BRMB, Birmingham's independent 'pop' radio station. The Carlton too felt the wind of change, and after 12 years became the Coliseum.

Moving pictures were pioneered at Curzon Hall, which eventually became the West End cinema (another site now occupied by TV studios!). There then followed a slow conversion as failing music halls switched to the new medium. First to go were the Kings Hall in Old Square and the Steam Clock in Ladywood. The former was entertainment's revenge on the long-forgotten capture of King's Street Theatre by the Methodists: King's Hall had been built as a place of worship. The first purpose-built cinema in Aston was the Aston Picture Palace in Lozells Road; the first in Birmingham was the Electric cinema in Station Street (both opening in July 1910). The Electric went through a series of names (Tatler, Classic, Tivoli) but in 1937 was only the second news cinema in the city. The News Theatre in High Street had been the first outside London in 1932. The first to show talkies was the Futurist in John Bright Street with *The Singing Fool*, starring Al Jolson, in March 1929. The Lozells Picture House was, on 8 January 1933, the first to show films on Sunday, an issue that provoked heated debate.

Few movements can have risen so high and fallen so fast as the cinema. By 1911, not long after the Cinematograph Act, there were seven cinemas in the city; by the outbreak of the First World War there were fifty-three. By the time the next war began, the number had almost reached 100, with a total capacity of around one hundred and twenty thousand. In 1937 planning permission for a new cinema in Nechells was turned down because there were five others less than a mile away. In the expansionist days they converted anything into a picture-house. Both the Lyric in Edward Street and King's Hall had been chapels; the Gaiety and the Metropole on Snow Hill had been music halls, while the Electric Theatre in Small Heath had been, and still was, part of the Co-op. The Masonic Hall on New Street, later the ABC, had been, not surprisingly, a masonic hall.

In the days of contraction (after the Second World War), they converted the picture-house into anything. The Savoy on the Pershore Road made parts for the Bristol Britannia aircraft, while Selly Oak cinema made Ariel motorbikes. King's Hall went through a spectacular series of changes after 1927, from flea circus and waxworks to slot machines and indoor market, before succumbing to the bulldozers. Saddest of all, the ABC on the Bristol Road was demolished to make way for a drive-in Macdonalds.

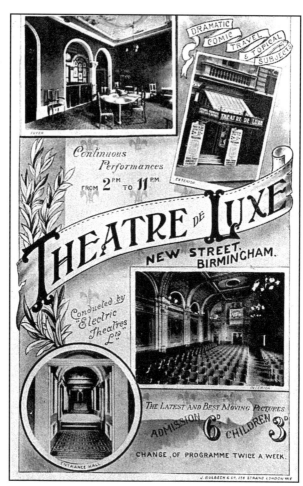

58. The Masonic Hall in New Street became the Theatre De Luxe in 1910. This was to be the first of many names: it was later called the Regent, the Forum and the ABC. The last film there was *E.T.* in 1983.

Much of this story could be repeated across the country, but in Oscar Deutsch's Odeon chain, Birmingham had a unique contribution to make. (A smaller Birmingham chain was that of the Jaceys.) The first was the Odeon in Perry Bar (now a bingo hall), which opened in August 1930; most impressive was the Odeon in New Street. When it opened its doors as the Paramount in 1937 (the film was *The Charge of the Light Brigade*, with Errol Flynn), it was the largest cinema in the Midlands, seating three thousand. Though used for many years as a concert venue (the Beatles appeared here), it remains a multi-screen cinema, though its proximity to the Bull Ring makes it vulnerable to redevelopment.

What was particularly striking about the Birmingham cinemas and a quality completely lacking in the handful of multiplexes that have replaced them was the sheer exuberance and eccentricity of the designs. They recaptured the spirit of Brummagem-ware, the town's legendary ability to forge and fabricate anything. The Beaufort in Ward End was built in

Tudor style, the half-timbered interior all done with painted plaster. The Alhambra on Moseley Road was the U.K.'s second 'atmosphere' cinema, designed to recapture (for no real reason) the feel of a Moorish palace. There were fountains in the Delicia, Gosta Green, and the Warwick in Acocks Green was designed as a medieval castle.

The history of popular music in 20th-century Birmingham is less a tale of rise and fall, as of splintering. Devotees of jazz, folk and pop all have their traditions, and few of them ever mix. As mainstream entertainment, jazz has its origins in the pioneering concerts at the Town Hall that began in 1946, followed in 1948 by the formation of a Rhythm Club and a Hot Club. But during the '70s and early '80s the tradition was kept alive more by pub-based jazz clubs, such as the *Barton's Arms* and the *Cannonball*. Consummate musicians like Andy Hamilton ploughed lonely furrows in those days. Yet in recent years, with the Jazz Festival and the opening of Ronnie Scott's in Broad Street, jazz has reclaimed its place at the centre of Birmingham's music scene.

Folk music has always been happiest in the pub, but although possessing the longest pedigree of them all, has struggled to survive into the '90s. However, alongside the tradition, themes of nostalgia and the rural, Birmingham of the '60s developed a powerful urban, campaigning folk, particularly at the Grey Cock Folk Club. The tradition survived into the '80s in radical theatre groups, such as Banner Theatre, founded by the B.B.C. radio documentary pioneer, Charles Parker. But Birmingham's radical theatre, never strong at the best of times, has found it difficult to survive in the days of national astringency for arts funding, and the city's commitment to main-stream 'prestige' art.

Pop music in Birmingham does represent something of a rise and fall. The city that produced groups like the Applejacks, The Moody Blues, The Move and The Spencer Davis Group in the '60s, and Black Sabbath and Led Zeppelin in the '70s, has had little impact in recent years, compared with Manchester or Glasgow. The key here would appear to be the decline in small live venues. The Barrel Organ in Digbeth, for example, where Dexy's Midnight Runners had their beginnings, was converted into an Irish theme pub. In the days of the four-piece band (and the rise of the Beatles), clubs like the Cedar Club on Constitution Hill, Rum Runner in Broad Street or the Carlton Ballroom (later Mother's Club) in Erdington gave new talent the opportunity to develop and rise.

The decline in the club or pub circuit (or even medium sized halls such as the Odeon or Hummingbird) is in ironic contrast to the emergence of stadium venues such as the N.E.C. Arena, or more recently the National Indoor Arena.

Birmingham's pop style, if it is possible to generalise, was heavier than the parallel movement in Liverpool, more likely to produce rhythm and blues in the '60s and heavy metal in the '70s. But to the punk era Birmingham gave Toyah, and to the new romantics it gave Duran Duran.

In more recent times, Birmingham's music has begun to reflect the city's multiculturalism. Joan Armatrading was the first major black artist to emerge from the city in the mid '70s, while UB40, formed in 1979, and Steel Pulse have helped to put reggae into the mainstream of British pop. The city has also become the main centre of Bhangra, a hybrid of dance rhythms and Indian music, while artists such as Apache Indian have begun to explore another hybrid form, mixing Caribbean and Asian rhythms interlaced with rap lyrics directly targeted at issues concerning the Asian community.

Chapter Twenty

Matters of Life and Death

The problems faced by the Corporation of Birmingham as it moved into the Victorian era were no different from any other: life and death, and how to avoid moving too swiftly from the one to the other. There were the issues of sanitation and health, disease and bad housing, improving the health of the people, the water supply. Solutions were not instant, but in some cases they were very radical indeed.

In 1848 the Public Health Act was passed, and Birmingham Corporation immediately requested that an 'Enquiry into the Sanitary Health of the Borough' be made, in order that a Local Board of Health could be established under the powers of the new Act. So it was that Robert Rawlinson visited the town in February and May 1849, and published his report later that month. The picture he painted was not as black as that of Manchester, Liverpool or London, but still there was considerable room for improvement.

By this date the population of Birmingham had risen to 220,000, of which almost one quarter lived in 2,000 courts in the town centre. It would be many years before this basic pattern was changed: by the First World War the number of courts had trebled.

Most of the courts were 'back-to-backs' or 'tunnel-backs'. A covered entrance led to a courtyard, bounded on three sides by houses and on the fourth by a high wall. The weekly rent for a 'house' of perhaps three rooms averaged from half a crown to 3s. 6d., though families frequently had one or more lodgers to supplement earned income.

It was the conditions in the courts that attracted Rawlinson's attention most of all. One court in Sheep Street, containing 12 houses, was partially flooded. Of another in Masshouse Lane a parish medical officer reported to him:

> The drainage is very bad; the water, mixed with ashes and filth from the dust-holes, extends itself up the court to the fronts of the houses, to approach which, to see patients, I have been obliged to walk on bricks placed for the purpose, and the poor have been unable to prevent the filth running into the house.

Public sewers were few and in many places drainage was non-existent. Those courts that had privies had too few of them and were:

> generally in a very conspicuous part of the premises, and it rarely happens that there is any door ... Ordure is consequently often kept in the houses, and emptied anywhere at nightfall; in other places, such as the Inkleys ... the door is opened, and it is thrown out without the least reference to the spot where it falls.

The impression is that many parts of the town had become an open sewer: the river Rea (once a place to fish for salmon) was in parts a Dead Sea as were the canals. Nor were

135

such conditions restricted to slum areas of the town: 'In the Hagley Road the gutters are receptacles of drains and filth till they become in a most putrid state, reeking with the contents of water-closets in the finest neighbourhood of Birmingham'.

The enquiry of Dr. Hill, Medical Officer of Health, into the conditions in the town centre in 1875, prior to the implementation of the Artisans' Dwellings Act, showed little apparent improvement on this situation: '... want of ventilation, want of light, want of proper and decent accommodation, resulting in dirty habits, low health, and debased morals on the part of the tenants'.

Hill's comments were graphically amplified by the Chairman of the Improvement Committee:

> In one case a filthy drain from a neighbouring court oozed into their little back yard; in another, the sitting room window could not be opened, owing to the horrible effluvia from a yawning midden just under it ... The house in which the little savings of an industrious man, £40, had been invested in the stock and goodwill of a greengrocery, was so frightfully leaky that, on being taken up into the back chamber, I found the ceiling had fallen down upon the childrens' bed, while the water had streamed through the bed on which the husband and wife slept, in the next floor, down into their only sitting room.

The consequence of all this was a terrible mortality rate, particularly among children, and particularly in the inner wards of St Mary's and St Bartholomew's. Overall, Birmingham's annual mortality rate in 1848 was 30 deaths per thousand people and rising. In the 10 years between 1851 and 1861, there were 34,517 infant deaths in a population of 290,000, and even in 1875 the death rate in St Mary's ward (26.82 per thousand) was twice the level of Edgbaston. The most extreme example in the Improvement Area was Bailey Street (perhaps it should have been called Death Row) where one in ten of the population died every year. The pattern of life was described by W. C. Aitken in 1866:

> Birmingham operatives marry early: the girl-wife becomes a mother, but, from early associations, she likes the manufactory better than her home—likes the company of the workers, and her earnings 'help to keep the house'. As soon as she can go to the manufactory after her confinement she goes (the absense rarely exceeds one month), and the infant is left the greater part of the day to be fed on artificial food, and is usually attended to by a child not more than six or seven years of age ... Children, healthy at birth, dwindle rapidly under this system.

Of course, this is to lump all the blame upon the working mother; there was enough disease to drag the child down, whether the mother was at home or not. Zymotic diseases (smallpox, diphtheria, whooping-cough, diarrhoea, etc.) were rife in the inner wards, killing around 1,700 a year by the 1880s, though by this date the *rate* was declining.

Deaths through smallpox had been in decline since the Borough Hospital for Smallpox and Scarlet Fever had been built in Winson Green in 1883-4. Treatment of the diseases was accompanied by a concerted campaign of vaccination. Indeed in the Winson Green area, formerly Birmingham Heath, were concentrated those institutions which constituted the under-belly of Victorian life: prison, fever hospital, asylum and workhouse. The Borough Asylum (or All Saints' Hospital) opened in 1850 and cost £53,000, but was extended soon after. Treatment of 'the insane' was parochial business, and parishes paid the Asylum 9s. a week to look after their charges. Parishes outside Birmingham paid 14 shillings. This was a complete reversal of the previous system, under which the poor law officers were obliged to send their patients to the cheapest hospital available, wherever it was. Aston was using a hospital near Northampton. In 1881 Winson Green Asylum was receiving around three hundred admissions a year, and the pressure for accommodation led to the building of Rubery Hill Asylum, opening in 1882. It should be said that the Victorians had a rather sweeping definition of the word 'insanity'. The case books of All Saints' show that many of the inmates were suffering from post-natal depression, epilepsy or alcoholism. Another cause frequently noted was 'religious excitement'.

Rawlinson's report identified a number of other causes of ill-health apart form over-crowding and the lack of sanitation. One was the parlous state of the water supply. The underground water supply that once attracted inhabitants to Birmingham was now highly polluted. This was true of both the numerous private wells and the public ones (Lady Well, Digbeth, Allison Street and Jamaica Row). The water sold by carriers from carts pulled through the streets was better, but the cost (a halfpenny for a can of 3½ gallons) was prohibitive to many. There was one water company in operation, serving about one third of the town, but mainly relying on the polluted river Tame for its supplies, and only supplying on three days a week.

It would be many years before this particular problem was solved. It was only under Joseph Chamberlain, in 1875, that the Corporation finally gained control over the water supply in the town. As Chamberlain himself told the Commons' committee: 'It seems to me absolutely certain that ... the power of life and death should not be in the hands of a commercial company, but should be conducted by the representatives of the people'. The total capacity taken over from the private company, from rivers and reservoirs, amounted to 200 million gallons, but with the increase in population and direct supply, it was soon not enough. Even after the construction of a large new reservoir at Shustoke, supply limped behind demand. Current supply, it was estimated, could last only to the 1920s and then, like the Tame, it would have to be abandoned and, like the Tame, it was already suffering from the problems of hardness and pollution.

As Chamberlain said, it was a matter of life and death. In September 1878, a fire at a confectioner's on Digbeth had resulted in the deaths of both the proprietor's wife and a maid-servant. One of the causes was an inadequate water supply. Two of the results were a reorganisation of the new borough fire brigade and a recognition that the problems of the current water supply needed radical new solutions.

Robert Rawlinson, in another report of 1871, had indicated that Welsh water might be a solution to Birmingham's problems. He indicated, following a similar proposal by Richard Hasard, that the source of supply might be the rivers Elan and Claerwen in mid-Wales. In 1890, with water now in municipal hands, Rawlinson's report was taken off the shelf.

Undoubtedly, the Elan Valley project (begun in 1894) showed Birmingham at the height of its municipal powers: the power to take long-term solutions and the power to direct considerable sums of money to them. (The cost of the whole scheme, including the purchase of land, was estimated at £6,600,000.) Birmingham bought the land, dammed the rivers and created its reservoirs. The area covered was 70 square miles, and the largest dam, Caban Coch, was 122-ft. high, and a similar width at the base. A wooden village, complete with school, library and hospital was built on the Brecon side of the Elan for the workers and their families. In spite of protests, no pub was built, though a Corporation canteen dispensed beer and tobacco. The full length of aqueduct and tunnel taking the

59.   The temporary village for workers and their families at Elan Valley. The whole project took 10 years but would solve the city's water shortage problems for centuries.

water to Frankley is 73 miles. On 21 July 1904 King Edward VII and Queen Alexandra officially declared the operation complete, and sent the first water on its journey to the Frankley filter-beds. By the following year, 12 million gallons a day were supplying all of Birmingham's needs. Ironically, the water was so soft that chalk had to be added to prevent corrosion, but it was said that the new drink was so superior to the old that it would no longer be necessary to add whisky to it.

A further issue, associated with the problems of water supply and public health, was earmarked by Rawlinson as needing immediate attention. As well as making inadequate provision for the living, Birmingham was not looking after its dead particularly well either. There were, in 1849, six Anglican burial grounds in the town centre, one of which (Park Street) was an annex to St Martin's. In addition, though Rawlinson does not mention them, there were cemeteries for Jews, Quakers, Baptists, Methodists and Congregationalists. Cohabitation between living and dead is not to be recommended on health grounds, and Rawlinson pointed out the pollution dangers of overcrowded burial grounds in population centres. Since no record was kept of where burials had taken place (at least in the Anglican churchyards), the sexton had recourse to the dreaded 'boring rod' to find space for 'just one more inside'. Families were often distressed to find that in burying one member the authorities were un-burying one or two more. The accumulation of a century or more of interments at St Philip's, for example, was clear enough in the height of the churchyard above street-level.

The understandable fear of being rudely awoken, not by a trumpet but a boring-rod, had already led one group of dissenters to go it alone and form the General Cemetery Company, with the intention of buying land for a new burial ground outside the town centre. It is difficult to believe that the gloomy retreat now known as Key Hill Cemetery was once 'the most picturesque of our cemeteries, the grounds being tastefully and admirably laid out in walks, with ornamental lawns and shrubberies'. But so it was when the first interment took place there in 1836. Here lie many of the Victorians that made Birmingham great (or notorious): Joseph Chamberlain, George Dawson, William Murphy (whose anti-Catholic campaign led to serious riots in 1867) and Mrs. Powell, 'the Female Blondin' (who fell to her death from a tightrope at Aston Lower Grounds in 1863), to name but a few.

Although Key Hill solved the immediate problem for non-conformists, it clearly did not suit the Anglicans. Consequently another company was formed and a Church of England cemetery was established on Warstone Lane, close to the Key Hill ground in 1848. The

60.   The General Cemetery, known as Key Hill, opened in 1836 and contains the graves of many of the city's Victorian greats. The caretaker lived in a flat under the chapel!

61.   Warstone Lane was the Anglican alternative to Key Hill. The lodge (seen on the horizon to the right) and the catacombs are still standing. St Michael's church has been demolished.

new cemetery contained catacombs, a place of burial previously only used at Christ Church in New Street, which did not have the space for a churchyard. Indeed, this was not the only link between the two institutions. When Christ Church was demolished in 1899, the 600 or so 'internees' (including John Baskerville) were transferred to Warstone Lane. In order not to disturb the city unduly, the transfers took place at night, an endless procession of funeral coaches making their slow progress out to the Jewellery Quarter. Among the many that now share a bed with Baskerville, we may mention Jacob Wilson, Birmingham's last town crier. On his death in 1882 the Markets and Fairs Committee paid £25 for the erection of a tombstone.

    Although the two new cemeteries were ideal for those who could afford to 'opt out', they remained a small-scale private solution to a large-scale public problem. As the burial grounds in the town were progressively closed by legislation, it became necessary for the Corporation once more to take 'the longer view'. Therefore it bought 105 acres of well-drained ground at Witton, and in 1863 the first Corporation Cemetery was open for business. Since the new burial place was to be available for all the citizens of Birmingham, it was necessary to sub-divide Witton between Anglican, Non-conformist, Catholic and Jewish burials.

Such were the changes and redevelopment taking place in the growing town that owned it that many of the early interments at Witton had been dead for some considerable time. Fifteen hundred coffins were moved here in 1882-3 from the Old Meeting House cemetery, swallowed up by extensions to New Street station. The latter was also responsible for much posthumous activity among the Jewish community. As their town centre burial grounds were lost to the railways, many burials were transferred to the new plot at Witton.

If the problems of water and burial were not enough, the Corporation had also to face the sticky problem of how to deal with 12 million gallons of sewage a day. In 1871 all of the waste matter that got as far as the main sewers found its way to the Saltley filtration works and ultimately into the river Tame. The council's actions were rightly hemmed in by local landowners, and a number of legal cases had been fought (and lost) over river pollution, most notably with Charles Adderley (later Lord Norton). The land nearby could be described as Birmingham's 'WC Fields'.

When Rawlinson visited, Birmingham was a 'midden' town. Few WCs emptied directly into the sewers; the rest, including refuse and ash, was collected directly from the courts and sold to farmers as manure. In 1853 the Corporation took over collections from private operators, appropriately under the Public Works Department. In 1876 it was transferred to the Health Department. By this date the 'Rochdale pan system', a more hygienic receptacle under the closet seat, was widely in operation. Once a week the nightsoil men collected both pans and tubs for ashes and other refuse and took them to the Corporation wharf in Montague Street. By 1885, the men were removing two million pans a year. Such were the technical improvements to the pans, the horse-drawn vans and the treatment works that Montague Street had become positively park-like with a shrubbery and flower-beds. From here recycled refuse could be bought, the rest being shipped away by canal.

Recycling was an issue at the heart of disposal even then. The ash could be formed into paving-slabs; indeed the paving in front of the Society of Artists headquarters in New Street was so produced. One grand scheme investigated but not put into action was to pipe the refuse away by aqueduct to Lincolnshire to improve the quality of the potatoes. This mirror image of the Elan Valley project was abandoned because of cost, but undoubtedly shows Victorian Birmingham's ability to think big.

By the mid-1870s it was thought that the back of the problems outlined by Rawlinson had been broken. Pan closet was steadily replacing midden, and running water was now piped to many courts, though only to a stand-pipe in the centre of them. Certainly the statistics were showing a marked improvement. But the problem of sub-standard housing remained.

Chapter Twenty-one

Libraries, Baths and Parks

If the Birmingham Council had little power in the field of housing reform, Parliamentary legislation was increasing its operational parameters in other ways. A series of acts on public baths (1846), libraries and museums (1850), and parks, allowed Victorian councils to provide something for the health and welfare of their people, even if domestic conditions remained in the hands of the private developer. The successes in these areas were the first sign that Victorian local government saw provision for the lower classes as central to its duties. After all, with increasing franchise, it could no longer afford to ignore them.

But first an early failure. One of the early decisions of the town council was to end the costly and inconvenient practice of sending prisoners to the county gaol at Warwick. Since Birmingham had its own Quarter Sessions (the first man convicted was one Thomas Allen, given two months with hard labour on 5 July 1839 for stealing a wooden bowl), it needed a borough gaol as well. Plans on the Pentonville model were drawn up as early as 1845, but it was not until 17 October 1849 that Winson Green Prison received its first guest. There were initially 336 cells (increased to 612 by 1885), and the full cost exceeded £60,000.

Many of the decisions as to the disciplinary system adopted and the appointment of officers were made by the Recorder, Matthew Davenport Hill, who will re-appear later as an educational reformer and as the brother of Rowland Hill, founder of the postal service. Hill recommended as first governor Captain Maconochie, R.N., an advocate of the reforming (rather than simply punishing) prison. In fact the first two governors were ex-naval officers. But it was the conduct of the second governor, Lieutenant Austin, R.N., that in 1853 brought a royal commission of enquiry down upon his head. The *Birmingham Journal* said of him:

> He is an extreme example of a class well known in the navy ... They scrub, they polish, they make toys of their ships, and by dint of minute regulations they make also machines of their officers and men ... He delights in gewgaw and glitter, paint and polish; and surrounding himself with conventional regulation, he considers the occasional infraction of this, however casual or accidental, a vital offence. His appetite for punishing such breaches of what he calls discipline is also insatiable ...

The occasion of the enquiry was the suicide of a 15-year-old inmate called Edward Andrews, the latest of 17 suicide attempts in the four years since the gaol had opened.

Much of the resulting report was an indictment of the Victorian prison system in general, but Austin's disciplinary code, or lack of one, had exceeded even that. Andrews' sentence had included hard labour, and at Winson Green this involved turning a meaningless crank 10,000 times per day to secure the victim his three meals. In the two weeks of his interrupted stay, Andrews had turned the crank a total of 126,000 times, but was unable to perform the daily quota of rotations, and was consequently put on a bread and water diet that had further weakened him.

Questioning of prisoners revealed that many and varied were the punishments inflicted on those guilty of indiscipline, including dousing with cold water, being attached to the wall by a leather collar and straight jacket, and having one's mouth stopped with salt. Austin's prior resignation did not save him from prosecution; he was sentenced in November 1855 to three months' imprisonment, chiefly for bad book-keeping!

But to return to happier matters, an Act of Parliament of 1846 empowered councils to provide public baths and wash-houses. On 12 May 1851 the first public baths in the town were opened in Kent Street. The architect, Daniel Hill, had also designed the Borough Gaol and the Lunatic Asylum. Initially, such institutions concentrated as much on washing and bathing as on swimming: they were more for cleanliness than for fitness. Kent Street contained 69 private and three plunging baths as well as the two swimming pools. The cost of a private bath (2d. for warm water and 1d. for cold) included one clean towel.

These were far from being the town's first baths; indeed there were three private baths already operating in Birmingham when Kent Street opened. In Snow Hill there were 'sulphureous, fumigating and medicated vapour baths' and more in George Street, Balsall Heath, 'plentifully supplied with pure spring water'. The claim was not quite accurate: they were condemned and filled in by order of the local health board in 1878. But by far the earliest were those at Ladywell off Hurst Street, dating from the 1720s, and said by Hutton to be the most complete in the kingdom. The swimming bath here was 118-ft. long and was surrounded by gardens; there were, by the 1830s, 10 other baths, segregated by sex, kept at a range of temperatures. In addition there was a separate bath for Jews, and others that provided spa water from Harrogate, Leamington and Cheltenham.

The Kent Street experiment was followed by public baths at Woodcock Street (1860), Northwood Street (1862) and Monument Road (1883). Kent Street also contained laundry facilities at a penny an hour, but these were little used. In 1878 they were converted into Turkish baths, a luxury also provided by Monument Road. There were also private Turkish baths on Broad Street, and above the Argent Centre in the Jewellery Quarter. This may seem a peculiarly Victorian institution, but the habit survived, at least in Kent Street, until after the Second World War.

Cottage Baths, which provided only individual facilities and no swimming, first appeared in Coventry Street in 1908, six for men on the ground floor and five for women above. An alternative to the tin bath in the living room, they were considerably cheaper than a cubicle at the public baths: a 10-minute spell in a cottage bath cost 2d. between the wars. Of course, the use of these declined with the improvement of housing conditions. Bournville was one of the first estates to specify a bath as a precondition of its housing, though this did not necessarily imply a bathroom.

What became apparent by the early 1880s was that public bathing appealed predominantly to men. The mixed nature of the swimming baths deterred many women from attending (only 1 in 26 of swimmers was a woman). To remedy this anomaly, in 1882 Kent Street opened for women only on three evenings a week, and proposals were made, but subsequently dropped, for a women-only pool.

In addition to inside pools, there were outdoor facilities at Cannon Hill (1873) and Small Heath Park (1883), though many were understandably reluctant to remove their

62. The Bird's Eye view of Birmingham in 1887. In the foreground are Mason College (left) and the Old Reference Library (right). Above the Town Hall can be seen the glass roof of New Street station.

clothes in such a location. Both were later closed by a combination of poor water quality and public indifference, though outdoor swimming remained possible at West Heath.

A spin-off from the building of locally-built facilities was their use as social clubs and assembly halls during the winter months. They were among the first community buildings in the city, and as such were used as recruitment centres during the First World War and first aid posts in 1939-45.

The 'fun-pool' has begun to replace the Victorian public baths in the city, replacing the attractions of tiling and terracotta with those of water-chutes and inflatables. Those on the Moseley Road in Balsall Heath represent a late survival of the tradition, and have been compared to 'swimming in Siena Cathedral'. They were promised during negotiations over the incorporation of the area into Birmingham in 1891, but only completed in 1907.

The gestation period for public libraries was a rather longer one. The Free Libraries and Museums Act of 1850 empowered councils to levy a halfpenny rate to maintain a library or museum, but only if two thirds of the rate-payers voted in favour of it. The referendum of April 1852 failed to obtain the two-thirds majority; then, as now, it was the level of the rates that carried most weight. As a result, it was not until 3 April 1861 that Birmingham's first public library opened on Constitution Hill. So popular was the idea now that new borrowers regularly queued for an hour to obtain their tickets, and a total of 5,422 joined in the first year. The initial plan was to create lending libraries for the four quarters of the town, together with a reference library 'to represent every phase of human thought, and every variety of opinion'. This scheme was in place by 1868: Adderley Park opened in 1864, the Central Lending Library in September 1865 on the same day as Deritend Library, and Gosta Green in 1868. A Shakespeare library opened, appropriately on the Bard's birthday, in 1868. This, as well as the Reference and Central Lending Libraries, was situated in Radcliffe Place (now Chamberlain Square), an area that was becoming the show-piece of Victorian Birmingham.

Although there were increasing problems of funding, the statistics of over 300,000 volumes borrowed per year suggested that the initiative was highly successful. However, the best-laid plans were reduced to ashes by a huge fire in the Reference Library on 11 January 1879, that turned the whole building into an inferno in 15 minutes. Despite the efforts of the mayor (who had to be restrained from dashing into the building to rescue books) and many others, the whole collection was practically lost. Only the illuminated *Guild Book of Knowle* was saved from a priceless collection of medieval manuscripts. In fact, most of Radcliffe Place was illuminated on that fateful afternoon. The fire was perceived as a national disaster, and donations of money and books flooded in, many of which form the basis of the current collections. In 1882 a new Reference and Lending Library rose phoenix-like from the ashes of the old.

Just as the public library movement had its roots in the private subscription libraries of the 18th century, so the art gallery and museum had its predecessors in the collections of curiosities and displays of art of an earlier age. James Bisset, famous as the author of a verse guidebook to Birmingham, had a 'Museum or Bazaar' on New Street, visited by Nelson in 1802. A similar institution at the end of the 18th century was Allin's 'Cabinet of Curiosities', on the site now occupied by the Council House. Allin sold new and second-hand clothes and shoes, but also advertised 'An Exhibition for the Curious Observer of Natural Phenomena', no doubt as a lure for potential customers. In 1805 he too advertised in verse:

But friends from the country, who hate for to travel,
O'er sharp-pointed stones, and to save tender feet,
I've opened a Ware house, by Fancy well stor'd,
Near Dunn's famous Swann, at the end of New Street.

63.   Allin's eccentric Cabinet of Curiosities stood at the corner of Ann Street and Congreve Street. The building's last tenants were the Suffield family, ancestors of the novelist, J. R. R. Tolkien. The watercolour is by Paul Braddon.

Charles Jones' 'Pantechnetheca', or General Repository of Art, in New Street (1823) allowed different manufacturers to exhibit their wares, and customers to buy them if they wished.

Individual paintings on the grand scale, usually depicting recent historical events, were also on display. An exhibition at the Theatre Royal in 1807 involved an animated portrayal of the Battle of Copenhagen with sound effects, while a huge depiction of the Storming of Seripatam was exhibited in Union Street in 1790. A building called the Panorama at the top of New Street specialised in large circular paintings, viewed from a platform in the centre. The line between art and commercialism was a blurred one: in 1749 the *Black Boy* public house in Edgbaston Street exhibited a model of the Temple of Apollo at Delphi, together with other classical representations. But the fact that the proprietor also threw in a magician doing card-tricks seems to undermine the educational nature of the experience! The first move towards a genuine art gallery comes in 1864.

Compared to local artists like Edward Burne-Jones (born in Bennetts Hill) or David Cox, the watercolourist, of Harborne, the name of Edward Coleman hardly makes the heart swell with pride. But Coleman's painting *Dead Game* has its place in history as the first work of art in the city's collections, and thus the forerunner of the priceless collection of buildings and works of art that constitute the Museums and Art Gallery. First exhibitions were held in the Central Library, but by 1878 the collection had outgrown this home and migrated to Aston Hall.

Part of the reason for its growth was the decision to create an Industrial Art Gallery, one of those distinctively Victorian concepts, though the Victorians had little to teach a man like Matthew Boulton of the links between art and industry. In 1849 the grounds of Bingley House on Broad Street had been the temporary home of 'An Exhibition of the Manufactures of Birmingham and the Midland Counties'. The exhibition was visited by, among others, Charles Darwin (who was attending the meeting of the British Association in the town) and Prince Albert. This early showcase of design and industrial art was taken up and amplified by the Great Exhibition of 1851 at the Crystal Palace.

Consequently, Birmingham's Art Gallery, once the opportunity to build it had presented itself, was to be as much a textbook of international design as a treasury of great works of art, and as such was extensively funded by industrialists like the Tangyes, Elkington and the glass manufacturer, Thomas Ostler. Ostler's firm provided the gigantic glass fountain that was the centrepiece of the Great Exhibition. Some, like Josiah Mason and Elkington, were art collectors already. The art gallery opened in 1885, occupying the space behind the Council House that had originally been earmarked for the law courts. The potentially prohibitive cost of building had been obviated by a cunning strategy: the Gas Committee used its extensive funds to build itself offices on the ground floor and to provide galleries on the floor above. It was a perfect example of art supported (literally) by industry.

The campaign for an art gallery came at a time of the rising influence of the Ruskinian Arts and Crafts Movement in the town, itself strongly associated with the Pre-Raphaelite Movement of which Burne-Jones was a central character. Birmingham, with a traditional (but declining) reliance on skilled artisans, was a natural seed-bed for such a movement. In 1885, the year of the art gallery's opening, the country's first Municipal School of Art opened in Margaret Street, followed in 1890 by a School of Jewellery in Vittoria Street.

The School of Art, behind which towered the figures of Burne-Jones and William Morris, led to an explosion of Arts and Crafts in the town, from workshops such as

64. The 1865 Industrial Exhibition at Bingley Hall, as seen by the *Illustrated London News*. The iron columns were surplus to the requirements of Euston station and installed here instead. The hall was irreparably damaged by fire in 1983.

Ruskin Pottery to associations of artists, craftspeople and designers like the Birmingham School and the Birmingham Guild of Handicraft. These designers found their work to the taste of Birmingham's ruling elite (men like William Kenrick, George Dixon and the Chamberlains) and to the wealthiest of the businessmen. The results can be seen throughout the city: the murals of Joseph Southall in the Art Gallery, Bournville Village, Joseph Chamberlain's home at Highbury and William Henry Bidlake's church of St Agatha (1901) on the Stratford Road.

The movement to provide Birmingham with public parks and gardens was another alliance between landowning wealth and Corporation organisation, and for once there is little in the way of predecessors, other than the 'paradise lost' of Vauxhall Gardens. The first public park was the gift of Charles Adderley in 1856, whose generosity was seemingly not undermined by a long-running legal dispute with the Council over pollution of the river Tame. Lord Calthorpe followed suit in the next year with the park that still bears his name. In neither case were the attractions limited to grass and trees. Adderley Park contained a small museum, while in Calthorpe Park two Russian guns captured from the Crimea were on display. This curious juxtaposition of the pastoral and the military was carried on in the 20th century, when a First World War tank was also on show there.

Aston Hall and Park, of which we have already heard much, fell into the Corporation's hands in 1864, shortly after the Female Blondin had fallen into the grounds. Unlike

65.   The School of Art in Margaret Street, designed by Martin and Chamberlain, was completed in 1885. A magnificent example of Victorian terracotta work, it is a Grade 1 listed building.

Calthorpe or Adderley, the largest of the municipal parks does not have the name of its donor: Cannon Hill Park was the gift of Louisa Anne Ryland in 1873, its original 57 acres having been landscaped and provided with boating and swimming pools at her expense. To a century dominated by 'famous men', Louisa Ryland gives a welcome counterweight: her gifts included both Cannon Hill and Small Heath Park, the Women's Hospital in Sparkhill, a donation towards the rebuilding of the General Hospital, and £10,000 towards the School of Art. Her generosity was self-effacing, sometimes anonymous, and always accompanied by constructive comment on organisation.

To the parks of the period we should also add the closed burial grounds. The annex to St Martin's churchyard in Park Street had long been a cause of complaint, with the frequent re-appearance of long-dead residents. In 1880 the grounds were re-opened as a park and children's playground, planted with trees, shrubs and flowers. (I admit that this takes some believing.) In 1894 much of it was lost to a widening of the L.N.W.R. line.

Much of the land donated or purchased by Birmingham was, as yet, outside the borough. Cannon Hill, Aston Park and the Lickeys were all outside, as were Lightwoods and Warley Park (purchased in 1902 and 1906 respectively). These two provided a 'green wedge' between the expanding Smethwick and Birmingham, and a useful check to further expansion. For Lightwoods Park the King donated two swans. Others, like Handsworth Park (1887) fell into the city's hands in 1911.

Working behind the lines of council policy were groups like the Birmingham Playgrounds, Open Space and Playing Fields Society, chaired by John Nettlefold, and committed to preserving open space and encouraging the cooperation of councils and landowners for their upkeep. In the early 20th century this group lobbied powerfully for the clearance and improvement of the Black Patch, a desolate piece of ground shared by Smethwick, Handsworth and Birmingham and occupied by gipsies. The land was cleared of its occupants (not without considerable resistance) in 1904, and laid out as a park in 1906. The same ideology that was creating 'Nettlefold Courts' (back-to-backs open at the front) was at work here: the belief that light, air and space were key factors in the improvement of conditions for the working classes.

We have yet to mention one man in connection with all this activity, and yet, as Joseph Chamberlain said of him: 'one who, perhaps more than any other, had set his mark upon modern Birmingham'. This was George Dawson, to whom must be attributed that ethos, known as 'the Civic Gospel' that underpins much of the Corporation's work in the second half of the 19th century.

Dawson was a London man, born in 1821 and educated initially at the same school as Charles Dickens. In 1843 he began preaching at Mount Zion chapel in Graham Street, but so wide and undenominational was his conception of the Christian message that in 1847 he found it necessary to create his own place of worship: the Church of the Saviour in Edward Street. So wide in fact that it included local government. Nothing sums up Dawson's conception of the duties, obligations and powers of civil authorities so well as his visionary address on the opening of the Reference Library on 6 September 1865:

> ... a great town exists to discharge towards the people of that town the duties that a great nation exists to discharge towards the people of that nation—that a town exists here by the grace of God, that a great town is a solemn organism through which should flow, and in which should be shaped, all the highest, loftiest and truest ends of man's intellectual and moral nature.

As his memorial at Key Hill succinctly expresses it, it was a matter of balancing and uniting 'duty' and 'right'. To the great families and politicians of Edgbaston he preached 'the gospel of public duty'; to the poor of the inner-city he said: 'Take your affairs into your own hands'. The new franchise of 1869 that propelled Joseph Chamberlain to power made such a balance possible, if not essential. Dawson's union of the classes resulted in the municipal drive of the 1870s. Before this the government of the town had been in the hands of the 'economists', more interested in keeping down the rates that flexing municipal muscles. What Dawson preached, Chamberlain and his associates performed.

George Dawson's was not a lone voice: H. W. Crosskey at the Church of the Messiah on Broad Street (Chamberlain's church) re-echoed the message, as did Dr. Robert Dale at Carrs Lane. Indeed it was Dale who perfectly expressed the new-found unity of religious and municipal message. Of one friend who mixed politics and religion he said that he: '... was trying to get the will of God done on earth as it was done in heaven just as much when he was fighting St Mary's Ward, just as much when he was speaking in the Town Council, as when he was teaching his Bible Class on the Sunday morning'. Nor was Dawson's the role of a mountain-top mystic. On issues such as the purchase of Aston Hall, the Free Libraries Act or the Freehold Land Society, he was an active campaigner, with the ability to move his audience emotionally as well as intellectually. No more appropriate place for his statue could be found than in Edmund Street, dwarfed by the great masses of the Council House, Library and Art Gallery, whose presence owes so much to his vision and energy.

Chapter Twenty-two

Municipalisation

Gas, electricity, water, transport: four facts of life that affect us all. We could summarise what has happened to the lot of them over the last 150 years in three words: municipalisation, nationalisation and privatisation. The last two are not necessarily of direct concern to a local historian; the first is vital and the high Victorian era was more so than any the age of municipalisation.

In 1874 a man with a trowel told the dignitaries assembled in what would shortly be called Victoria Square: 'I have an abiding faith in municipal institutions, an abiding sense of the value and importance of local government'. The man was Joseph Chamberlain, and he was laying the foundation stone of the new Council House. The Council House scheme itself reflected the sea-change in councillors' attitudes since the 1850s. Land on Ann Street

66.   An artist's impression of the new Council House, partly accurate. The entrance to the art gallery and clock tower were later re-designed. The architect was Yeoville Thomason; the mosaic over the entrance is by Salviati.

had been earmarked for development since 1853, but financial uncertainties put the idea on hold until 1871, when a competition was held to choose an appropriate design. The 29 entries hardly began to compare with the 179 that Sheffield received. But even then professional jealousies and disagreements delayed the choice again. It was widely believed that Chamberlain and Martin's gothic design was the best, but others felt that a classical form would be more suitable for the surroundings. Finally, 21 years late, the first stone of Yeoville Thomason's building was in place, with all the others to follow over the next five years.

If local government in Birmingham was born when the Corporation finally took over from the Street Commissioners in 1851, it reached maturity, appropriately, about 21 years later. The man who took it to unforeseen heights of power was a Londoner. Joseph Chamberlain was born there on 8 July 1836. At the age of 18 he came to Birmingham to work for his uncle's

67.   Joseph Chamberlain (1836-1914). His vision transformed the conservative town of 'the economists' into a 'new Athens' of municipal expansionism.

screw-making business (later to become G.K.N.) in Birmingham. The new firm of Nettlefold and Chamberlain was to become the largest screw-making company in the country.

Joseph Chamberlain's entry into politics came with his election as a Liberal councillor for St Paul's Ward at the local elections of 1869, the first under the new extended franchise. Within four years he had been elected mayor, and was preparing to unleash dramatic changes on his adopted town. 'The town,' he promised in an oft-quoted remark of that year, 'shall not, with God's help, know itself!'

It is easy to exaggerate Chamberlain's contribution to local government in Birmingham. After all, we have seen that the pre-Chamberlain Council had already instituted major reforms in terms of social provision, not to mention the earlier work of the Commissioners. Chamberlain's contribution was in taking the Corporation finances onto a new level, enabling the Corporation to undertake massive projects such as Elan Valley and the Improvement Scheme. Simply put, it was to apply the economics of the market-place— massive borrowing, take-overs and shrewd long-term planning—to local government. We need to look at three chief areas of Corporation expansion. The first, which we have already discussed, was taking control of the water supply. The second was a similar move to municipalise the gas supply.

Much had happened in the gas industry since Murdock's time. Two companies were operating in the town. The first, which had creamed off much of the lucrative business of the town centre, was the Birmingham Gas Light and Coke Co., formed in 1819. The location of its first retort house gave Gas Street its name. The second, formed in 1825 to take in much of the Black Country and the roads into Birmingham, was the Birmingham and Staffordshire Gas Light Company. In 1845 a second Act extended the latter company's control to almost the whole of the current Borough of Birmingham. An uneasy *ménage à trois* was the result, with the Corporation paying over the odds for street lighting, and having little say as to distribution, brightness and hours of operation. Rawlinson had pointed out in 1849 that charges seemed to be unduly high, blaming them on the presence of two companies with two sets of underground pipes and overhead costs. It has to be said that local government and private companies have never worked desperately well together at the best of times.

Chamberlain's proposal in 1874 for a municipal take-over had two reasons behind it. Firstly, he argued that all state monopolies should be in the disinterested hands of elected representatives. Secondly, the profits that accrued from ownership could be turned to major capital projects, without additional burdens on the rate-payers. Even the increase of the Borough debt to £2½ million was not necessarily a bad thing. As has been said before, if you owe the bank £200, they suspend your account; if you owe £2 million, they put you on the board.

The Gas Bill was passed in July 1875, and the Corporation made profits of £34,000 in the first year. In 10 years the Gas Committee supplied 600,000 private and 10,000 public lamps. The Corporation employed 200 lamplighters, committed to do their rounds whatever the weather. But in that first decade of municipal control, almost £250,000 profits could be directed towards public works.

So successful were the new arrangements, and so energetically did the Gas Committee promote the service, that wide-scale use of electric lighting was slow to emerge in the city. The Town Hall, and the shops and offices in a small area of the city centre, were supplied with electric lighting as early as 1889 (the first generator was in Dale End). Impressions were favourable, particularly since indoor gas lighting gave a rather smoky yellow light, and the heat generated led to much fainting in the upper galleries of the Town Hall.

The Corporation took over the electric supply in 1899, but electric street lighting was little in evidence before the First World War. Indeed, there were still some oil lamps in use in Market Street. It was between the wars that electric discharge mercury lighting began to be systematically installed on the city's streets. By 1972 there remained only 180 gas lamps in Birmingham, and they were fading fast.

The concept of a town council that borrowed much, thought big and acted fast was not to end with the Gas Undertaking. Far from it. By the summer of '75 Chamberlain had turned his attention to the issue of 'redevelopment'. Under the terms of the Artisans' Dwellings Act (1875), any town with a population over 25,000 was empowered to buy condemned property (after examination by the Medical Officer of Health) and deal with it as it saw fit. On 27 July of that year, Chamberlain proposed the setting-up of an Improvement Committee:

> It might run a great street, as broad as a Parisian boulevard, from New Street to the Aston Road; it might open up a street such as Birmingham had not got, and was almost stifling for the want of—for all the best streets were too narrow. The Council might demolish the houses on each side of the street, and let or sell the frontage land, and arrange for rebuilding workmen's houses behind, taking the best advantages of the sites, and building them in accordance with the latest sanitary knowledge ...

68. An early photograph of the corner of Newton Street and Corporation Street. Attempts to revive the earlier commercial mix of Corporation Street have emerged in recent years.

The only snag here was that the Act did not empower councils to build any housing. No matter—let the Scheme commence.

The Improvement Scheme would take in, or take out, many of the poorest streets (but by no means all of them) in the town centre: Upper Priory, the Minories, Thomas Street, London 'Prentice Street and the Gullet, to name just a handful. We have already seen something of the conditions in this impoverished area. Suffice it here to add the comment of the chairman of the Committee in October 1875: 'The rubbish and dilapidation in whole quarters have reminded me of Strasburg, which I saw soon after the bombardment'. The 'great street' would be cut from New Street through to the faded glories of Old Square, before joining the route of Lichfield Street at its junction with Newton Street. A second street through to Colmore Row had to be abandoned because of the cost of the intervening land, and a third to Dale End (Martineau Street) was delayed until 1886. A railway tunnel to link New Street with Snow Hill had also to be scrapped.

Demolition work from the New Street end began in August 1878 and, by January 1882, Corporation Street, as it became known, had reached Old Square. The scheme was estimated to cost £1½ million, but sale of leases in what was to be Birmingham's premier shopping street was expected to reduce the overall burden on the rate-payers to around £½ million: which was termed 'a price well worth paying'.

The first lease of land (in January 1878) was for a women's hospital in the Priory, and the scheme later included the Grand Theatre, *Cobden's Hotel* and the Corporation

69. The Victoria Law Courts, designed by Sir Aston Webb and Ingress Bell after a competition. The foundation stone was laid by Victoria and the building opened by her son. The statues are by the socialist artist, Walter Crane.

Street Winter Gardens, bringing the refined delights of Bournemouth to Birmingham. Further along, a site was found for assize courts, which the Council had originally intended to place at the rear of the Council House. By combining under the same roof assize and magistrates courts and a police station, the Corporation could at last rid itself of the antiquated and restricting Public Offices in Moor Street. A design competition was won by Aston Webb and Ingress Bell of London, the entries being judged by Alfred Waterhouse, who had earlier judged the Council House competition. It was to be one of the grandest of the city's terracotta palaces, the richly decorated material that dominated Birmingham architecture towards the end of the 19th century. The foundation stone was laid by Queen Victoria, in the middle of her nationwide Jubilee tour, on 23 March 1887, in token of which the buildings were named the Victoria Courts. They were officially opened by the Prince and Princess of Wales on 21 July 1891, and welcomed their first criminals nine days later.

The New Theatre, renamed the Grand, opened in November 1883, and stood next to Old Central Hall (later known as King's Hall) in Old Square. Both buildings converted from variety theatre to cinema, the Grand finally ending up as 'The Grand Casino Ballroom' before its demolition in 1960.

Joseph Chamberlain's use of the word 'boulevard' was no doubt significant; it smacked of Napoleon redesigning Paris and, if that enterprise had undertones of (enlightened) dictatorship, there were enough critics of the scheme to suggest that the former mayor was driving a bulldozer over the rate-payers, and that the finances of Corporation Street were not as rosy as its supporters alleged. Unarguably the rates did rise (by about 2s. in the pound), but they were rising before that anyway. Traders in Birmingham's traditional shopping streets—New Street and High Street—complained that attention and trade was shifting to the new street and leaving them high and dry.

But it was the argument over re-housing that was most difficult to answer. According to the initial calculations, the resident population of the area had been 16,596, all but 3,000 of whom were working-class families. There was no provision in the Act for the Corporation to find them alternative housing, other than to earmark sites for private developers. But by the middle of 1885 only 62 houses had been built, and 653 lost. Finally, in 1889, the Council moved to erect 22 two-storey, three-bedroom cottages in Ryder Street, followed by a further 81 in Lawrence Street, Old Cross Street and Duke Street in 1891. Rents for tenants 'of good class' ranged from 5s. to 7s. 6d. a week. Thus the area now under Aston University was Birmingham's first, very modest, 'council estate'.

PUTTING ON THE SCREW.
(The Improvement Scheme.)
" It is now estimated that another £100,000 is wanted,"
—Is the present revised estimate a final one, or may we
expect that some time hence another £100,000 will be
found necessary.—*The Birmingham Daily Post.*

70. A cartoon from *The Dart* of 1882 expressing worries that the Improvement Scheme could only be achieved by squeezing the rate-payers. *The Dart* remained a fiercely anti-Chamberlain magazine. Chamberlain, of course, knew all about screws from his career with G.K.N.

By 1933, 40,000 council houses would have been built, but the days of such mass enterprise were far distant in the 1890s. Initially the council put a block on further back-to-backs and tried renovation and improvement instead. The first Chairman of the Housing Committee, J. S. Nettlefold, gave his name to the improvement known as 'Nettlefold Courts', demolishing the houses to either side of the tunnel entrance to form an open court. The town council and the slum-dwellers seemed to be seeing daylight at last.

What the Improvement Scheme had shown was the ability of Birmingham Corporation to act radically when the occasion arose. The question of sub-standard housing was not one that was yet perceived as a crisis, despite what Rawlinson had said 40 years earlier. In consequence, measures were piece-meal and small-scale. Municipalisation, the flavour of the month as far as how people lived was concerned, would not be a concept to be applied to where they lived for some years yet.

While the city council was placing a first tentative toe in the water of urban conditions and artisans' dwellings, one business at least was pursuing its own radical solution to inner-city congestion. Chocolate, in spite of the cholestorol, was about to become the centrepiece of a very healthy lifestyle, but we need to go back a couple of generations first.

On 1 March 1824, the following advertisement was placed in *Aris's Gazette*: 'J.C. is desirous of introducing to particular notice Cocoa Nibs, prepared by himself, an article affording a most nutricious beverage for breakfast'. The 'J.C.' in question was John Cadbury, and the address was 93 Bull Street. This was not, in fact, the beginning of his chocolate manufacture—he was only breaking up roasted beans at this stage—but that was to follow soon after. One of Birmingham's economic success stories was just beginning.

John Cadbury's life and his business interests in many ways encapsulate the whole Cadbury culture. A Street Commissioner and Overseer of the Poor, he was a member of the 'Steam-engine' sub-committee that looked at ways of reducing atmospheric pollution in Birmingham. He also took up the cause of chimney sweeps, or 'climbing boys', campaigning for the use of mechanical cleaners to replace this exploited under-class. And most crucial of all, of course, he was a Quaker and leader of the Temperance movement. This blend of business acumen and social reform remained central to the Cadburys throughout the 19th century.

In 1847, when his premises in Crooked Lane had the G.W.R. tunnel cut through it, John Cadbury re-located to Bridge Street. The Bull Street shop passed to another branch of the family, eventually to become Barrow's Stores, one of Birmingham's premier grocery businesses. The Bridge Street factory was soon to contain many of the elements to be

71. *The Dart*'s cynical view of 'the new Birmingham' of Joseph Chamberlain's imagination. The transformation scene was the spectacular end of every Victorian pantomime.

developed later at Bournville. *Chamber's Journal* published in 1852 a description of the place: a chimney that did not give off smoke and a workforce (mainly women) that received a weekly half-day holiday in the summer months, as well as permission to attend evening classes twice a week. Cadbury's was the first firm in town to enforce the Saturday half-day closure.

Campaigns for the reduction of factory and shop hours (and pubs, come to that) were a common feature of Victorian social reform. When George Cadbury altered summer working hours at Bridge Street (6.00 a.m. to 2.30 p.m.) in 1865 and introduced fines and rewards for punctuality, he argued:

> This we do as a more convenient business arrangement. But we also believe it promotes the health and comfort of those employed—introducing habits of punctuality, early rising, and, what is more important, early retiring to rest; thus escaping much of the temptation which abounds during the late evening hours.

The lease on Bridge Street was for 35 years, and by the late '70s was running out. John Cadbury's sons, George and Richard, were then running the firm and began the search for a new site. It was in June 1878 that they purchased 14 acres of land between Stirchley and Selly Oak. It was almost a green field site, but not entirely open: both the Birmingham West Suburban Railway and the Worcester and Birmingham Canal ran nearby. The name Bournbrook, suggested by the Georgian hall that stood across the road, was soon changed to Bournville, a French-sounding name being more marketable.

When the firm moved to Bournville, cocoa was the main product. In 1880 sweet manufacture began, and the first exports were shipped to Australia, followed by much of the rest of the Commonwealth. Early in this century came Cadbury's Dairy Milk (1904), followed by Milk Tray (1915) and Roses (1938). Merger with Schweppes took place in 1969. Little of the original factory of 1879, and none of the first 24 workers' cottages, have survived, such has been the expansion of the firm and the village in the intervening years. The land around Bournbrook Hall, for example, became the Girls' Recreation Ground. The last occupant of the hall, which came down in 1907, was William Martin, whose architectural partnership with John Henry Chamberlain produced a generation of Birmingham schools.

It was in 1895 that George Cadbury purchased land near to the factory, with the intention of building a model village. Cadbury outlined the chief reasons behind the scheme to the first Garden City Conference, held at Bournville in 1901. The object was that of: '... alleviating the evils which arise from the insanitary and insufficient housing accommodation supplied to large numbers of the working classes, and of securing to workers in factories some of the advantages of outdoor village life, with opportunities for the natural and healthful occupation of cultivating the soil'. Alexander Harvey, the greatest of the Estate architects, added to the reasoning in *The Model Village and its Cottages* in 1906: 'The cultivation of the soil is certainly the best antidote to the sedentary occupations of those working in large towns ... Many believe, indeed, that with its encouragement the abuse of the social club and public-house will be materially lessened, and one of the greatest social evils of the time disappear'. Consequently, the first leases stipulated that no house was to occupy more than a quarter of its grounds, and gardening skills were encouraged and refined by evening classes. The idea was to reverse the financial flow of recreational activity. Instead of squandering it on booze, the educated worker could produce, on 1901 calculations, a produce yield of 1s. 11d. per week.

By 1900 an estate of 300 acres had been bought, and the first 300 houses built. The whole property was then transferred to trustees—the Bournville Village Trust—who continue to hold overall control of the Village and its development. And though some speculative building crept in on the Stirchley side of the Estate, a virtual monopoly of the contracts by architects like Harvey and Bedford Tyler assured high quality of design. Harvey made clear his detestation of:

> Desolate row upon row of ugly and cramped villas, ever multiplying to meet the demands of a quickly increasing population, where no open spaces are reserved, where trees and other natural beauties are sacrificed to the desire to crowd upon the land as many dwellings as possible, and where gardens cannot be said to exist—such are the suburbs which threaten to engulf our cities.

The result in Bournville was domestic architecture essentially nostalgic in character, much influenced by Voysey and the Arts and Crafts Movement. The style is seen best in the public buildings around the Village green (what could be more nostalgic than that?), the 'medieval' Rest House of 1914, the Day Continuation Schools of 1925 and Junior School, with its distinctive carillon, of 1904. In that year, statistics from the medical officer of health showed that deaths in Bournville were running at 6.9 per thousand; in Birmingham the figure was 19 per thousand. The Bournville experiment, it seemed, was working.

Bournville heralded a number of 'garden suburb' schemes locally. In Bordesley Green the Ideal Benefit Society inaugurated a 'workmen's garden colony' in 1908, consisting initially of 225 houses and shops, and others at Handsworth Wood and Moseley in the '20s and '30s. Also in 1908 Harborne Tenants Ltd, under the chairmanship of the housing pioneer J. S. Nettlefold, built around five hundred houses between High Street and Lordswood Road. The scheme is now known as Moor Pool Conservation Area.

But as important as the experiments at Bournville and the Ideal Village were to town planning, they did not begin to face up to the issues of mass housing. Indeed they provided an escape route from it: a deposit on a property in Bournville amounted to £75 minimum, and the cost of a house in Bordesley Green remained way beyond the means of most. Courts or terraces were the only available choice for many, if choice they had. But the expansion of the city after 1911 widened the possibilities considerably.

Chapter Twenty-three

Schools and Hospitals

Until the Education Act of 1870 schooling was one of those little luxuries that few families could afford. Indeed a survey of 1838 revealed that only one in five of the town's children received any kind of day schooling. As with the hospitals that we will come to later, most early Victorian schools fall into one of two categories: private or charity.

For those that could afford it, King Edward's on New Street and the Blue Coat School by St Philip's remained the chief attraction for the parents of Anglican children. The Protestant Dissenting Charity School in Graham Street received 'poor female children' and in most cases turned them into domestics. Better-off girls could gain an education in the arts of music, deportment and the kind of lifestyle to which they would become accustomed at one of the many small private 'academies' dotted about the town and surrounding areas. Victoria Road, Aston boasted no less than six of them, and there were upwards of 250 altogether. Most were run by a woman or sisters, and indeed it was one of the few career opportunities for older women, whether married or single.

The charity school was still a relatively rare bloom at the beginning of the 19th century. The Female School of Industry in Queen Street received poor girls: '... who are taught to read, knit and sew, and instructed in such other Duties as will be the means, it is hoped, to qualify them, whatever may be their future Situation in Life, to become good and faithful Servants, and useful Members of Society'.

As with any charitable or centrally funded venture, value for money was a prime concern. The educational system devised by Joseph Lancaster 'on a new, expeditious and cheap plan' offered just this. By using older children as monitors, one teacher could run a school of 400 or more children. Certainly it was cheap: one teacher and one classroom per school, but it accommodated a range of ages and levels of literacy. Four hundred was the size of the Lancastrian Free School that opened in Severn Street in September 1809, offering instruction in reading, writing and arithmetic. As a report proudly claimed in 1812: 'All the boys in the school, with the exception of those who are in the sand class, are in the daily habit of writing upon slates, and of these there are 50 who write also on paper'. Religious instruction was emphasised, but of a non-denominational kind; indeed a small number of the boys attended the synagogue.

The same 'monitorial system' was used in schools promoted by the National Society for Promoting the Education of the Poor in the Principles of the Established Church. The first National School to open in Birmingham (1812) was in Pinfold Street. In 1814 there were 450 boys, and around two hundred girls on the floor above. All applicants had to be nominated by subscribers (a means of ensuring that the children were Anglican), and education was limited to the '3 Rs'. It was but a brief interlude between the crib and the factory.

72.   Education on the cheap. The Lancastrian or Madras system used monitors (those standing) to teach younger children. Parents were invited to see the system in operation at first hand.

At a time of educational experiment, the work of Thomas Wright Hill deserves particular note. Hill opened a school called 'Hill-Top' in Gough Street in 1803, later moving to 'Hazelwood' on the Hagley Road, where it was run by his two sons, Matthew and Rowland. The distinguishing element of Hill's school was 'to teach our pupils the arts of self-government and self-education'. At a time when democracy was still a rare commodity in society, Hazelwood was a school run by a committee elected by the pupils, and misdemeanours were judged and punished by a similarly elective magistracy that changed every month. In addition, the boys had their own token currency that could be earned by academic performance or charitable works (and lost by bad behaviour). These could be traded in for additional holidays. Not only that; the school was the first to have a science laboratory and gas-lighting, as well as central heating. Rowland Hill's experiment was widely appreciated: there were visits to the school by Wilberforce and De Quincey, and the philosopher, Jeremy Bentham subscribed to the school magazine. Hazelwood received pupils from as far afield as Greece and Spain, and it was only Rowland's retirement through ill-health that forced its closure in 1846. He went on to invent the postage stamp instead.

But for the unprivileged many, the choices were less stimulating. Ragged schools, such as those founded by William Chance in Windmill Street (1845) and Digby Street (1848), provided basic elementary schooling for around two hundred children. Most ragged schools were attached to and founded by local Anglican churches, though not necessarily excluding dissenters. A report on 'progress' at St Philip's ragged school in Lichfield Street in 1847 gives some idea of what was on offer for the hundred or so children:

> They are under the care of an experienced master; their little tasks appear more as a recreation than otherwise; they are watched over carefully; their faults patiently and kindly corrected, so as to win them by persuasion and gentleness from the idleness and errors into which they may have unfortunately fallen; and every other day they receive a substantial meal.

The 'substantial meal' was itself a guarantee of a good attendance. The intention at Lichfield Street was to create an 'industrial school', training its tiny charges (through making and mending clothes and shoes) in a life of labour. Sure enough, in 1849 the school moved to become Gem Street Industrial School, accommodating 330 boys and girls (of seven years and over) in three classes. The training and education was free, though an attached asylum for orphans charged £8 a year. A time capsule placed beneath the foundation stone explained that: 'The system of education provides that the children be taught trades and industrial occupations, besides reading, writing, arithmetic, and Christian knowledge'.

Piecemeal as this process was, a further educational survey of 1868 revealed that around 39 per cent of children aged five to 15 were now engaged in full-time education, double what the figure had been 40 years earlier. However, the older the child was, the less likely that you would find him or her in school; the ability to earn money began early, and the average time spent in school was consequently only about two years. This survey had been commissioned by a new pressure group, the Birmingham Education Society, founded in 1867 under the leadership of George Dixon. For the next few years Birmingham was to be the centre of a national educational debate, with men like Dixon, Chamberlain, Jesse Collings and Dawson at the heart of it. The outcome, though not entirely as they would have wished it, was the Education Act of 1870, and for the first time elementary education became compulsory in England.

The debate reflected two growing trends in Birmingham and the nation as a whole: secularisation and municipalisation. The Education Society, and later the Birmingham-based National Education League, argued that education had too long been in the hands of denominational bodies. What was needed to solve the partial system that the churches and charities had created was free compulsory education in the hands of the local authority, and funded by the rates and central government. But hardly had the National Education League set up its impressive structure of town branch committees than Forster's Education Act came onto the statute book.

The League found the government's measures half-hearted and hemmed about with compromise. Not only did it fail to oust the denominational schools (replacing them with School Boards only where current provision was inadequate), it also failed to bite the bullet of free schooling. Charges were initially 3d. a week for children over seven years of age, and 2d. for those under seven. Birmingham School Board fought a long-running campaign with Disraeli's government to get the fees reduced, finally abolishing them in 1891.

What Forster's Bill had produced was a two-headed beast. The elected School Board, independent of local government but reliant on its rates, challenged a long-established denominational system over a range of issues: fees (the latter did not wish to see their charges undercut by Board Schools) and the nature and desirability of religious or sectarian teaching. And because of the nature of the first elections, the radical town council found itself facing a conservative School Board, with little prospect of peaceful *cohabitation*. John Bright, the local M.P., told Forster that: 'There is much hot water in Birmingham on the education question'. It certainly made the first School Board elections unusually vitriolic.

However, there was little to be done but to run with the system, flawed as it may have seemed. The first Board School opened at Bloomsbury in March 1873, catering for 1,059 pupils (boys, girls and infants), and by 1880 there were 28 schools, with provision for 28,787 children. Many of the early schools were designed by the local firm of Chamberlain and Martin, following a common pattern of assembly hall surrounded by classrooms. Most also have a distinctive tower, part of the 'air-conditioning' system felt to be vital for the combination of healthy mind and healthy body.

There seems no doubt that the Birmingham School Board led the country in its energy and organisation, providing tarred playgrounds and some kindergarten teaching, and widening the curriculum to include science, cookery and woodwork. But it became clear that a single structure of funding and control was, in the end, preferable. The Education Act of 1902 abolished the School Boards and transferred their powers to the local authority. The fact that a Board member, George Kendrick, became the Chairman of the new Education Committee, suggests considerable continuity in its aims and objectives.

Until 1944, of course, it was not compulsory for children to pass to secondary education, though a number of 'Higher Grade' schools such as Waverley Road (1892) and, six years later, George Dixon (formerly Oozells Street) allowed poorer children to do so. The first nursery school opened at the Birmingham Settlement in Summer Lane in 1919, but it was not until the 1940s that provision in this field markedly increased. In Victorian times adult evening classes and Sunday schools filled a little of the gap.

As education became increasingly subject to national legislation in the 20th century, the distinctive nature of Birmingham schools began to fade. Periods of economy in the 1910s and 1930s sandwich one of considerable expansion in the 1920s, when new housing estates, specifically intended for young families, needed many new schools. Forty new elementary schools were built between 1923 and 1935. To include a statistical summary of the current state of primary and secondary education in the city would be to condemn this book to instant redundancy: so fluid is the present position, with opting-out and perhaps longer term changes to the funding of state education on the horizon. Perhaps we should finish where we began, with King Edward's and Blue Coat. The latter continues in Harborne, while the former, now comprising a number of schools, still occupies pride of place in the private sector.

Progress in adult education was, if anything, slower than that in elementary schooling. Both the Mechanics' Institute (1826-42) and the Polytechnic Institution (1843-8) folded through lack of resources. The Midland Institute was to be more successful, both in its fundraising and its survival. Even before its establishment, Charles Dickens raised £227 from three readings of *A Christmas Carol* in the Town Hall, appropriately at Christmas 1853, the author becoming one of the first honorary members of the new institute. The aim of the institute, according to the Act of 1854 that allowed the Corporation to grant land for building, was 'the advancement of science, literature and art', and the completed institute was to include a library, newsroom, exhibitions and many lecture courses. Dickens called it 'a Temple of Concord which will be a noble example to the whole of England'. The foundation stone in Paradise Street was laid by the Prince Consort in 1855, the finished building being the first element in Birmingham's 'education quarter' around the Town Hall.

Directly opposite the Midland Institute was another educational establishment: Queen's College, a residential college for medical students, founded by William Sands Cox in 1828. This was the first institution in Birmingham with the power to grant degrees, as an external arm of London University. This was the foundation that in many respects under-lies Birmingham's first university, though it was Mason College, the result of massive donations by Josiah Mason, that provided its first home. Josiah Mason's Science College was erected in 1880, incorporated as a University College in 1896, and finally made a university in its own right in 1900. It need hardly be said that its first chancellor, Joseph Chamberlain, was more than instrumental in the college achieving university status. The first principal, Oliver Lodge, watched the gradual transfer of the university from its central but restricted site in Chamberlain Square to the new one in Edgbaston, a move that was only completed in 1961. It was at the old site, however, that two of Britain's prime ministers were educated: Stanley Baldwin and Neville Chamberlain.

Mason College was to be the first of three Birmingham institutions to make the transition from college to university. In 1964 the old College of Technology at Gosta Green became the University of Aston in Birmingham, now simply Aston University, during a period when central government was targetting Birmingham for increased technological education. No prime ministers to list amongst its alumni, though it can claim Alfred Bestall, illustrator of *Rupert the Bear*! Indeed, Birmingham can claim to have contributed more than its fair share to the reading matter of the young: Thomas the Tank Engine hails from Kings Norton, and the author of *The Hobbit* (J. R. R. Tolkien) spent his childhood in the city.

73. Josiah Mason (1795-1881), founder of the college that became Birmingham's first university and the orphanage at Erdington where he is buried. His pen company was producing almost five million nibs a week.

More recently, in 1992, Birmingham Polytechnic became the city's third university as the University of Central England in Birmingham, or U.C.E. for short. The latter has many roots in 19th-century soil: Cadbury's Day Continuation School at Bournville, the Municipal College of Art in Margaret Street and the Midland Institute itself.

The progress of Birmingham's Victorian hospitals reveals the same three strands of private provision, charity and rate-supported. The latter category was represented by the workhouse, which also provided a rudimentary education for its child inmates. Once the Birmingham Union Workhouse had moved to the Dudley Road site in 1851 it expanded at an alarming rate (and with alarming rates). Initially designed for 1,100, it had doubled in size by 1881, and had 63 employees on the pay-roll. Given that the poverty that drove people to the workhouse could be the result of age and illness, it is not surprising that much of the building was given over to sick wards, and that in 1889 a separate Workhouse

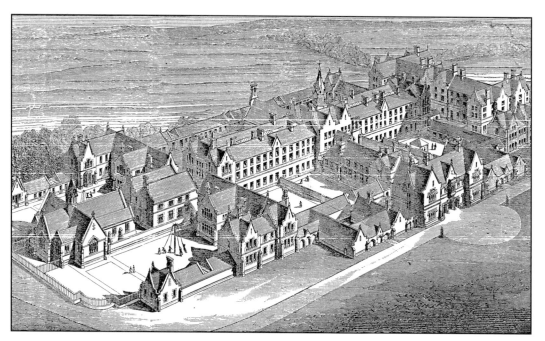

74.   In the 1850s Birmingham Workhouse moved from Lichfield Street to Winson Green. The main entrance faced onto Western Road. Note the two separate may-poles for girls and boys.

Infirmary had to be built. Designed by W. H. Ward to the model recommended by Florence Nightingale, one corridor a quarter of a mile long linked the nine 'pavilions'. One thousand one hundred beds were divided between such exclusive categories as 'bad leg ward', 'old female epileptic ward', 'venereal ward' and 'itch and de-lousing ward'.

The Workhouse Infirmary was the only one of the city's hospitals directly supported on the rates. Compared to this, the voluntary or charitable hospitals were small indeed. The *Medical Directory* of 1907 shows the General Hospital as containing 346 beds and the Eye Hospital as having one hundred and five. The other seven were smaller still. All, however, had much larger out-patient departments. Most of these were designed for a particular group (the Women's or Children's Hospitals) or part of the body (Ear and Throat, Eye, Dental etc). Only one (the Homeopathic) was radically different. A Homeopathic Dispensary opened in Great Charles Street in 1845, but the hospital, designed by Yeoville Thomason, opened on Easy Row from 1875.

By the Victorian period the General Hospital already had a long tradition. Funded by charity events (such as the Music Festivals and the Aston Fêtes of 1856), subscriptions and donations, by 1872 it had treated a total of 740,000 patients. A break-through in its funding had been the introduction of the Hospital Sunday Fund in 1859 and, more importantly the Hospital Saturday Fund, with work-place collections that eventually changed to a form of medical insurance. In 1897 the General moved from its original site in Summer Lane to the terracotta palace in Steelhouse Lane. Once more Louisa Anne Ryland was a major contributor to the £200,000 that the new buildings cost.

A hospital 'for the gratuitous relief to the poor in all cases of diseases of teeth' opened wide at 13 Temple Street in 1857. The Dental Hospital then established is now the oldest in the country. Despite the inconvenience of only having two chairs and sharing offices with a newspaper and a building society, 269 teeth were removed in the first year, all without the help of an anaesthetic. It was only after the Dental Hospital moved to Broad Street in 1871 that a chloroformist was appointed and nitrous oxide went some way to alleviating the pain of separation.

Much medical attention was lavished on Broad Street. In 1842 a Lying-in Hospital was established here to provide maternity care for poor women. In 1868 it converted into a charity service offering care at home. This accommodation was taken over by the Birmingham and Midland Free Hospital for Sick Children, established in 1862 by Dr. Thomas Pretious Heslop. The diet sheet reveals that in 1882 those on a 'milk diet' received two pints of it a day, along with eight ounces of bread and dripping. Fresh vegetables were served twice a week 'when practicable'. In 1917 the hospital moved to Ladywood Road.

To William Sands Cox, whose practice in Temple Row was only three doors away from Heslop's, we owe the Queen's Hospital, a teaching establishment attached to Queen's College, and based in Bath Row from 1840. Until 1875 admission was by subscriber's ticket only, after which it became free. In 1941 it became the Birmingham Accident Hospital and Rehabilitation Centre, the first of its kind in Britain.

A Hospital for Women was set up in the Crescent in 1871, aimed at patients of the middle income range. All women whose family earnings exceeded 30s. a week were expected to seek private care elsewhere, while the poorest had to be referred to the House Committee: the Workhouse Infirmary was still their more likely destination. After 1878 the

75. Homeopathy was still in the mainstream of medical treatment in the Victorian period. The hospital in Easy Row (opened in 1875) received around five thousand patients a year.

76. The first eye hospital opened in 1823 in Cannon Street, later moving to the former *Royal Hotel* in Temple Row. Admission was by subscriber's ticket. In 1882 the far-sighted governors planned a new hospital in Edmund Street.

in-patient and out-patient departments separated, the latter moving to a new home in the Priory, as part of the Improvement Scheme. The residential half was one of the first of the city hospitals to re-locate to the suburbs; it moved to premises provided by (yet again) Louisa Ryland in Sparkhill.

It was the crisis of medical provision as a result of two world wars that was the impetus to major change in the running of hospitals. In 1930 the workhouse hospitals came under council control, but the fully integrated system that was required had to wait a little while yet. In 1934 the Prince of Wales laid the foundation stone of a new Medical Centre, close to the University in Edgbaston. When the centre was visited by the King and Queen in 1939, it was given the name 'The Queen Elizabeth Hospital'. Increasingly the Q.E. has become the focus of development in hospital care in Birmingham, and the future of the remaining city centre hospitals is doubtful. Some, however, such as the Children's and Accident Hospital are regional, if not national, institutions and are likely to survive. Evolution will no doubt take its toll, as it always has.

Chapter Twenty-four

Entertainment Without Music

The root of all crime, the cause of ill health, or simply an antidote to the drudgery of everyday life? Few institutions in Birmingham posed as many questions as the public house. At the top end of the market (metaphorically speaking, for most of the pubs near the Bull Ring were definitely at the bottom end of the market), the grander public houses and hotels provided much needed meeting places in the town centre. After all, the town council met in the *Woodman* prior to the building of the Council House, and the inaugural meeting of the Kennel Club took place in the *Grand Hotel*.

It was the rise of the beerhouse, licensed to sell ale but not spirits, that gave most cause for concern. By 1890 almost half of the city's 2,178 licensed premises were beer-houses, three times the number there had been 50 years before. Almost all of them brewed their own beer. Thus was alcohol brought within the means of even the poorest. Alcoholism itself was a relatively limited problem; it was the squandering of scarce resources that provoked a moral backlash. A Birmingham broadside described the ill effects of the continuing tradition of St Monday (or 'fuddling day'):

> St. Monday brings more ills about, for when the money's spent,
> The children's clothes go up the spout, which causes discontent;
> And when at night he staggers home, he knows not what to say;
> A fool is more a man than he upon a fuddling day.

> *Chorus*
> For it's drink, drink, smoke, smoke, drink, drink away,
> There is no pleasure in the house upon a fuddling day.

The Birmingham Temperance Society had been founded in 1830, reinforced by later movements such as the Gospel Temperance Mission of 1882 and the Birmingham Coffee House Company, which aimed to offer a cheap alternative place of resort to the pub. The establishment of town missions in the slums by a number of the non-conformist sects was also an attempt to provide a non-alcoholic place of recreation and education for the poorer classes. Digbeth Institute, founded by the Carrs Lane Congregationalists in 1908, offered meeting-rooms, a café, billiards room and a kind of rudimentary 'citizen's advice bureau', as well as evening classes and worship. The place closed in 1954, but continued to play an important social role as the misnamed 'Digbeth Town Hall', particularly as a venue for public meetings. It is now a night-club (with alcohol) and venue for live music.

The Temperance and church-based movements were only one of a number of assaults on the demon drink. Another was the creation of 'alcohol-free zones'. Much of the Calthorpe

77. The *Dog and Duck* or, more popularly, the 'Bark and Quack' at Holloway Head. Behind it stands Chapman's windmill. Both were demolished in the 1870s.

estate in Edgbaston excluded pubs and, most famous of all, Cadbury's relocation to Bournville was an ideal opportunity to create a community and a culture that was tee-total.

But the dominance of the self-supporting beerhouse was coming to an end by the 1870s. After 1869 it was necessary for a beerhouse to be licensed; the magistrates tightened their grip and new influences were at work within the town council. In 1876 the council authorised a new 'pub watch' by special officers, and in 1881 Major Bond, the chief superintendent of police, introduced what became known as the 'quiet drunkard' order, whereby anyone found drunk, whether misbehaving or not, was arrested. The latter scheme had to be abandoned as unworkable, but not before an irrevocable breakdown in relations between Bond and the Watch Committee.

As the number of licensed houses levelled off, and then declined, so a number of larger brewers began to swallow up the publican brewers, and the system of tied houses was born. By 1890 the largest of the common brewers, Holt Brewery, had 155 houses, followed by Henry Mitchell with 86 and Ansell and Sons with sixty-four. Henry Mitchell, and his future partner William Butler, had both begun as publican brewers; Mitchell at the *Crown Inn* in Smethwick, Butler at the *Crown* in Broad Street. Their merger in 1898 created another giant to rival Holt's, and all brewing was switched to Mitchell's Cape Hill works, which had begun brewing in 1879. The process of merging gathered pace into this century. In 1958 Birmingham was down to six independent brewers: Ansells, Atkinsons, Dares, Davenports, M&B and Frederick Smith. And the takeovers have continued, as local companies have become national ones. Now no beer is brewed at all in Birmingham. The anonymous balladeer who sang the following would turn in his grave:

> For Ale are we famous, clear, wholesome and strong,
> One drop of it now would enliven my song.
> Had my good Mother's milk tasted like it, I vow
> I ne'er would have left, but kept sucking till now.

The alternative to beer, of course, was alcohol-free drinks. Complaints about the dreadful quality of ginger beer in the Victorian era were rife: let's try something else. Tea was ale's fellow-traveller, first served in bars and places of recreation like the *Apollo Hotel* in Moseley Street. Men like Thomas Ridgway, dealer in tea in the Bull Ring during the early 1830s, and J. H. Brindley, who founded the Priory Tea and Coffee Co. in 1893, were part of a wide network of distribution, gradually turning tea from a communal drink to a domestic one. The Temperance Society in particular seized upon tea as an ideal product to promote in opposition to alcohol and, brewed in huge urns, it was sold at fundraising meetings. Coffee could never really compete when it came to mass production like this.

Most successful of all the Birmingham tea merchants was William Sumner, whose beginnings were as a grocer and druggist in the Bull Ring in 1820. The medicinal element became crucial when John Sumner marketed 'Typhoo' tea from his premises in High Street in 1903, the site now occupied by Waterstone's bookshop. By brewing only the edge of the leaf of a Ceylon variety, Sumner produced a brew that was low in tannin and could be sold as 'the tea that doctors prescribe', a cure for nerves and indigestion. The 'tipps' was the result of a printer's error, which was too distinctive to abandon. The company subsequently moved to Castle Street (off High Street) and, in 1924, to a canal-side location in Bordesley Street. Thither came around three thousand chests of tea per week, the unromantic end of a journey from distant Ceylon. Right up to the Second World War packing was done by hand by women. The works were extensively damaged by the same bombing raid that destroyed the Prince of Wales Theatre, but the tea lived on, merging with Cadbury Schweppes and then re-emerging as Premier Brands Ltd. in 1986.

Society was also beginning to find sources of entertainment that did not revolve around the public house. Early in the 19th century much 'sport' ended in something getting killed. A 'pit' in Smallbrook Street was the chief venue for cock-fighting until the 1820s, and there were many others, at least until the Prevention of Cruelty to Animals Act of 1835. A cocking in Smallbrook Street between 'the Gentlemen of Warwickshire and the Gentlemen of Worcestershire' in May 1809 involved a total of 102 cocks. Dog fights were common around Vaughton's Hole, as well as in the notorious upper rooms of pubs. Bear-baiting had already been the subject of legislation, but continued to be practised, particularly around the Heath. In 1828 a crowd of 1,000 at Little Hockley Pool was dispersed from a baiting, but Handsworth continued to be the local centre, particularly during the Wake.

The scattered nature of such communities made enforcement difficult; nearer to Birmingham, opposition to the sport was more effective. In 1798 the Chapel Wake, a celebration of the foundation of St Bartholomew's chapel, was due to include a bull-baiting behind the *Salutation Inn* on Snow Hill, but was stopped by intervention by the volunteer militia. The organisers changed venues to the Heath, but were again caught. Curiously, the one innocent party—the bull—was arrested and imprisoned!

The last of these 'innocent' pleasures was probably ratting, usually held in pubs, which continued to generate betting and prosecutions throughout the Victorian period.

Contrary to expectation, there is no direct evidence of bull-baiting ever having taken place in the Bull Ring, but the two annual fairs there were the focus of just about every other form of entertainment imaginable. The Pleasure Fair, held in June, and the September Onion Fair occupied most of the streets of the lower part of town, including Dale End, High Street, Smithfield and Digbeth. Until 1851 both were announced by the town crier and preceded by a procession of high and low bailiffs and a musical band.

The Onion or Michaelmas Fair in particular was Birmingham's equivalent to Nottingham's Goose Fair or London's St Bartholomew's. If the arrival of the first crops of onions had been the excuse in the 18th century (piled up as high as houses in Bull Ring), it was the side-shows that provided the main attraction for many. Here were gathered annually the wax-works, swing-boats and booths full of the unfortunates who did not fit into the category of what the Victorians considered 'normal': fat, bearded, short and ugly. Daniel Lambert, the world's fattest man, began his career (presumably by eating) in Birmingham, while Nanetta Stocker, an Austrian migrant who was also the world's tiniest woman, is buried in St Philip's churchyard. In the absence of permanent zoos, Bostock's and Wombwell's circuses and menageries provided locals with their only glimpse of animals more exotic than a pigeon or a bull terrier.

Birmingham's surprising lack of a zoo has often been a bone of contention and an opportunity for entrepreneurial skills. Morris Roberts, an ex-prizefighter, opened one in Balsall Heath in 1873, but its superannuated animals were not so far gone that they could not escape into the surrounding streets. It closed three years later and became a skating rink. Cannon Hill Park also converted its short-lived zoo into a nature centre for native British animals and birds.

However, the wild-life zone that was the Onion Fair (both human and animal) was increasingly the subject of adverse comment as the 19th century progressed. The lobby that would later propose that no public houses be erected in the whole of the Improvement Area, was already voicing its disapproval of the drunken behaviour and disruption to trade during the six days and nights of the fairs. In 1861 the entertainments were confined to the immediate vicinity of the Bull Ring, and in 1875 abolished altogether. This was, however, not quite the end of the matter. The Horse Fairs continued in the street named after them at Whit and Michaelmas, while a three-day Onion Fair, now limited rather literally to onions, remained a pungent place in the autumn. The fairground entrepreneurs simply moved their event out of the area of council jurisdiction to the Old Pleck at Aston. Here it stayed, under the watchful eye of Pat Collins, until the Aston Expressway was cut through the site.

The fading of Vauxhall Gardens left something of a gap as far as outdoor entertainments went, a gap finally filled by the formation of the Aston Park Company to run the Hall and grounds, before eventually transferring them to the Corporation. The new Park was opened by Queen Victoria on 15 June 1858, but the Queen was to be involved in Aston Park's affairs again in 1863, when the death of a female tightrope walker brought the new grounds into disrepute. She wrote to the Mayor, expressing her horror that: '... one of her subjects—a female—should have been sacrificed to the gratification of the demoralising taste unfortunately prevalent for exhibitions attended with the greatest danger to the performers'. The mayor might have replied that the Prince of Wales was not averse to watching this kind of thing. Instead, the council saw to a speedy takeover of the park in 1864.

For those who could reach it, Aston Hall and Grounds offered all you could wish in outdoor and indoor entertainment. A season ticket could be bought for one guinea, allowing unrestricted access to indoor events. It was Birmingham's equivalent of the Crystal Palace, with a stage (Holte Theatre stood inside the Great Hall from 1879-86), an aquarium, skating rink and cycling track. The Pageant of 1838 had its historical precedents: in 1860 historical tableaux included chariot races and gladiatorial contests, while Britannia took her pet lion for walks round the Park to advertise the event.

Another unusual event in Aston Lower Grounds was the second ever floodlit football match between Birmingham and Nottingham, some years before the sport became organised into the now familiar leagues and cups. The Birmingham Football Association was founded in 1875 and, in 1889, 12 of the local teams formed the Birmingham and District Football

78. The grounds of Aston Hall were used in the 1850s for charity fêtes, raising money for hospitals. By 1857 the charity in question was the hall itself, as moves were made to buy it for the Corporation.

League, the second oldest in the world. A year earlier, the first English Football League had included as founder-members both Aston Villa (who finished runners-up) and West Bromwich Albion (who were sixth). William McGregor of Aston Villa was the chief instigator of the idea. A second division was introduced in the 1892-3 season, with Small Heath among its members.

Strange are the beginnings of these local, if not national, institutions. Founded in 1874, Aston Villa began life as a team connected to the local Methodist circuit. Their local rivals followed in 1875: Small Heath, or Small Heath Alliance, or Birmingham, or Birmingham City, was a spin-off from the Holy Trinity Cricket Club in Bordesley, looking for winter exercise. There are enough histories of the two clubs to chart their ups and downs without this volume adding to them. Suffice it to say that the Villa appears perennially tortured by its success, the Blues by its failure. Villa's triumph over Anderlecht in the European Cup Final of 1982, however, remains the pinnacle of achievement by any football side in the West Midlands.

Success in the other football code has been more intermittent. The city's premier rugby club, Moseley, was founded in 1873 as an offshoot of Havelock Cricket Club, moving to its current home at the Reddings seven years later. At the time of its centenary, Moseley was probably at its height, followed by a steady decline in the '80s and '90s that was the common experience of many of the Midland clubs. Cricket in Birmingham has altogether more ancient origins. The earliest recorded game took place on 15 July 1751 at Holte Bridgman's Cricket Ground, at the Apollo in Aston. Aston remained the centre of the game locally for many years, W. G. Grace making his first appearance at the Lower Grounds in 1871. Games at the Lower Grounds were often of a very curious nature: one match pitched a team of one-armed war veterans against another of one-legged players. Nor was the tradition of 11-a-side always adhered to. In 1878 an Australian side came to Bournbrook, fresh from having bowled out the M.C.C. for 33 and 19. Pitted against a team of 22 local players from the Pickwick Club, they found it understandably harder going.

Warwickshire County Cricket Club was founded in 1882, principally on the initiative of William Ansell, as a mixture of what he called 'democratic Birmingham' and the 'county element' of gentlemen and army officers. Lord Calthorpe offered them a piece of 'rough

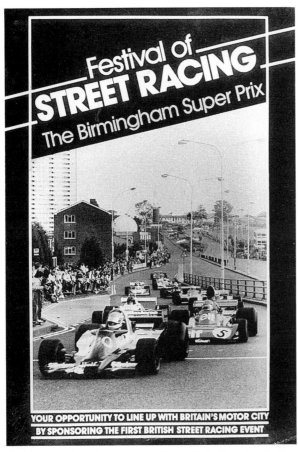

Festival of
STREET RACING
The Birmingham Super Prix

YOUR OPPORTUNITY TO LINE UP WITH BRITAIN'S MOTOR CITY
BY SPONSORING THE FIRST BRITISH STREET RACING EVENT

79. Birmingham's answer to Monte Carlo lasted only five years, having failed to capture the sporting headlines. The first race (1986) was brought to a spectacularly abrupt end by a hurricane.

grazing land' in Edgbaston, and the first match on the County Ground was played in June 1886, watched by 3,000 people. In that first season the visiting Australians played at Edgbaston twice, against Warwickshire and an England XI captained by Grace. The first test match, however, had to wait until 1902. Although the Australians were bowled out for 36 in their first innings, it was the English weather that came out on top, the game ending in a mudbath for players and spectators alike. (Many were trampled under foot during the rush into the ground on the last day.) The event made a loss of £2,000, even before the claims for damages to clothing came in. An inauspicious start to the career of one of the world's great test match grounds.

Despite the presence of Edgbaston, Birmingham's climb into the first division of international sporting cities has been a long one. In the early '70s the city had thoughts of bidding for the 1982 Commonwealth Games, centred upon an indoor sports stadium on the site of the former Snow Hill station. The move partly stemmed from the successful staging of group matches at Villa Park during the 1966 World Cup. But this, like the bid for the 1992 Olympic Games, fell on internationally deaf ears. On both occasions the city received little moral, and no financial, support from central government. Equally unsuccessful as a long-term project was the Birmingham Super Prix, the U.K.'s first street-based motor race. Its five-year run ended in 1990, having failed to secure significant private backing, and its distant aim of gaining Grand Prix status unachieved. The birth-place of Nigel Mansell was not yet ready to stage his races.

But the 1980s also brought some notable successes. The Snow Hill scheme was unexpectedly reincarnated as the National Indoor Arena that opened in 1992, the premier indoor athletics stadium in the country. And the continued importance of the N.E.C. arena as a sporting venue has been supported by major improvements to the Alexandra Stadium, the city's outdoor athletics track and home of the Birchfield Harriers.

Chapter Twenty-five

City of a Thousand Trades

The industrial metropolis that Birmingham had become by the mid-19th century had its romantic as well as its tragic side. On one side were the products of world famous industries: the transatlantic cable, the Crystal Palace fountain, the Orient Express. On the other was the reliance on child, or cheap female labour, the increasing pollution of atmosphere and water supply, the more than occasional fatal accidents in the Gun Quarter. One explosion at Ludlow's Ammunition Works in Witton (December 1870), for example, was the subject of a lurid street ballad:

> The General Hospital ne'er contained
> More human forms by fire inflamed.
> There fifty females, roasted, lie
> In agonies to groan and die.
>
> When armies meet in wilful war,
> We expect they'll reap in blood and gore;
> But when industry plies her hand
> We reckon not of death's demand.

It was a century that would radically change the nature of employment and manufacture, particularly in the transition from workshop to factory, a transition already foreshadowed by Soho. The introduction of steel and of steam power altered the means and volume of production, but there were other industries that simply fell victim to changing taste. Henry Clay, a former employee of John Baskerville in the japanning business, had patented in 1772 a new technique of sheet papier-mâché, but the new material, much heralded in its day, did not long survive him. Today's innovation is tomorrow's museum piece.

The supremacy of the 'Brummagem gilt button' was also a thing of the past by the 1860s. By then around six thousand were still employed in the industry, only a third of the number of 30 years earlier, though mechanisation meant that Birmingham was still manufacturing in excess of 600 million a year. Fashion had rejected the old gilt button, but there were plenty of other pearl and linen and glass and metal buttons to keep the business going. Here was an industry that perfectly juxtaposes the romantic with the mundane. The raw materials came from all four corners of the world: 'vegetable ivory' from Central and South America, mother-of-pearl from the East Indies, the Persian Gulf and the Red Sea, ivory from Africa. The workers came from all four corners of Birmingham, but were mostly women and children. Women's wages (about 8s. a week) averaged a third of men's, and that of young children could drop to as low as one shilling a week. It was not uncommon for girls as young as six to be employed in the industry, and equally young boys found jobs as 'nut crackers', breaking open the shells of vegetable ivory nuts. Conditions may not have been as oppressive as in the mills or down the mines, but exploitation was nevertheless rife.

Other industries were still on the increase. Umbrella manufacture, a business almost unknown before the 19th century, was dominated by Birmingham firms. In the 1860s the statistics of employment were: 258 girls, 214 women, 154 boys and 120 men. A number of manufacturers simply built the 'furniture', the frame being covered elsewhere, usually London or Manchester. Others imported the covering cloth too, Alpaca wool from Peru and Chile being a popular material after 1851.

Many of Birmingham's industries began the century in their traditional quarters, which in some cases would remain their home until the present day. One of the most unusual was the 'Vinegar Quarter' around Aston Cross. Here were based a number of industries that relied on the area's hard water, such as brewing and vinegar or sauce makers. Ansells closed their brewery there in 1981, exactly one hundred years after opening it; HP Sauce remains in its original location. The city that had such a reputation for its metal industries is apt to forget its contribution to the table. Even as late as 1951, industries engaged in food, drink and tobacco production were still employing 23,000 people. One of the late Victorian success stories was Bird's Custard. Alfred Bird built his Devonshire Works on Deritend in 1890 principally for the production of the immensely successful 'custard not made with eggs'. Alfred Bird & Sons were fast-food manufacturers before their time, expanding into instant puddings (Instant Whip) and coffee (Maxwell House), before moving out of the city in 1963.

80. Alfred Bird's 'egg-less custard' was a domestic necessity—his wife was allergic to them. The works on Deritend, established by his son, are now an arts complex, appropriately called 'The Custard Factory'.

The Jewellery Quarter, confined almost exclusively to the 'golden triangle' north of St Paul's church, contained in the 1860s around 20,000 employed in the gold, silver, gilt and toy trades. At its peak before the Great War the trade employed perhaps 50,000, the largest industry in the city. Here was a trade that epitomised our idea of Birmingham industries of the early industrial period: small, specialised and open to anyone with the appropriate skills. As J. S. Wright said in 1866:

All that is needed for a workman to start as a master is peculiarly-shaped bench [known as a peg] and a leather apron, one or two pounds worth of tools (including a blow-pipe), and for material, a few sovereigns, and some ounces of copper and zinc. His shop may be the top room of his house, or a small building over the wash-house, at a rent of 2s or 2s 6d per week, and the indispensable gas-jet ...

From such unpromising surroundings came the rings, pins, lockets and so on that passed via a 'factor' to the shops of London. The firm of Charles Smith and Edwin Pepper, whose works have now become the Jewellery Quarter Discovery Centre, gives a good indication of the rise and progress of such businesses. Beginning in 1899 as a small workshop in the garden of two terrace houses on Vyse Street, it specialised in making gold bangles and cuff-links. The terrace was later replaced by an office front, but the workshop remained relatively untouched until the family shut up shop in 1981.

The Discovery Centre was an act of loving reconstruction; the problem of preserving what remains of the Quarter, while at the same time allowing its businesses room for growth and change, is a trickier one.

Preservation is no longer a viable option with the Gun Quarter, the Quarter having shrunk to one or two streets behind Lancaster Circus. At the time when Samuel Timmins published his snap-shot of the industrial mid-lands, *The Resources, Products and Industrial History of Birmingham and the Midland Hardware District* in 1866, it retained much of that small workshop atmosphere still evident in parts of the Jewellery Quarter. More even than the jewellers, the gun-makers were an interdependent 'co-operative' of many skills, as the gun itself contains lock, stock and barrel. The trade employed about 7,000, equally divided between manufacturers and assemblers or 'setters up'. Their close relation-ship (and the use of child labour) are evident: '... the lads may be seen, one with half-a-dozen stocked guns on his shoulder, conveying them from the stocker to the screwer; another with a tray full of locks for the polisher; a third on his way with a few barrels to the Proof-House; and so on'. But already by the 1860s increased com-petition and mechanisation had begun

81.   Kynoch's in Witton was one of a number of Birmingham companies to take up bicycle manufacture. But the First World War saw the firm once more concentrating on munitions. By 1918 Kynoch's were producing 30 million cartridges a week.

to lead many away from the 'cottage industries' of the Gun Quarter. A joint stock company, known as Birmingham Small Arms, built its Small Heath Factory in 1861, beginning with military arms and then diversifying into cycles and motor bikes. Similarly expansive was the firm of Kynoch's, moving from percussion caps in Great Hampton Street to the famous Lion works at Witton in the 1860s and later becoming the Metals Division of I.C.I. The international nature of the gun trade may be seen in the 1891 visit of Chiefs Huluhulu and Umfete, two envoys from Southern Africa, to both B.S.A. and Kynoch's. The anonymous balladeer with a liking for beer that we have already quoted was singing in about 1810:

> Our swords and our guns thro' the world are the best,
> As our foes to their sorrow can truly attest;
> With Birmingham Bayonets, Birmingham Ale,
> No true British spirit was e'er known to fail.

Smethwick was never a 'quarter' in the same way as the Gun or Jewellery Quarters were, but a number of Birmingham's major manufactures were concentrated there. The Tangye brothers set up their huge Cornwall Works in 1855, making hydraulic machinery that found a market throughout the world. One of the earliest orders was for the jacks that launched the *Great Eastern*. Another of the Tangye successes was differential pulley-blocks, manufactured from 1859. The King of the Belgians used one in the 1860s to lower or lift himself from one floor of his palace to another and Garibaldi employed them to re-mount artillery. Nearby in Spon Lane, Chance Brothers took over a crown glass factory in 1824, before moving into the booming sheet glass market eight years later. Here they produced almost a million feet of glass for the Crystal Palace. James Chance also broke into the lighthouse market, previously a French monopoly, manufacturing the optical equipment for lighthouses on Shetland, Innistrahal in Ireland, Great Orme's Head and Gibraltar.

Two more industrial giants were not far away either. New production methods in the 1850s, as well as take-overs, turned Chamberlain and Nettlefold (later G.K.N.) into the country's leading screw-makers. The Patent Nut and Bolt Company, which had taken over the London Works in Smethwick in 1864, also became part of G.K.N. in 1902.

The large factories in Smethwick were still the exception, rather than the rule. Even by the 1870s, firms employing more than 500 workers were still a rarity. One was the Victoria Works in Graham Street, the steel pen factory of Joseph Gillott, the leading name in an industry where Birmingham led the world. Here was an industry whose turnover had been transformed by machinery, producing an estimated 14 million nibs a week. It was also an industry dominated by female labour, roughly six to one women to men, not including the packaging work which would also have been predominantly female.

Not far away, in Newhall Street, was the works of Elkington's, pioneers in electroplating. The invention that revolutionised the plating industry was made by Joseph Wright, a Birmingham surgeon. Wright's was a discovery with many applications, from the silver plating of cutlery and nut-crackers to the bronze plating of statues. The statue of Robert Peel, which stood at the top of New Street, was the first, but was rapidly followed by a succession of famous plated names that found their way to South America, Mauritius, Calcutta, Pall Mall and Queen Square, Wolverhampton. Prince Albert alone was 'done' seven times. It is hardly surprising that Elkington's Works, employing around one thousand workers, was a famous Victorian tourist attraction. The Science Museum that replaces it is equally so.

Steel wire was another of those Birmingham monopolies with a thousand applications. Joseph Webster of Penns Hall, Sutton Coldfield cornered the European market in piano wire in 1824, and it is sobering to think of the great continental musicians that relied on this humble Birmingham product. But even this product was found to have its limitations and it was only after a merger with James Horsfall that the firm of Webster and Horsfall produced the hard, unstretchable wire that gave them the edge over their rivals. At their works in Hay Mills the firm produced the strong but delicate wire necessary for needles, pianos and umbrella frames. Later, in the 1860s, the product was adapted for more robust uses such as undersea cables. The transatlantic telegraph cable was completed by 250 workers over 11 months, using 30,000 miles of wire. Hay Mills was evidence that what George Cadbury achieved at Bournville was not entirely original. James Horsfall built a school for the children of his workers, and in 1873 endowed a church, St Cyprian's, to serve the community. The company still survives at the same site.

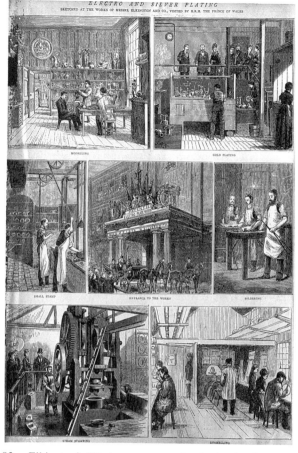

83.   Elkington's Works were a popular destination for royal visitors. The Shah of Persia (1889) and the future Edward VII (1891) toured the factory.

Three industries, as much as any, show the changes in technology and work patterns of the end of the Victorian era. Electrical appliances found a natural home in the city, as the new power source found increasing applications in lighting and transport. The General Electric Company's headquarters at Witton and Joseph Lucas's works were only the peak of a Birmingham mountain engaged on the production of dynamos, meters, transformers and suchlike.

The story of Joseph Lucas is one of those recurring Birmingham tales: the barrow boy made good. A hawker of paraffin in Hockley, he set up a business making buckets, before producing the 'King of the Road' lamp for the expanding cycle market in the 1880s. By 1948 Lucas's were employing over 17,000 workers, specialising in electrical components and lamps for the car and cycle markets.

Like the firm founded by Joseph Lucas, George Kynoch's company moved far beyond what its founder had envisaged. Kynoch's had begun with percussion caps, but even by the time that George Kynoch died in 1891 (having debunked to South Africa to escape financial difficulties), the firm was involved in brass, copper and steel castings. By 1903 there were 10 factories, six of which were in or near Birmingham, with an immense range of products, from cycles, paper and soap to railway fog signals, tubing and gas engines. As one production line shut down (cycles and soap), so another started up. In 1919 Kynoch's pioneered the use of the zip fastener in Europe. Ten years later, when the company changed its name to I.C.I. Metals, it was well on the way to becoming a multi-national.

Many Birmingham industries, though initially independent from, steadily became reliant upon the transport revolution that moved from cycles and trams to cars as the 20th century progressed. And more than most, they have suffered from the transfer of motor manufacture out of the city. At the beginning of the 20th century, transport, in a transitional phase, offered an extraordinary wealth of possibilities. Public transport moved through a series of changes from steam and electric tram to trolley and motor bus, while personal transport leapt from bicycle to motor-cycle to automobile with extraordinary rapidity.

Some firms, like the Dunlop Rubber Company, moved into the city to take advantage of the large skilled workforce or because of proximity to related industries. Its massive Fort Dunlop Works was still employing over 10,000 workers in 1954. Others, such as the Austin Motor Company, were indigenous. Herbert Austin left the Wolseley Tool and Motor Car Co. in 1905 to form his own company at Longbridge, unveiling his first 25-30 hp car in the following year. By the end of the decade a thousand workers were producing a range of models. But three models in particular have given Longbridge its important place in the history of the industry. The launch of the four-seater Austin Seven in 1922 made Austin the world leader in the light car market. There followed many years of intense competition with the Oxford-based Morris Company, ending with the merger of the two in 1952 as the British Motor Corporation. A generation after the Austin Seven in 1959, the Mini (designed by Alec Issigonis) again transformed the fortunes of B.M.C. The Mini's reputation for economy and style was built upon with the launch of the Mini Metro in 1980, by what had then become British Leyland.

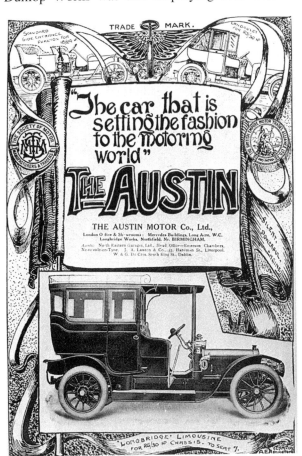

One of the reasons for Birmingham's economic boom in the 19th century must have been the relatively tranquil nature of labour relations. Unionised labour was relatively rare

83. Herbert Austin drove his first car out of the Longbridge gates in April 1906. Around 120 models were sold in the first year.

in the predominantly small workshops of the city, a situation that led to the re-location of
the stove grate trade from Sheffield, where trades unions possessed considerable power.
The other side of this coin was the dominance of 'sweated' labour, particularly among
women and children. 1889 was an exception to the general rule; in that year the gasworkers
struck successfully for an eight-hour day and 3,000 bedsteadmakers came out for higher
wages. Troubles in the latter industry led to an unusual alliance between the Bedstead
Manufacturers' Association and the Bedstead Workmen's Association in 1891 to regularise
prices and share profits more equitably. The cohabitation owed much to the work of
W. J. Davis, the secretary of the Brassworkers' Union from 1872 to 1921.

However, the period leading up to and following the First World War saw more
organised resistance to wages and conditions, and legislation to prevent disruption. In 1910
the Trades' Council launched a campaign against sweating in the city's baking industry,
and Birmingham workers were heavily involved in the 1911 Rail Strike and the 'Midland
Labour War' of 1913 over a 23s. minimum wage. The high water mark of union power
in the city was the early 1970s, when Longbridge was the centre of a number of disputes.
But most notably, during the 1972 Miners' Strike, a crowd of around 15,000 workers
prevented vehicle access to stockpiled coke at the Saltley Depot.

The development of industry also demanded a stable banking system and place to
display goods and execute transactions. Such support services grew in parallel with industry itself. The Exchange Building in Stephenson Place of New Street opened in 1865,
offering traders common ground to negotiate deals, as well as much needed office and shop
space. Five years earlier, Bingley Hall had opened in the grounds of the old Bingley House
as what would now be called an exhibition centre. Iron columns, surplus to the requirements of Euston station, were its principal architectural distinction. Holding up to 25,000
people, it was used principally for agricultural and trade shows (including the annual Dog
Show, Cattle Show and Chrysanthemum Show), as well as being the only venue apart from
Curzon Hall capable of accommodating an indoor circus. The country's first purpose-built
exhibition hall was gutted by fire in 1983, to be replaced by the first purpose-built convention
centre.

In banking, Birmingham can claim to have established, or had a hand in the establishment of, four national institutions. Taylors and Lloyds was founded in 1765 with a branch
in Dale End. Lloyds (the link with Taylor was lost in 1852) was the only one of the
original private banks to survive the financial crisis of 1826 that led to the establishment
of provincial branches of the Bank of England. The Birmingham Banking Company was
the town's first and largest joint stock bank but fell in the 1860s. Its headquarters, designed
by Thomas Rickman, survive on Waterloo Street. More successful was the Birmingham &
Midland Bank of 1836, which, like Lloyds, became one of the four clearing banks. The
first branch was in Union Street; the oldest surviving (now a bookshop) opened opposite
the Exchange in 1869. The Birmingham Town and District Bank of 1836 became part of
Barclays, while the Municipal Savings Bank, founded by Neville Chamberlain, became
part of T.S.B.

Chapter Twenty-six

The Changing Bull Ring

Nothing shows the changing face of Birmingham better than the Bull Ring, the traditional heart of its commercial life. When we last left it, the Street Commissioners were pulling down the ancient houses around St Martin's and concentrating all market activity in Smithfield and the Bull Ring.

In February 1833 the foundation stone of the Market Hall was laid. One of the first great occasions held there was a dinner for 4,000 poor people to celebrate Victoria's coronation on 28 June 1838. The architect was Charles Edge, who completed the Town Hall, but the new covered market dwarfed even that building. It was 365-ft. long and the interior contained room for 600 stalls. The installation of gas-lighting in the hall transformed the nature of market shopping; no longer was sunset the signal for stall-holders to shut up shop. In fact, Saturday evenings were the busiest time of the week. It was, in some ways, a precursor of the modern shopping centre, with its 'water feature' in the shape of a great bronze fountain (installed in 1851) and the famous clock, with its figures of Guy, Earl of Warwick, the Countess, a retainer and a Saracen. The clock was made by William Potts and Sons of Leeds and originally graced the Imperial Arcade in Dale End. It was transferred to the Market Hall in 1936, but was destroyed by bombing on the night of 25/26 August 1940. On the negative side, the hall was also a pickpocket's paradise. When the 1853 commission of enquiry into the Borough Gaol visited the juvenile ward, the majority of boys confessed that they had learnt their trade in the Market Hall.

The fish market, one of Birmingham's most popular institutions, was built on the site of the *Nelson Hotel* (formerly the *Dog Inn*) in 1869, and a covered vegetable market was completed in Jamaica Row in 1884. By this time over 200,000 carts of produce were reaching the markets every year. The rise of vegetables, dead meat and fish made up for and (partly caused) the decline in livestock, though even by the 1880s over 3,000 horses and 60,000 pigs were on sale at Smithfield in the average year. Birmingham's decline as a centre for horse trading (at least, in its original sense) is seen in the dwindling of the once crowded Horse Fairs, held at Michaelmas and Whit in the street that bore that name. At the last one in 1911, only 11 horses and one donkey attended!

The Horse Fairs were the last survival of the two medieval fairs, held annually at least since 1529: the June or Pleasure Fair, and the Michaelmas or Onion Fair. Their decline and fall was a sign of the new age into which Birmingham was moving. Increasingly fair-goers found their sense of fun the subject of disapproving looks from the Town Council. Until 1851 they had been announced by the Town Crier and a procession of 'fair walkers' that included the High and Low Bailiffs. After this date the Crier was limited to less ceremonial and more practical operations, like weights and measures testing in the market.

84. The Market Hall, designed by Charles Edge, opened for business in February 1835. The fountain was a farewell gift by the Street Commissioners on their retirement in 1851. It was later moved to Highgate Park.

Despite being an agricultural event asociated with the arrival of the first onions of the season, the Onion Fair was much more than that, filling most of the town with theatrical booths, fun-fairs and menageries. As many as three menageries (Bostock's, Wombwell's and Mander's amongst them) provided most of the population with their only opportunity of seeing a wild animal. In fact, if we overlook the gingerbread, the alcohol, the ice-cream and the swing-boats, the whole occasion was a most 'educational' one. There was the chance to see a giraffe or a superannuated lion, or to visit 'Napolion's Palace' or the 'Roil Famely Waxworks', or to sample the delights of a 45-minute adaptation of *Macbeth* down in Jamaica Row, and all for a penny.

But an increasing number of 'the people's representatives' thought the six day self-indulgence that the fairs brought with them 'a great annoyance to sober and quiet people' and an indefensible interruption to normal business. As early as 1781, William Hutton had called the Onion Fair 'the lowest of low amusements: riot, drunkenness and mischief'. In 1861 the fairs, instead of being allowed to swamp the town, were limited to the Bull Ring and Smithfield area, and in 1875 were banned from the town altogether. In fact, the magic of the Onion Fair was already beginning to lose a little of its glitter:

Through the streets I was wandering here and there,
When I came on the spectre of Birmingham Fair:
The roads they were sloppy, the night it was damp,
And the puddles reflected each paraffin lamp.
'Mid the din and the glare, as I stood in the slime,
I dreamed a dream of the olden time,
When, a careless youngster, I used to stray
To the Fair! - To the Fair! for my holiday.
But somehow the shows look shabbier now
Than of old, e'er these lines were across my brow;
The knights, and their dames, have a tawdry air;
And the wild beasts look tame in their wooden lair.
The gingerbread's stale, and the nuts are a snare;
Whilst kicking and punching's the fun of the fair.   (Anon.)

From 1875 the Onion Fair was confined exclusively to onions, but the entrepreneurs of the travelling shows simply moved to a site beyond the Council's clutches: the Old Pleck near Aston Church. Here it remained (as Pat Collins' Fair) until the Aston Expressway was driven through the site in the 1960s.

85.   The much lamented Bull Ring that vanished with the '60s redevelopment. Only the church survives in the Bull Ring of today. The appeal of the place was as much for the street preachers as for the cheap vegetables.

The popular belief is that the decline of the Bull Ring began with its redevelopment after the First World War. Evidence shows that even the Victorians of the 1880s were pining for the Bull Ring of their youth. The increase in high street shopping and the more effective collection of tolls was beginning to drive many of the 'characters' away from their traditional patches. Even the Victorian press looked back nostalgically to 'Billy the Laceman', with his six-foot laces tied to a stick, or to 'Jemmy the Rockman' who sold 'composition' for coughs and colds. A survivor into the 1870s was Henry Holmes, who dressed as Napoleon to sell 'the only French sausage rolls in Brum'.

What took their place on the fringes of the market were the fringes of society, purveyors of matches, toy umbrellas and dried flowers, operating through a wholesaler, who supplied their wares for a few coppers. Their descendants were the barrow boys who were finally evicted in 1964.

The Victorians created the Bull Ring that survived, relatively untouched, until the Second World War. Nelson's statue became the focus, first for quack doctors, then for soap-box orators and preachers like 'Holy Joe' or 'Jimmy Jesus'. 1960 saw the last appearance of 'Old Charlie', whose sign-boards turned him into a walking biblical text. And long after the Chartist Riots, the Bull Ring was always the focus for political protest, from the frozen-out canal boatmen of 1875 to the unemployed marchers of 1922. The Rag Market was the meeting-place of Oswald Mosley's New Party in 1931, the scene of violent confrontations with demonstrators.

The combination of Rag Market, Woolworth's, barrow boys and street traders made the area cut-price territory for the working class, with highly flexible opening hours. Market stalls, lit by hazardous naptha flares, often remained open till midnight, with auctioning of produce under way by 10.00 p.m. Despite the abolition of the fairs, the fairground atmosphere persisted, and the Bull Ring remained as much a place for entertainment as for shopping.

As with many of the city's institutions, it was the Second World War that put an end to the old Bull Ring, as much through the changes of habits and geography as from the damage it caused. On the night of 25/26 August 1940, the Market Hall was reduced to an empty shell by incendiary attack, and though it hung around for another 20 years (as an open market and the venue for occasional exhibitions), the umbilical cord between Birmingham and its Bull Ring had been cut. The families separated by evacuation and war service would never again make their Saturday night expeditions to that noisy but exotic world.

As early as 1940 Herbert Manzoni had drawn up proposals for an inner ring road, of which the redevelopment of the Bull Ring was an integral part. Here, and indeed in the plans as late as 1958, the Market Hall was to be retained. The current route of the ring road reflects the late decision to demolish, the space vacated by the old hall being left as gardens, named after the same visionary city engineer. In 1963 the decision was made not to replace the Market Hall clock. But there was room for just one more 'character' in Manzoni Gardens: the 23-ft. gorilla, lent by the Peter Stuyvesant Foundation, that spent six months there in 1972. Its popularity did not persuade the Council to spend £22,000 on making it a permanent exhibit. After a spell advertising used cars in Camp Hill, King Kong moved to Edinburgh.

Joseph Chamberlain would probably have proposed that the Bull Ring redevelopment be a municipal operation; these were different times. Government restrictions on capital expenditure effectively handcuffed local government at a time when closer involvement on redevelopment might have been preferable. Eleven companies tendered bids and designs for a new Bull Ring; the city elected to go for that of Laing's, which borrowed substantially from previous designs by the architect, James A. Roberts. Roberts' plan included one particularly unusual feature: a round office-block 12 storeys high to sit on the top of the old hill above the market. Later revisions took it to 25 storeys and deleted the roof-top restaurant. Other proposed features, such as a cinema and crèche, also found their way into the waste bin.

The scheme's solution to the hill was a series of stratified levels, linked by escalators and underpasses, that let the shopper down slowly from New Street to the open market. At the bottom was a 23-acre air-conditioned shopping centre, 350,000 ft. of retail trading space, an office block, multi-storey car park and bus station. Work began in the summer of 1961.

Reading the glossy promotional literature that accompanied the plans and announced the opening of the Bull Ring Centre in May 1964 is a sobering experience. They promised (using the buzz-words of their time) 'continental' restaurants, all-the-year-round garden displays, 'stiletto-proof' flooring. Every other word had 'style' suffixed to it (continental-style, pagoda-style). But central to the marketing was the price: it was the '£8 million Bull Ring' and the '£1 million Rotunda'. It was the perfect shopping experience, all under one roof.

86. Birmingham's most popular piece of public art—King Kong—has been lost to the city. It now stands in Edinburgh's Grassmarket.

What went wrong with this pioneer in shopping centres? Certainly, as with much of Birmingham's post-war development, it was dangerously ahead of its time. Much of the R & D was based on American models, which were a generation ahead of their British counterparts. Secondly, the shopping focus and traditions of Birmingham were changing. This was a long-running problem: no one knew where the centre of Birmingham was, least of all the planners and, as the focus shifted from Bull Street to the Bull Ring to High Street to Corporation Street and so on, social patterns were always one step behind. But a crucial mistake was the failure of nerve regarding the bus station. Instead of being the central terminus for Corporation buses, the bus station at the Bull Ring was used only by out-of-town Midland Red buses. Indeed the new ring road diverted bus routes away from the Bull Ring.

Of course, the higher rentals that an £8 million development brought with it made the traders less tolerant of 'teething problems'. Subways and broken escalators made the public less inclined to take the plunge down into the Bull Ring (as opposed to the former incline), and dramatic as the Rotunda looked, it remained a 'dead building' as far as shopping went and an interruption to that crucial continuity between upper and lower town. An early indication of dissatisfaction was the closure in 1965 of Mecca's Mayfair Suite. Announcing the decision to move out, Eric Morley dubbed the new Centre stony, austere and lacking sparkle: 'With regret, I think the Bull Ring as it stands at present lacks atmosphere'.

The future of the '60s Bull Ring is assured: it will be demolished. However, the form of the 'next solution' remains a subject of intense controversy. The Bull Ring's traditional appeal has led to the kind of emotive argument rarely seen in a city that pays little attention to sentiment when planning issues are at stake. Groups such as the 'Birmingham for People' movement have used the Bull Ring as the focus for a wider campaign to balance popular needs against the plans of big business. Each generation creates its own Bull Ring, and grows increasingly nostalgic for the one it has left behind.

Nevertheless, the market area remains the hub of wholesale trading. In spite of various attempts to move the markets out of town (a site was acquired at Castle Bromwich in 1948), and more recently to Heartlands, it has maintained its close attachment to the Bull Ring, a link cemented by the grant of £1.3 million by the European Community in 1974 towards a new wholesale complex.

The question of whether the Bull Ring Centre was Birmingham's, or Britain's, first shopping centre depends on what you mean by 'shopping centre'. As early as 1875 a company was formed to provide a row of shops above the G.W.R. tunnel between Colmore Row and Temple Row. The Great Western Arcade, lit for the first time in 1876, provided 42 shops on two levels below a huge chandelier. One of the original stores, Ashmore's shoe shop, stayed there until 1993. There were further arcades too: the Central, the Imperial of 1883, the Colonnade and the City Arcade of 1897 all made Birmingham 'an Arcadian town', as the *Mail* called it in 1882.

The department stores too provided a 'total shopping experience' under one roof. In 1885 Chamberlain persuaded David Lewis to open a new shop on his 'Parisian boulevard', and Lewis's remained there until its closure in 1991. It opened to a fanfare of trumpets and on the first day 40,000 shoppers crowded through its doors. At night, a revolving electric light

87.   The Beehive Warehouse in Albert Street, part Victorian department store, part rabbit warren. Opening in 1870, the building almost reached its centenary.

signalled the arrival of Lewis's to an entranced people. To two generations of Brummies Christmas and Lewis's went together like Morecambe and Wise.

The key to building shops in the 1950s was to combine retail and office use (actually an idea that the Great Western Arcade had tried), such as the new £6 million Rackham's store on Corporation Street that opened in 1960. But by the '60s the department store seemed to be an animal on the way to extinction. In 1969 the Debenham's group announced the closure of its Marshall and Snelgrove's store, whose presence in New Street dated back to 1926. Indeed, the '60s became a depressing litany of big store closures: Kean and Scott's century of trading in Corporation Street closed its final chapter in 1969 and Henry's, owned by B.H.S., ended a 36-year association with Birmingham in the same year. The store that perhaps more than any epitomised 'shopping under one roof', the Beehive, closed for the last time in February 1972. Opened in Albert Street in 1870, it was the last of the family department stores in the city centre and had only moved to 'bigger and better' premises on Priory Ringway five years before. Like the cash in its innovatory compressed air distribution system, it had finally gone down the tubes.

For 'department store' read 'shopping complex', for the loss of the one to the city centre has been the gain of the other. In the case of the Co-op, it was a direct replacement:

88. An aerial view of '70s Birmingham. The inner ring road (below the Rotunda) isolated the Bull Ring market from the commercial centre.

the last Co-op in the city centre became in 1987 the Pavilions, named European shopping centre of the year. The 'generation gap' between shopping centres is a short one. Between the Bull Ring and the Pavilions came the Birmingham Shopping Centre of 1973, occupying the 7½ acres above New Street station. This had some of the ideas of the old (piped music, 'permanent' tiled floors, wide malls) with some of the vocabulary of the new (people 'through-put', 2.5 million per month feed-flow). The result was a product that had to be re-launched in the mid-'80s as the mysteriously spelled 'Palisades'.

Other shopping centres have since arrived to the city centre: Fletcher's Walk, part of the Paradise Circus complex, the Plaza and Avatar's Arcadian development, occupying the site of the Ladywell Baths behind Hurst Street. The latter recovered the concept of 'cinema and shopping complex' lost to the Bull Ring, but suffered from the isolation from the city caused by the 'concrete collar' of the ubiquitous Ring Road.

The impact of out-of-town shopping, particularly evident in the popularity of the Merry Hill Centre near Brierley Hill, has come dangerously close to closing many of the Black Country towns as shopping centres. In Birmingham, a little more distant, the effect has been to suspend expansion, though with well publicised casualties: the city centre now contains no supermarket. City planners see increased pedestrianisation and improved public transport as two routes to the regeneration of the centre. The problem is: how to make people vote with their feet, and not with their cars.

Chapter Twenty-seven

Greater and Greater Birmingham

In 1888, to mark the 50th anniversary of Incorporation, Birmingham Council took the long overdue decision to request the Queen to grant the place city status. Victoria answered in the affirmative in January 1889. Elevation was in many respects a cosmetic exercise; Chamberlain light-heartedly objected to the move, saying that it would only make the Town Clerk more pompous than he was already. But it was symbolic of a new mood of expansionism within the council, and of a place that was moving with self-confidence towards the 20th century. Politicians like Joseph Chamberlain, George Dixon and John Bright were making Birmingham's voice heard in Westminster just as it had been heard in the old reform days. But things were changing nearer to home, too. Two years earlier the first overtures had been made (and rejected) to the surrounding authorities to join a larger conglomerate.

The districts around Birmingham were already well aware of their neighbour's growth. Just as Birmingham now owned huge tracts of land that had been donated or bought for leisure use (Aston Park, Cannon Hill, the Lickeys), its workers were also spreading far beyond the cramped inner city. By the late 1880s terrace houses (the building of further back-to-backs had been outlawed in 1876) had created a tightly packed ring around the centre. With the exception of Winson Green, they were almost all outside the borough boundaries: Sparkbrook, Balsall Heath, Small Heath, Saltley and Nechells had all seen Birmingham expanding into Warwickshire and Worcestershire. In Lozells the Freehold Land Society enabled subscribers to break out of the world of the back-to-back that their origins propelled them towards. Like a stone dropped in a pond, the ripples of population growth were spreading far and wide. Those who could afford it were moving further out still, to the old villages of Moseley or Handsworth.

Places like Witton and Small Heath had become, after the re-location of firms like B.S.A., G.E.C. and Kynoch's, industrial centres in their own right. They were followed by Cadbury's move to Bournville, and Austin's to Longbridge.

Improvements in suburban transport were opening up many areas to commuter housing long before they became officially parts of the city. When the first train left Harborne station on 10 August 1874, bedecked in red, green and white flags, another Staffordshire village was roped in. Similarly the opening of the line to Sutton in 1862 led to the 'discovery' of Erdington. Between 1881 and 1911 its population rose from just over 2,500 to 32,500. The same story could be told of Handsworth and Balsall Heath.

From the 1870s a spider's web of tramways also pulled the suburbs ever closer to the inner city. The 1861 Birmingham Improvement Act enabled the Corporation to lay down tramways but, like a privatised rail network, the vehicles themselves were initially run by private companies. On 20 May 1872 the first horse-drawn tram went into operation between Colmore Row (then called Monmouth Street) and Hockley. A second route down the Bristol Road was opened four years later, and 1882 saw the introduction of steam trams. The latter may have spared the horses, but not the passengers or pedestrians. They were 'monstrously heavy, outrageously noisy ... and most offensive to the sense of smell', as a Moseley resident complained in 1885. In addition, they spilt water on the streets which froze in cold weather, and frequently mowed down children. Otherwise they were fine. Even so, there were tears in a few eyes, not necessarily caused by pollution, when the last steam tram ran on the last day of 1906. 'Killed by an electric shock', the souvenirs said.

The search to find a user-friendly alternative was a long one. Cable tramways were tried on the Hockley to Bournbrook line in 1888, and electric cars powered by accumulators ran on the Bristol Road in 1890. A clerk on the staff of the former was the future star of the music hall, George Robey, then still known as George Wade. Neither system proved successful, and in 1900 electric overhead wires were introduced. This was to be the prize-winner that covered the city's skyline until the 1950s. The first Corporation tram ran from Steelhouse Lane on 4 January 1904, and by 1911 the Corporation had control of all the tramways in the city. But a new replacement for the tram was already on the table. In 1922 the Nechells route was the first to be converted to the 'rail-less' overhead system known as the trolley bus. Conversion of the Hagley Road (1930) and the Coventry Road (1932) followed. Progress could be very uneven, though. In 1907 Hagley Road reverted from the unreliable petrol buses to horse-drawn, residents only being won over to electric trams in 1913. But if the disappearance of familiar tram-lines under asphalt was depressing

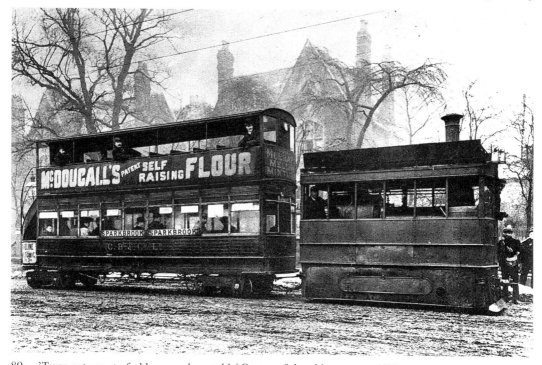

89. 'Twas not sweet of old, as our love told / On top of the old steam car / When a wondrous breeze made us cough and sneeze / With a smell like rotten eggs and tar! A steam tram on the Stratford Road line.

for traditionalists, the Council was making a fortune out of the scrap iron: not a commodity to be sniffed at in the run up to the Second World War.

The introduction of penny fares made trams the key to a commuter boom, and the extension of routes to the *Swan*, or to the *Fox and Goose* in 1913, opened up new areas such as Yardley and Washwood Heath. Both hotels allowed commuters to store their cycles (for 2d.) before continuing their journeys by tram. Yardley was now building houses at the rate of 800 a year. Many of the tram routes ran across borough and district boundaries, obliging local boards and councils to cooperate rather better than they had sometimes done in the past. In the same way, the three Poor Law Unions set up in 1834 had grouped the villages around Birmingham into sometimes curious alignments. Yardley was part of the predominantly Warwickshire Union of Solihull; Handsworth was in the West Bromwich Union; Deritend and Bordesley were part of the Aston Union, though they had been in the borough of Birmingham since 1838. There were other links, too: Yardley's gas and water supplies came from Birmingham, though it was outside the city until 1911, and Balsall Heath and Harborne were part of the parliamentary borough of Birmingham, but still run by local boards. The map of mid-Victorian Birmingham was a highly confusing one.

From 1891 Birmingham set about simplifying the map. From the time of Incorporation in 1838, Edgbaston, Deritend and Bordesley had been part of the borough. In 1891 the rate-payers of Harborne, Saltley and Balsall Heath voted in favour of incorporation. Such decisions were predominantly, if not completely, influenced by the wallet (comparing the School Board and Poor Rates) and by the promises of better facilities made by Birmingham. It was a civilised but expensive wooing: Harborne got its promised public library (a converted masonic hall), Balsall Heath a library and swimming baths. The latter's baths cost a total of £33,000 and were not completed until 1907, the council finding the water to be an inconvenient 700-ft. down!

Quinton was the next to go in 1909. Although Worcestershire County Council spoke of 'pillage and robbery', the population of the area was very much in favour; half of them worked in Birmingham as it was. In the same year the Boundaries Commission published a report recommending that Aston Manor, Erdington, Handsworth, Kings Norton and Northfield and Yardley be added to the city. At a stroke the move would treble the size of Birmingham and turn it into the second city in England, with a population of 850,000. Again, over half the householders were already working in the city.

The chief objections, when the scheme reached Parliament, came from Handsworth, Kings Norton and Yardley, but the promise of differential rating solved most of those. The Bill passed through the Lords in May 1911 and Greater Birmingham was born. The Domesday village team had almost reached the top of the Premier League.

If it took the Greater Birmingham Act to turn Birmingham into a major city in the eyes of the statisticians, its presence as a major political force in the country had long been accepted. Back in 1868, under the franchise laws, Birmingham returned three members to Parliament. Since the electorate were only allowed two votes, and all candidates appeared on the same ticket, it took some impressive organisation and tactical voting to ensure that the three winners were all Liberals. But then, Birmingham was a solidly Liberal town, and the Liberals were well organised. At the height of their power in 1876-7 it was hardly worth a Conservative contesting a municipal ward; in 1877 all 17 Liberals were returned unopposed.

The situation owed much to the personality of the unofficial leader of the Radical Liberals, Joseph Chamberlain, to the formation in 1877 of the Birmingham-led National

Liberal Federation, and to the Birmingham 'caucus'. The caucus was a large circle of party activists, led by Chamberlain, pressing forward its radical policies both at a national and local level. To its opponents the Birmingham Two Thousand were a 'party within a party', terrorising Parliament and making its members 'slaves of the all-powerful dictator of the hour'. There was not much doubt who the dictator was. To its supporters it was the most effective way of bringing the will of the majority to bear on its representatives: democracy was not only for election time. It was more than reminiscent of Attwood's Union.

By the early 1880s, with the caucus behind him, Chamberlain was perhaps the most powerful politician (and one of the most radical) in the land. After the 1885 General Election, Lloyd George wrote that: 'this victory is all due to Chamberlain's speeches. Gladstone had no programme that would draw at all'. Even though Randolph Churchill had given John Bright a good run for his money in 1885, Liberal power in Birmingham was unassailable.

What happened in March 1886 was as extraordinary a turnaround as modern British politics had seen: Joseph Chamberlain walked out on the Liberal party. The split that spoilt the party was over the issue of Home Rule for Ireland. For Chamberlain, self-government for Ireland meant no more than local government; for Gladstone it was an Irish Parliament, with powers over everything except the armed forces and foreign policy. However radical Chamberlain's policies were over electoral reform and municipalisation, he was an imperialist at heart, and Home Rule meant the dismemberment of the Empire. Most of Chamberlain's Birmingham colleagues followed him, and a new party, the Liberal Unionists, was born. Together with the Conservatives they brought down the Gladstone government. Given this new shared agenda, it would not be long before a formal alliance between Unionist and Conservative was formed. In March 1891 Prime Minister Salisbury and Chamberlain shared a platform for the first time in Birmingham; in 1919 the two parties were effectively merged.

William Gladstone did not give up without a fight. In November 1888 'the Grand Old Man' bravely decided to speak in Chamberlain's citadel itself. In one of the largest indoor political meetings ever seen, Gladstone spoke for two hours at Bingley Hall. Joseph Chamberlain's decision to visit America prevented a memorable confrontation, but the occasion was remarkable enough for another reason. A journal, *Political World*, had the speech recorded on an Edison phonograph, specially shipped from New York, to play back at later political meetings. It was the first time that a political address had been recorded. As the local magazine, *The Dart*, proclaimed:

> The phonograph has come, it can repeat
> Each word as spoken by the voice of man,
> Carried afar in every distant street.

The party political broadcast had arrived!

Thirteen years later, another future Prime Minister was to make an ill-advised trip into the lion's den. On 18 December 1901 Lloyd George spoke at the Town Hall in opposition to the Boer War, which Chamberlain supported. The result was widespread rioting and the death of one protester from a police baton. Lloyd George was smuggled from the hall in a policeman's uniform, while at least one enterprising trader was selling half-bricks to throw at him.

That dramatic resignation of 1886 was to affect politics in Birmingham and the country for the next 50 years. Joseph Chamberlain's career was far from over, and two

90.   The only known photograph of the whole Chamberlain dynasty. Neville is on the left and Austen in the centre. Seated is Joe's American wife, Mary Endicott (right). The picture was taken in the grounds of Highbury.

sons, Austen and Neville, would prolong the dynasty, both in Birmingham and the cabinet, until the Second World War. Joseph Chamberlain's position over tariff reform was to further sub-divide his new party, but even after his debilitating stroke of 11 July 1906, Joe's influence remained powerful. Three days earlier his 70th birthday had been the cause of celebrations and a floral cavalcade through the city worthy of any royal visitor, and such was his reputation in Birmingham that he continued to be elected by the Birmingham West constituents for the next eight years, though he was no longer able even to write his name. His power survived particularly through Austen, who was Chancellor of the Exchequer (1903-5 and 1919-21). 'Damn those Chamberlains', said Lord Derby in 1910, 'They are the curse of our party and of the country.'

At one time Birmingham supplied five cabinet ministers, including the two younger Chamberlains, a record for one city. It was not until 1924, ten years after Joe's death, that a Conservative/Unionist suffered his first reversal in the city in a Parliamentary election. In that year Herbert Austin was sensationally beaten, and Neville Chamberlain only squeezed past Oswald Mosley after two recounts. But it was not until Neville's resignation as Prime

Minister in 1940 that, after a period of 64 years, a Chamberlain no longer sat in the House of Commons.

Joseph Chamberlain died on 2 July 1914 and was buried, after a private funeral, at Key Hill Cemetery.

A month later, Europe was thrown into the worst conflict it had ever seen. Around 150,000 men from Birmingham marched to the Fields of Flanders, and 12,400 never returned. The introduction of the City Batallions, backed up by increasingly strident propaganda, made recruitment an offer few could refuse. In the first week 4,500 men signed up. Workers in the Jewellery Quarter were among the last groups to recruit in numbers, and they were subjected to much vitiation in the press before they emerged from their workshops.

The depletion in the work-force at home broke long-established patterns of employment, with women stepping over the unofficial line into heavy industry, and boy scouts (around 450 of them) working as bell-boys on the trams. As many as 15,000 women came to work in a city that was crucial to the successful conduct of the War. The Women's Volunteer Reserve found themselves in a variety of occupations, from making munitions to cultivating allotments.

There were other strangers settling down in the city, too. The German invasion of Belgium brought some 4,600 refugees from the Low Countries, initially to a reception centre in Islington Row, then to local families or larger homes like Harborne Hall. Long before the E.C., the Cercle Belge Café gave a European atmosphere to the city. Likewise, the invasion of Serbia in 1915 brought around 30 Serbian boys to Selly Oak, where they remained until 1919.

Clearly Birmingham's factories had a vital contribution to make. B.S.A., which made the Lewis gun, was producing 10,000 guns a week, and Kynoch's 25 million cartridges and 300 tons of cordite. They were already engaged in munitions; others, such as Longbridge, switched production to shells and armoured vehicles, at the same time increasing the work-force from 2,800 to 25,000. The Mills hand grenade was a Birmingham product. Even the Quaker firm of Cadbury's increased production to supply food for the troops. In March 1918 a visiting journalist described a city that had 'transformed itself', though at the same time concealing the identity of the firms themselves:

> Jewellers abandoned their craftsmanship, and the fashioning of gold and silver ornaments for the production of antses and shells; world-famous pen-makers adapted their machines to the manufacture of cartridge clips; and railway cariage companies launched out with artillery wagons, limbers, trucks and aeroplanes, and the chemical works devoted their energies to the production of the deadly T.N.T.

The factories of Birmingham would never be the same again.

Birmingham's military importance made it an obvious, though distant, destination for the zeppelins, but the heavily enforced restrictions on lighting made the city a difficult target. Indeed, the whole zeppelin episode could have been considered more of a comedy of errors, had not the half-ton bombs threatened such devastation. The first raid on 31 January 1916 found the Black Country with its glow from the foundries a more convenient target; the second on 19 October 1917 narrowly missed the Austin Works at Longbridge, one bomb demolishing an out-building, before inflicting severe damage on a number of fields. The last raid by five zeppelins took place on 12 April 1918, but anti-aircraft guns made the pilot of L60 nostalgic for the Fatherland and keen to rid himself of his cargo. Two bombs made a considerable impact on Robin Hood Golf Course and Manor

Farm, Shirley. It is said that the only casualty in the zeppelin raids on the city was Mrs. Cadbury's pet monkey, and even that died of a heart attack.

Even without the help of enemy bombs, much of Birmingham was changed by the War. Chamberlain's old home at Highbury and the University buildings in Edgbaston became military hospitals, while Rubery Hill treated soldiers with shell-shock. The art gallery was converted into a depot for the Lady Mayoress's committee, engaged in the collection and distribution of clothing. There were even tanks in Victoria Square, promoting Tank Bank Week. Campaigns to encourage people to invest in the war effort (Tank Bank, Dreadnought and Big Gun Week) realised a total of nearly £17 million. Friendly rivalry between towns gave the collections something of a football championship feel, with Birmingham just pipping Manchester to the prize of a commemorative, but not particularly useful, tank.

One savings scheme that survived long after the War was the Municipal Savings Bank, first suggested by Neville Chamberlain in 1915. Initially limited to a contribution directly from the wages of those in employment, it paid a fixed interest of 3½ per cent, the majority of the income going directly to the government. Chamberlain met with fierce resistance from the established banks and from the Treasury, but the institution opened on 29 September 1916 as the first Municipal Savings Bank in the country. 'The real problem', said Chamberlain, 'is how to make a man save who hasn't saved before.' But so successful was it, attracting 30,000 new investors by the end of 1917, that the bank was made permanent in 1919. By 1938 it had 450,000 depositors and its funds were a vital element in subsidising the municipal housing drive of the inter-war years. Neville Chamberlain himself laid the foundation stone of its new headquarters in Broad Street in October 1932; the building and the bank now being part of the Trustee Savings Bank. Appropriately, given its origins, the T.S.B. has also moved its headquarters to the former post office in Victoria Square.

On 11 November 1918 that same square was filled by people, as the news of the Armistice spread through the city. It would be similarly filled by bereaved relatives and grateful survivors for many Novembers to follow. As the Lord Mayor announced to that vast crowd in 1918: 'Today marks the beginning of a new era in human development'.

Chapter Twenty-eight

Homes for Heroes

Two issues preoccupied the city in the immediate aftermath of the War: how to provide a fitting tribute to those who died, and a better life for those who didn't.

A war memorial could, the planners argued, be part of a wider civic scheme that included new council offices, a mansion house for the Lord Mayor, a Natural History Museum, new Central Library and a concert hall. The city had already spent around £100,000 acquiring property on Broad Street for such a scheme. Well, in more affluent times that might be so, but the 1920s were not a time for grand civic initiatives. There were more pressing concerns for public money to be devoted to. The Hall of Memory scheme, consisting of a building to house the Book of Memory and an arcade, was pared down to £35,000; it would at least have the honour of being the first element in the great new civic square.

Made of Cornish granite and Portland stone and adorned with figures by Birmingham-born sculptor Albert Toft, the Hall of Memory was officially dedicated by Prince Arthur of Connaught on 4 July 1925. On that first day, 30,000 waited patiently to file through the doors and pay their respects. It remains the focus of Birmingham's Poppy Day, though the arcade has since been transferred to the Peace Garden which opened in 1992 in the bombed out ruins of St Thomas, Bath Row.

The rest of the civic centre idea progressed slowly. At the outbreak of the Second World War, a Masonic Hall (now Central TV) and the Municipal Bank had been completed on one side of Broad Street, and council offices (Baskerville House) were nearly finished on the other. And that was that for a while: the library would have to wait another 35 years and the concert hall 50 years.

With the War over, Birmingham was facing a major housing crisis. At a demonstration by 10,000 ex-service men in May 1919 one spokesman spoke of 'discharged men ... living in houses where seventeen people slept in two rooms, ten in one attic'. The Housing and Town Planning Act of 1919 obliged councils to turn their attention to working-class housing; with the huge expansion of the city in 1911 lack of space was no longer an excuse.

For the next 20 years houses seemed to be appearing everywhere. Around 105,000 were built before 1939, just under half of which were council houses. It was an era of experiment: the all-gas house, the all-electric house (in 1932), and all-concrete houses. Herbert Austin even tried 250 wooden bungalows at Hawkesley Mill. The City Council sent a delegation to Germany, Austria and Czechoslovakia in 1930 to investigate the possibility of flats. It had already tried out a tenement scheme in Milk Street in 1900 (a move opposed by the Trades Council) and three-storey flats at Garrison Lane in 1927. The result was the ill-fated Emily Street flats of 1939, a scheme that had to be demolished.

92. One of the rejected designs for the Hall of Memory. The memorial was to be the centrepiece of a municipal development that included a planetarium, museum and concert hall.

The incorporation of Perry Barr into the city (it had first been approached by West Bromwich) in April 1928, and of Castle Bromwich and Sheldon in 1931, allowed Birmingham to build huge housing estates, the size of a small town. As early as 1928 the possibility of an airport at Sheldon had been broached; within five years of incorporation there were 1,070 houses there, and the site of the proposed airport had moved outwards to Elmdon. The Kingstanding estate, the largest of the '30s developments, had 5,000 municipal houses by 1939. At the other extreme, both of the city and planning initiatives, Hall Green became an estate that was developed privately. Houses here cost around £600 each.

The explosion in house building was not without its hiccups. In 1926 a three-bedroom council house was available only to 'good tenants', and a 'good tenant' was defined as earning £4 a week, effectively placing it way beyond the means of many. Nor did the building of the early '20s begin to make up for years of inactivity. By 1926 the 13,000 houses built were only just keeping pace with the population growth, and not making any impression on an inheritance of slums. A survey of 1936 showed that there were still 38,773 back-to-backs in Birmingham, 13,650 without water and 51,794 without separate toilets. Furthermore, the great new estates may have been the size of towns, but they did not have the community facilities of them. The dash for housing was leaving social planning far behind.

At least Corporation control of public transport allowed it to adapt the network to the expanding city. In 1922 the Corporation introduced the first closed-top trolley-bus, but the motor bus began to overtake both the trolley-bus and the tram by the end of the decade. In April 1926 the Outer Circle bus route was introduced, a 25-mile journey providing inter-connections between the city's radial tramways. Given the undeveloped nature of some of the country lanes, the service had to run on motor-buses. By the outbreak of the Second World War, Birmingham's omnibus fleet was the largest in the world, and an annual total of 400 million passengers were using Corporation bus and tram.

The economic expansion of the city suffered badly from the recessions of the early '20s and '30s. By 1921 there were 51,361 unemployed in Birmingham, and a further 16,000 on short-time. By 1931 that number had risen to 62,000. Having expanded its industry to levels unimaginable before the War, Birmingham found the subsequent contraction hard to take. Nationally, around 1,200,000 jobs had been lost. The General Strike of May 1926 focused attention on a social tragedy, but the government survived.

The ability of Birmingham's industries to switch production and develop new products had been proved during the War, and that flexibility protected them against the worst of the recession. It is, however, easier to put one's economy on a war footing than to return it to peace-time production.

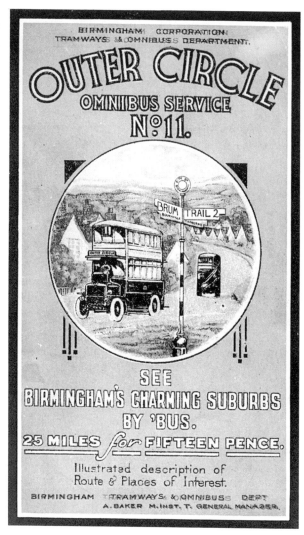

93. Birmingham Corporation's unique outer-circle bus service began running in 1926. The route is 25 miles long and now takes two hours to complete the trip.

Many firms found the going tough. The future of Longbridge was secured only with the arrival of the Austin Seven in 1924. Costing only £168, it and the Morris Minor made a major impact on the small car market. The growth of the motor cycle and aircraft industries similarly protected many Birmingham firms. When the 'green shoots of recovery' began to appear in 1931, the city was at the forefront of growth. By 1937 unemployment was down to five per cent.

The inter-war years witnessed a major growth in the supply of electricity, and the reorganisation that led to the introduction of a National Grid in 1926 recognised Birmingham as the centre of the Midlands area. This was some achievement, for the city had been slow to adapt to the new source of energy. Municipal ownership of supply began on

1 January 1900, two years after Aston Manor had taken over its supply, but the advent of a 'Greater Birmingham' and the growth of the tramways revealed that the city was undergenerating. During the Great War Birmingham 'borrowed' from the private generating station attached to Fort Dunlop, but plans were developed for two new 'modern' stations. Coincidentally, both were completed in 1929, though work on Nechells 'A' had begun before the War. Larger by far was Hams Hall 'A', constructed on land previously owned by Lord Norton near Coleshill. Its two cooling towers were the world's highest. By the mid-'30s Birmingham was supplying electricity to about 162,000 customers, and the new capacity of Nechells and Hams Hall would have a major role to play in supplying industry during the Second World War. About 70 per cent of power would be directed towards the war effort.

94. Another failed design. The proposed Council House on Broad Street recognised the need to centralise council services. It was even to include a 'hall of weddings'. The naked male statue was too shocking and had to be removed.

When the ex-Lord Mayor of Birmingham and now Prime Minister, Neville Chamberlain, made that fateful radio broadcast on 3 September 1939, there must have been a strong sense of déjà vu. Many of those sights and sounds familiar from the earlier war were here again: War Weapons Week, royal visits, the Lady Mayoress's Fund, air-raid precautions, allotment cultivation. But this time the people of Birmingham were digging in for a long war; there was no 'over by Christmas' delusion this time.

The politicians of the city had taken a lot of convincing that war was on its way. The Unionists had remained faithful to the policy of appeasement of their former colleague, while the Labour opposition moved reluctantly to the idea of another military build-up. By the time that the first German bomber unexpectedly dropped its bombs on Erdington, more out of frustration of not finding anything more strategic to drop them on, the whole system of A.R.P. stations, fire-watchers, Anderson shelters and the rest was just about ready for action.

Birmingham's first war had been fought largely at a distance; this time it would be different. Technology had brought the Midlands within range of the German war machine, and Hitler knew the importance of the area as a munitions centre. There might have been strong reasons for transferring munitions production further north, away from such a vulnerable target, but Birmingham's metal-based industries and adaptable skilled work-force still made it the obvious headquarters.

During the three years before 1939, four shadow aircraft factories had been established in the Birmingham area, only serving to make the city even more vital to the war effort and a target for the bombers. In July 1937 Rover's shadow factory at Acocks Green began to produce engine parts, particularly for the British Hercules, followed by another in Solihull. In June 1938 the first of about 2,700 aircraft rolled off the production line at Austin's shadow factory in Cofton Hackett. Largest of all was that at Castle Bromwich, run by the Nuffield Organisation and then by Vickers. Occupying 345 acres and employing up to 15,000 people, it was the largest of all the British shadow factories, producing a total of 11,000 Spitfires and 300 Lancasters.

The shadow factories were reliant upon many local components manufacturers. Radiators for Hurricanes and Spitfires came from Serck Radiators on the Warwick Road, and all their carburettors were initially made by S.U. Carburettors, also on the Warwick Road. Gun turrets were made at Lucas's, armoured vehicles at Metro-Cammell and amphibious craft at Morris, to name but a few. As in the Great War, B.S.A. and Kynoch's (now part of I.C.I.) reverted to military production. Around half of the precision weapons used in the War came from B.S.A., while huge quantities of ammunition were produced at Witton. In total about 400,000 of Birmingham's population were engaged in munitions work.

Such work made Birmingham an obvious, even essential, target for the Luftwaffe. But so successful were the black-outs and the dispersal of factories that they made the rest of the city highly vulnerable to misdirected raids. Bombing was rarely random, but it often looked that way. As a military operation, the Luftwaffe would no doubt consider the Midlands raids of dubious merit, only B.S.A. receiving the kind of bombing that was intended. In contrast, over 2,000 people in the city were killed, 3,000 seriously injured and 5,000 homes destroyed. In all there were 77 enemy raids between August 1940 and April 1943, the great majority at night.

Chief Raids of the Blitz

8/9 August 1940	A lone bomber hits Erdington. One person killed.
25/26 August 1940	City centre raid destroys Market Hall. 25 killed.
24/25 October 1940	City centre hit by incendiaries. Marshall & Snelgrove's store burnt out.
25/26 October 1940	Single bomb kills 19 in the Carlton cinema in Sparkbrook. The Empire Theatre also destroyed.
14/15 November 1940	Raids on Coventry.
19/20 November 1940	Heaviest raids yet. 350 bombers cause 400 deaths, 50 of which are at B.S.A.
22/23 November 1940	200 bombers cause over 600 fires, particularly in Tyseley and Saltley. Three-fifths of the city deprived of water.
11/12 December 1940	Longest raid of the War, lasting 13 hours. 263 people killed.
9/10 April 1941	Last serious raid of War. 250 bombers destroy the Prince of Wales Theatre and the corner of New Street/High Street. 1,121 dead or injured.
28/29/30 July 1942	900 killed or injured.
23/24 April 1943	Last raid of War.

It would come as scant consolation to those injured or made homeless by the Blitz, but the damage might have been much worse. The Luftwaffe failed to follow up its successes, particularly after the 22/23 November raids, when damage to the water supply rendered the city helpless. Again the dispersal of factories and people from the inner city lessened the potential impact of the raids. Nevertheless, a total of 5,129 high-explosive bombs and 48 parachute mines fell on the city, and 140,000 houses suffered damage, if only superficially. It might have come as some consolation for the sufferers to know that, in May and July 1942 in their own Elan Valley, R.A.F. bombers were practising with a new type of bomb that would have such a spectacular impact on German dams in the following year.

The Blitz did, of course, have a huge impact on family life. The first evacuation of children took place on 1 September 1940, when 25,000 children, 4,000 teachers and 12,000 mothers and children left the city. But the scheme was voluntary and many lonely parents subsequently retrieved their infants or simply kept them at home. A second mass evacuation took place in November and December, when a further 22,000 children left for pastures new. Into 1941 'trickle' evacuation continued into south Wales, Staffordshire and the East Midlands.

Yet the combination of drift back by evacuees, and the lack of compulsion in the operation meant that 175,000 children remained in Birmingham to face the joys of home teaching, school bomb shelters and rationing. The effect of rationing was diminished a little by the extension of school meal provision and by the city's 59 British Restaurants, offering 'basic but wholesome' meals. This was a preferable name to 'Communal Feeding Stations', though the latter probably summed up the food on offer more accurately. In 1944 they provided almost 11 million meals and around half continued as Civic Restaurants, run by the Corporation, in the years of austerity after the War.

Preparing for the peace began long before the end of hostilities, indeed long before there was a certainty of victory. Proposals such as Bournville Village Trust's *When We Build Again* (1941), with its green belt and satellite towns, show that dreams of the future grew naturally from the nightmares of the present. On the other hand, the future's nightmares were also on the drawing-board: in 1943 the Public Works Department revived the idea, first broached in 1917, of an inner ring road as 'indispensable ... when traffic once again resumes a normal basis'.

Many of the arterial roads had already been widened (Pebble Mill Road was the first dual carriageway in 1920) to cope with the actual, and anticipated, increase in road traffic. The city centre remained at crisis point, and the need for flexible transit between Birmingham's interconnected industries made such a road almost inevitable.

The German bombers made the redevelopment easier, and the Council applied the 'Corporation Street' principle to what remained. Buy up the frontages, widen the road and lease the new frontages for lucrative new shopping and office development. The new road would be neither 'an urban motorway, nor principally a traffic street, nor a shopping street', but a combination of all three. It would be many years before the scheme was completed, or even off the ground. Government restrictions on capital expenditure prevented any work taking place until, in 1953, permission was given for the widening of Digbeth and Deritend.

On 8 March 1957, demolition began on Smallbrook Street to begin the ring road proper. It was a spectacular opening: the first charge of gelignite, detonated by a government minister, sent press and dignitaries running for cover, and one to hospital. Smallbrook Ringway was begun, taking down one of the city's oldest cinemas (the Scala had opened in 1914) in its bold neo-classical sweep up to St Martin's Circus. In its place, across the road, came the Albany, the first new hotel in Birmingham for 88 years. So dominant was the motor-car that the Hill Street subway was the first in the country that forced pedestrians to cross a road underground. Ironically, this subway, by the 1990s an intimidating point of access to the theatre-land of Hurst Street, was removed in 1993 in a move to re-assert the priority of the pedestrian over the car.

The first stretch of the Inner Ring Road was opened by Ernest Marples in March 1960, and the circle completed in January 1971. The final cost was around £33 million. An unfortunate slip of the tongue by the Queen at the opening ceremony in April 1971 obliged the Council to name the whole road 'Queensway', rather than just the tunnel from Suffolk Street to Great Charles Street.

The Inner Ring Road was the first, but by no means the last, of the radical road building plans of the post-war era. The Birchfield Road underpass of 1962, the first in the country, streamlined the route to the north. And in May 1972 the Aston Expressway, with its seven-lane tidal flow, opened a direct route to the new motorway interchange at Gravelly Hill. The latter, graphically nicknamed 'Spaghetti Junction', remains a potent symbol of the age of the car, and an internationally known image of Birmingham itself. An earlier, prefabricated sign of things to come, was the Camp Hill flyover. Built in days in 1961, it was demolished in weeks in the late '80s.

Birmingham's love affair with the road was an obvious consequence of a city with so much invested in the motor industry, made even more attractive by the 75 per cent government grants that such schemes received in the post-war period. The decision was not made without some consideration of alternatives: an underground railway (in 1947) and rapid transit (in 1956). But the high cost of a tube line ruled it out, even though the £13 million compared roughly with the provisional cost of the inner ring road and less than half its actual cost. When the last tram made its way from Steelhouse Lane to Erdington on 4 July 1953, Birmingham became the largest city in the world without any form of electric public transport.

By the late 1980s it had been recognised that the Ring Road and Expressways were not the 'total solution' that they had promised to be in the 1960s. In traffic terms they had become a victim of their own success. Such was the build up and reliance of traffic on them that a far from inconceivable scenario of four or five break-downs or accidents at key points (such as the Great Charles Street tunnel) could grid-lock the city in a matter of minutes.

Such a possibility, together with the recognition that cities are for people as well as cars, led to a number of strategic initiatives. Electrification of the Cross-City railway line, the introduction of bus-only lanes on arterial roads and the consideration of rapid transit in the form of Midland Metro based at the newly re-opened Snow Hill station all indicated the renewed importance of public transport in the 1990s. Another was the initiative in 1992-3 deliberately to interrupt and slow down traffic flow on the Inner Ring Road, by introducing traffic lights and pedestrian crossings on Great Charles Street and Smallbrook Queensway. This, together with the pedestrianisation of a large portion of the shopping district in 1992, implicitly discouraged traffic from the city centre.

95.   Broad Street between the wars, looking towards Easy Row. On the left are the Church of the Messiah, the *Crown* and the Prince of Wales Theatre.

As much a symbol of the new mood as any was the redevelopment of Victoria Square, the heart of Birmingham's public life. The area had been opened up by the demolition of Christ Church in 1899. In 1930-1 it had been the test-tube for an experimental new solution to traffic-flow known as 'the gyratory system', a system so complex that the newspapers printed maps to explain to pedestrians how to cross it. In 1970 plans to drive a new multi-carriageway through it were narrowly avoided, resulting only in the demolition of Galloway's Corner on the site of Christ Church. Another campaign was necessary (in 1978) to head off plans to demolish the 1890 post office building. Finally, in May 1993, a fully pedestrianised Victoria Square was opened by the Princess of Wales, complete with fountain and art-work by Dhruva Mistry and Anthony Gormley. It represented another stage in the 'Europeanisation' of Birmingham city centre (paved piazzas, tree-lined boulevards and public art) and the end (at least, for a while) of a century of planning proposals.

Chapter Twenty-nine

What Went Wrong with Tomorrow?

In 1960 Alderman Frank Price, the leader of the controlling Labour Group on the City Council, published a series of articles in the *Evening Mail* on 'The New Birmingham'. As a historical document, the articles perfectly encapsulate that confidence and clarity of vision that powered the city off the grid of post-war austerity. Of the area that became Newtown, Price quoted Rawlinson's 1849 description: 'foul fetid courts, insanitary, ill-built houses and squalid streets'. He wrote of attractive pedestrian precincts, high point block flats with a sense of grandeur, and swaying trees down Summer Lane. When Birmingham won a 'City Challenge' grant of £37.5 million towards a complete renovation of Newtown in 1992, Rawlinson's description was still remarkably accurate. The '60s shopping centre was 'the worst in Europe', and the whole scheme impressed a government minister as 'worse than anything in Eastern Europe'. Clearly Paradise had been found and then mislaid again.

Behind much of Birmingham's post-war redevelopment stands the powerful figure of Herbert Manzoni, the visionary City Engineer and Surveyor, a sort of George Dawson driving a bulldozer. Much of the city that the '50s and '60s created began in his twinkling eye in the early 1940s. Ultimately though, he provided an engineer's solution to the problems of housing and transport, not an architect's: 'As to Birmingham's buildings, there is little of real worth in our architecture. Its replacement should be an improvement, provided we keep a few monuments as museum pieces to past ages'. Of the structures that replaced them Manzoni was no more sentimental, feeling that a modern building's life-span should be no more than 20 years anyway. In the case of some of the city centre's less awe-inspiring constructions, such as Bush House on Broad Street (1956), even 20 years smacks of the over-sentimental.

The overall strategy of the post-war years needs to be looked at from three directions. The development of new roads we have already discussed; alongside this was the need to provide enough homes for a city of one million and to recreate a substantially ruined city centre.

Birmingham's population passed one million in 1931, and in 1948 it replaced Glasgow as the second city of the U.K. A housing strategy had to take account both of the increasing population and the necessary demolition of much sub-standard housing in the inner area. The 1944 Town and Country Planning Act provided the powers, and by 1946 the city was moving towards compulsory purchase in the five designated 'new towns' or Redevelopment Areas: Nechells and Duddeston (part of the area now known as Heartlands), Bath Row, Summer Lane, Ladywood and Gooch Street. In all almost 100 acres and 30,000 houses were targeted for demolition and redevelopment.

96.   High-rise homes in Bromford Estate. Squeezed by green belt on one side and an increasing population on the other, the city adopted the solution of high-density housing. But flats have created more social problems than they have solved.

So complete was the recreation of these areas that many were renamed, with local people suggesting possible names. The area around Gooch Street became Highgate (it might have been Belgravia, Calthorpe or Forest Island); the Bath Row site became Lee Bank (and not Churchill Rise or Great Chamberlain); Summer Lane was now Newtown. The historical continuity hoped for in the old names was belied by the total break with the past that actually resulted. This was 'the new Birmingham'.

The statistics make impressive reading. Between 1945 and 1970 Birmingham had demolished 55,000 homes (especially after 1966) and built 81,000 new ones, with a peak of 9,000 in 1967, far in advance of any other single authority. But such an achievement would not have been possible without the introduction of high-rise accommodation, largely on the initiative of the Chief Architect, Sheppard Fidler. Fidler recognised (around 1952) that the luxury of 'endless space' provided by Greater Birmingham was an illusion, made the more so by stricter laws to protect the Green Belt. Birmingham was using up space too quickly, and needed to bite the bullet, so long avoided, of flats.

The first high-rise blocks were at Tile Cross in 1953. The former Castle Bromwich airfield, purchased in 1959 and renamed Castle Vale, accommodated a population of

20,000, many of whom lived in multi-storey blocks. In order to keep as many people as possible within their Redevelopment Area, the flats got taller and taller, culminating in the two 32-storey blocks at Lee Bank. However, by the time that the city began to develop the Water Orton estate (renamed Chelmsley Wood) in 1963, opposition to high-rise accommodation greatly altered the nature of estate design.

Almost before Harold Macmillan had left the site of the new 12-storey blocks he had opened in Nechells in 1954, residents noticed that lifts were not working and the rents were much higher. Alderman Price spoke with pride of the famous 'Garcey refuse disposal' chutes; tenants got nostalgic about back yards and dustbins. And while the planners talked of 'neighbourhood units', the press spoke of 'concentration camps'.

Meanwhile, the city centre was undergoing a sea-change, too. But if the five 'new towns' were suffering from over-planning, the central area was falling victim to the lack of an overall plan. By parcelling up blocks of the city centre and inviting tenders from the developers, the Corporation effectively abrogated overall responsibility for co-ordinating and harmonising the result. It was more important to get sites occupied and rated than to engage in protracted arguments over planning and design. The London and Edinburgh Trust, whose proposed redevelopment of the Bull Ring met such opposition in the 1990s, must have longed for such a developer's paradise! At the same time post-war euphoria took the architect's language to new heights, in more than one sense of the word. 'The city needs buildings like Marilyn Monroe,' said one, 'but without the curves'.

The Big Top site at the corner of New Street and High Street was one of the first broken dreams of the new age. Redevelopment had begun on the night of 9 April 1940, when the Luftwaffe simplified the job of the planners. For the rest of the War, the area became the centre of the Brighter Birmingham movement, an attempt to keep spirits high as the bombs fell and theatre companies thought it unwise to travel. Behind dwarf conifers and a decorative façade stood the 'Big Top', offering all the fun of the fair, the circus and the Halle Orchestra. Where shoppers now jostle in Boot's, a lion-tamer was unpleasantly mauled in 1945 ... and not a chemist's in sight.

By the 1950s plans were afoot for various office and retail developments, including C & A, Marshall & Snelgrove and a 32-storey skyscraper. But multiple ownership inevitably led to architectural compromise, and the resulting seamless and uninspiring block was described by Pevsner as 'a bad joke'. There was little here of which the Corporation could be proud, except perhaps the innovatory service tunnel that ran alongside the inner ring road, allowing delivery access at basement level. When completed in the late '50s, the Big Top gave the city centre its first shopping centre and its highest building.

The Corporation was more directly concerned with its dream of a civic centre on Broad Street. William Haywood's scheme, which had overtones of Mussolini's Rome, had been approved in 1944, but probably had little chance of completion. Almost the only element that survived was William Bloye's civic column, depicting a naked metal-worker. But civic decency was offended, and even this had to go.

In 1965 a revised scheme shuffled the pack, locating the Repertory Theatre in what became Centenary Square, with a residential element, in the form of four tower-blocks behind. The proposed new Central Library was to be at the centre of a new development called Paradise Circus on the Inner Ring Road. By then the old University building, Mason College, had been demolished, allowing the new library to rise as the old one fell. Despite a public enquiry, the Central Library opened by John Bright in 1882 was replaced by the

Central Library opened by Harold Wilson in 1973. What the latter gained in space and efficiency, it undoubtedly lost in romance and beauty. Closely modelled on the inverted ziggurat of Boston Town Hall, it was once memorably described by the Prince of Wales as resembling a place where books were incinerated, not borrowed. Nevertheless, with its seven floors and 2,500,000 books, it is one of the largest public libraries in Europe, and a remarkable sign of the '70s City Council's continuity with the Civic Gospel of the Victorians. Such a development is probably inconceivable now.

The Central Library was the work of an architect who, more than any, set his seal upon the architecture of the new Birmingham. John Madin, a contemporary of James Roberts (designer of the Rotunda, the *Albany Hotel* and much of the Bull Ring) at the Birmingham School of Architecture in the '40s, rose through the Calthorpe Estate redevelopment to design a series of important buildings such as the Post and Mail Building, the Central Library and Pebble Mill, the local headquarters of the B.B.C. Together, Madin and Roberts were as influential a pair of architects as Chamberlain and Martin had been in the last period of civic expansion.

From the beginning of the 17th century, Birmingham had been a town that derived much of its energy from the influx of newcomers. The Quaker families of the 17th century, the influx of Irish, Welsh, Italian and rural English families in the 19th, and even the temporary shelter of Belgians during the Great War, had added their peculiar cultures to the melting pot that was Birmingham. Soon after the Second World War, the appeal of a city with jobs to offer exerted its influence even further afield.

Before the War Birmingham had few colonial migrants, most of whom were skilled medical workers from India. By 1991 it had the largest ethnic percentage of population in the UK: 206,000, amounting to 20 per cent of the total. Before 1961 immigrants from the Caribbean far exceeded those from the Indian sub-continent, a statistic that has since been reversed. But all these communities initially shared a similar pattern: the arrival of a single or married man, followed later by a family. By 1952 the total of migrants from the Commonwealth had reached 4,600, of which over half were from Pakistan. The later '50s saw the proportion of Afro-Caribbean arrivals rise considerably. The 1962 Immigration Act, the first to restrict immigration substantially, increased the movement of whole families into Birmingham as the open door policy was increasingly slammed shut.

As with Irish immigration in the 19th century, many of the newcomers originated from geographically concentrated areas of the Commonwealth, as news of those who had successfully made a new life spread between families and neighbours. A growing economy, still predominantly industrial, that needed unskilled labour welcomed them. And with an unemployment rate that averaged less than one per cent throughout the 1950s (around half the national average), there appeared to be jobs for all. Only in the field of public transport was there much sign of friction, when in 1954 the Transport Committee recruited large numbers of immigrants to work on the buses. Here the local workers, predominantly Irish, resented the cuts in overtime hours that a larger workforce implied.

If the situation in the factories gave the impression of racial harmony, it was in the search for a place to live that many immigrants met with prejudice and discrimination. One West Indian testified to having spent his first month in Birmingham (in 1942) living in a phone-box on the Dudley Road! City Council policy, oscillating between the fear of racial conflict and the trust in racial harmony, moved significantly from ghettoisation through integration to recognition of cultural difference as the century has progressed. The third

97.   Birmingham Central Mosque on Belgrave Road. The mosque was planned in 1961 but the project was dogged by financial difficulties. It was only in 1982 that the golden dome was triumphantly placed on the minaret.

stage, conceived during the '80s, was perhaps as much a reflection of the failure of the other two policies, though it is one that had expediency on its side and fitted neatly into the city's development plan to promote distinctive quarters of activity and culture.

Ghettoisation was perhaps an inevitable consequence of housing policy in the post-war period. From 1949 applicants for a council house had to be resident in the city for five years. Therefore, as the indigenous population were moved out into the municipal 'new towns', it was in the middle ring of Handsworth, Aston, Sparkbrook and Balsall Heath that the new settlers were concentrated. This situation at least allowed the City Council to target resources accurately, and lessened the fear of racial conflict. The different communities rarely ever met.

In 1959 the Liaison Officer for Commonwealth Immigration shone a torch on this policy. The city's 35,000 immigrants (two-thirds of whom were Afro-Caribbean) were crammed into around 3,200 houses in the middle ring. Not only was the accommodation sub-standard, it made the goal of integration almost impossible to achieve: 'The immigrants are living in tight pockets turning inwards to themselves and it would seem intent on creating a "little Jamaica", or the like within the City. I believe that this trend, unless checked, will have serious consequences'. The situation outlined here was, or would be, equally applicable to the Pakistani and Indian communities that arrived later. If anything, the closer family organisation of the latter groups increased it. If the ability to speak the language of their new home was a sign of integration, then the statistics were not promising. A survey of elderly people in Handsworth/Soho area in 1981 revealed that 88 per cent of elderly Asians were unable to speak English.

The early settlement pattern of the 1950-70 period was still reflected in the distribution of Asian and Afro-Caribbean people in the '90s. Most were still living in the middle ring wards of Soho, Handsworth, Aston, Small Heath and Sparkhill. The highest concentration in 1981 was in Sparkbrook ward (50.8 per cent of all residents), dropping to less than two per cent in the Sutton wards. Mobility is dependent upon money, and with unemployment and deprivation still proportionately higher among the ethnic communities (unemployment in the '80s was roughly three times that among the white population), this situation had not altered much by 1991.

The distinct and distinctive nature of the Asian culture especially changed many of the shopping streets of areas like Balsall Heath and Sparkbrook. The springing-up of Asian

98.   The Birmingham of the '50s was to see the growth of many new cultures. New settlers came to the city from the Caribbean, India and Pakistan, Somalia, Malaya, Cyprus and Yugoslavia, to name but a few.

businesses, and especially the growth of shops selling Hindu garments and jewellery or Halal meat, video-rental shops and restaurants specialising in Bangladeshi and Pakistani cuisine in the '70s and '80s has had a remarkable effect on a city with a reputation for greyness. Indeed the development of the *balti* (the word was originally a disparaging term for the Kashmiri or Punjabi *karahi* or *wok*) has given the city an unexpected standard-bearer in distinctive cuisine.

The presence of single males from India and Pakistan had an unexpected effect on Birmingham's declining cinema industry. As the general cinema-going public slumped in the 1960s and many picture-houses closed, a number found a new lease of life (or rather a stay of execution) as Asian cinemas. The Waldorf in Sparkbrook, the Alhambra in Balsall Heath and Villa Cross Picture House all survived in this way. The earliest was Pringle's Picture Palace in Gooch Street, demol-

99. Birmingham's first Chinese restaurant was the Tong Kung at Holloway Head which opened in 1956. The first generation of restaurants were all 'chop suey houses', a pale reflection of genuine Chinese cuisine.

ished as part of the Highgate development. The growth and arrival of families lessened that need in the later 1970s, replaced by a thriving video market in Asian language films.

Nothing revealed the problems of alienation, deprivation and ghettoisation more than the Handsworth riots of 9-10 September 1985. In a scenario not dissimilar to the Brixton riots of the same year and the Los Angeles riots of 1992, conflict between predominantly black youths and the police at Aston Cross led to widespread rioting and looting in Lozells. And as with the Korean community in Los Angeles, it was another minority, the Asian shopkeepers, that suffered most from the break-down in law and order.

The enquiry led by Julius Silverman was one of many attempts to uncover the causes of the riots. At the surface there was the long-standing frame of confrontation between Afro-Caribbean youths and the police (less severe rioting had taken place in 1981); deeper were educational and social problems leading to the unemployment and a sense of alienation felt by many black people, but particularly young males.

During the '80s and '90s the City Council undertook a more pro-active role in fulfilling the duties of the 1976 Race Relations Act: 'to promote equality of opportunity and good relations between persons of different racial groups'. The purchase of the former Aston Hippodrome as a centre for Afro-Caribbean arts, the commitment to including at least two per cent of people from the ethnic communities in its workforce, and the promotion of multi-ethnic events such as the Birmingham (formerly Handsworth) Carnival suggested a new policy of creating 'integration with individuality'.

Chapter Thirty

The Rebuilding of Birmingham

What did Birmingham have to offer to the world in the early 1970s? A great deal still relied on the traditional ingredients of blood, toil, tears and sweat. With 307,000 jobs in manufacturing (compared to 277,000 in service industries), the city was still heavily reliant on a sector that was about to decline rapidly. In July 1973, the firm whose slogan had once been 'One in Four is a BSA' disappeared in a desperate series of mergers which did not save Norton-Villiers-Triumph either. One hundred and twenty-two years of manufacture fell victim to Japanese competition, and with it the British motor cycle industry as a world force.

The fall of B.S.A. was a sign of things to come: in the next 10 years Birmingham would lose around 150,000 jobs, almost all in manufacturing. All the Victorian and Edwardian giants would be cutting back in their workforce, either because of new technology, mergers or loss in market share.

The merger of the Leyland Motor Corporation with British Motor Holdings (including Austin) in 1968 created a massive industry with a workforce of 170,000, but a turnover that hardly matched the profits of the separate companies. By 1974 B.L.M.C. was on the verge of returning its first ever losses, and needed a cash injection by central government. The bewildering sequence of mergers (beginning with Austin and Morris in 1952) had created an industrial giant, but one with two many arms. A multiplicity of unions, fragmented bargaining structures, inequitable rates of pay and poor industrial relations led to the company's poor performances in the '70s. At Longbridge, a management team led by Sir Michael Edwardes (and nicknamed 'The Kremlin' by the workers) was faced by a highly unionised workforce led by union convener Derek Robinson (nicknamed by the press 'Red Robbo'). Longbridge seemed to epitomise all that was worst in British industrial relations. Robinson's dismissal in 1979, not resisted by the workers, heralded a period of restructuring and computerisation. B.L., as it had then become, was ready for a high-profile relaunch with the advent of the Metro, but not at the level of employment seen in the '60s.

What had happened at B.L. was paralleled elsewhere. In 1984 four out of every five redundancies were in manufacturing, as Lucas, Metro-Cammell, Cadbury and Rover all shed jobs. You didn't need to read the statistics to recognise that times were changing; the dark and broken windows at Ansell's Brewery at Aston Cross, or Talbot car works in Small Heath, or the Lucas factory at Great King Street were evidence enough.

It was clear that the kind of manufacturing diversification that stimulated Birmingham's growth in the 19th century needed to be interpreted more widely. Such a belief, long before it became a strategy, coincided with moves to establish a National Exhibition Centre in Birmingham. This was a long-established bee in the council's bonnet. It was generally believed that Bingley Hall, a magnificent Victorian achievement in itself (built in six

100. The Lucas Works in Great King Street celebrates the coronation of George VI and Queen Elizabeth in 1937. It has since been declared surplus to requirements and closed.

weeks in 1850), was no longer the place to display and market the skills and products of the 1960s. London had a similar opinion of Earl's Court and Olympia. From as far back as the First World War the city had planned to build an exhibition hall on the Broad Street complex (where Central TV now stands), but negotiations had dragged and a comprehensive civic centre looked unlikely. When the last British Industries Fair was held at Castle Bromwich in 1957, pressure to find a modern replacement intensified.

From around 1960 a battle of lobbying between Birmingham and London, familiar from the 19th-century competition over guns and brass, was joined. The Midland city met intense opposition from the C.B.I. and from vested interests in the capital, who saw London as the only conceivable location for a National Exhibition Centre. But the possibility of such a Centre at Northolt had met with less than enthusiastic support from the Greater London Council, while Birmingham had identified an ideal site at Warren Farm at Bickenhill. The arguments over the relative merits of a Birmingham, or London-based Centre continued well into the 1960s.

It was not until 1970 that the city finally received firm government support, followed by a £1½ million grant, support that survived the change of government in 1970. Progress depended on the provision of adequate support services, namely a new intercity station to serve the Centre, hotel accommodation on site and an upgrading of the nearby airport. British Rail's agreement to build Birmingham International station on the line to London (opening in 1976) comes in stark contrast to its later decision not to support the International Convention Centre with a similar station 15 years later. Construction began in February 1973 and the N.E.C. was officially opened by the Queen four years later.

By any standard the N.E.C. has been an unqualified success and a massive boost to the local economy. Twelve halls covering 125,000 square acres included an arena (opened in 1980) for sporting and musical events, arranged around Pendigo Lake. The advantages of a relatively unrestricted site allowed the city to add three new halls in 1989 and to continue to expand into the surrounding fields in the 1990s. In its first 10 years the N.E.C. had directly or indirectly generated around 4,000 jobs and attracted £59 million of inward investment. Its proximity to Birmingham Airport (linked by a revolutionary hover-train called Maglev) provided the stimulus for the £62 million International Airport in 1984 and a second terminal in the early 1990s.

So far, indeed, did the success of the N.E.C. exceed expectations that the city used it as a platform for more risky gambles in the '80s and '90s. The bids for the 1992 Olympics and for a national football stadium, both based on the N.E.C. site, and the construction of a city centre exhibition complex on Broad Street have involved Birmingham in high-profile marketing in an uncertain world.

You can spend millions promoting your city and giving it a place on the world map, then one event can blow it apart. Just as the first stages of construction were underway at Bickenhill, Birmingham suffered its worst peacetime disaster. At 8.18 and 8.20 p.m. on the night of 21 November 1974, two I.R.A. bombs exploded in city centre pubs near to the Rotunda. As one witness in the Mulberry Bush described: 'I didn't actually hear the explosion. The lights just sort of flickered and then went out and I was being carried through the air'. Such was the force of the explosion that two youths who had been passing the pub were killed by debris blasted into the street. The simple combination of a battery, two clocks and 30 lbs of explosive turned the *Tavern in the Town* into a pile of rubble and bodies, the horror increased by the fact that the pub was below ground level. Ironically, the barmen were Irish. One recalled: 'There was an almighty blast and there were screams and shouts from everywhere. The ceiling fell in and the bar blew back at me ...'. The 21 deaths and 168 injuries made it the worst mass-murder in British history. Many of the victims were Irish; one man, John Reilly, lost two sons. The bombs at the *Mulberry Bush* and the *Tavern in the Town* were the culmination of a campaign of I.R.A. bombings in the city that had begun in August of the previous year. They were followed by outbreaks of anti-Irish sentiments; the Irish Centre in Digbeth and Irish pubs were fire-bombed, Longbridge workers demonstrated and Irish workers were sent home for their own safety. Within a week the Prevention of Terrorism Act had been rushed through Parliament.

It was in this climate that six Irishmen from the city were arrested and later found guilty of the killings at Lancaster Crown Court in August 1974. Their convictions were only the beginning; allegations of ill-treatment at Winson Green and mishandled evidence persisted, and the case of the Birmingham Six gave the I.R.A. the kind of propaganda coup that the pub bombings could never provide. After a prolonged campaign, the Birmingham Six were released in March 1991.

The National Exhibition Centre stands in the outer ring of the modern city of Birmingham. Anyone catching a train from Birmingham International into the city will rapidly pass into the inner ring. It is as much a journey from Birmingham's future into its past: a world of Victorian terraces, abandoned factories and badly deteriorating '60s estates. It was this inner zone that attracted and has continued to attract the attention of the economic strategists from the 1970s into the 1990s. But a hundred years after Chamberlain's Improvement Scheme, the Birmingham of the 1970s could no longer generate the finance to act unilaterally on the inner zone, even if direct action from the centre was still advisable.

From 1977 the City Council, West Midlands County Council (formed in 1974), central government and the Birmingham Area Health Authority entered into an economic alliance to target resources into this core area as part of the Inner City Partnership Programme. There were signs that some earlier lessons had been learnt. Funding was used both for direct investment in roads, and for 'enveloping', a pioneering scheme to improve the quality of the existing housing stock externally, while encouraging residents to improve them internally. If this sounded like Nettlefold revisited, at least it stemmed from the recognition of the positive qualities of the existing environment, rather than from the financial impracticality of wiping the slate. Much of the rest of I.C.P.P. funding was devoted to the voluntary sector and private initiatives, stemming from a belief that the regeneration of a community starts from within.

Many such initiatives continued into the 1990s. Influenced by the success of the Black Country Development Corporation, a private Urban Development Agency was established in 1988, covering about 2,300 acres in the East Birmingham area. Westminster encouraged, indeed compelled, local authorities like Birmingham to see that a combination of private investment and public money was the only way forward in large-scale regeneration schemes of this kind. Ironically, the more successful the city became in generating funding from within, the less deserving became its case when it came to central government funds.

Increasingly in the later '70s and '80s, the European Community helped to plug the gap left by central government. E.C. grants for capital projects such as the Wholesale Markets (£1.3 million), the Small Heath by-pass (£3 million), Camp Hill (£3.5 million), Snow Hill tunnel (£2.5 million), and above all the International Convention Centre (£49 million) went a long way to make up for the neglect of Birmingham in the early years of E.C. membership. The region's 'assisted area' status was an economic prize long fought for, but again one which depended upon failure.

The legacy of planning and expansion in the '60s was a costly one. Despite the decline in the city's population (falling below one million in 1987), Birmingham was facing another of its periodical housing crises. Construction and design faults meant that by 1988 over half of the city's tower blocks were in need of attention, and indeed continued disatisfaction with high-rise living led to the replacement of such towers at Castle Vale by lower density housing.

In the city centre, too, the mid-'80s showed a change in attitude. The City Centre Symposium or Highbury Initiative of March 1988 made a number of recommendations for improving the quality of life, shopping and everything in the centre of the city. Central to this was the breaking of the 'concrete collar' of the inner ring road, whose presence symbolised the supremacy of traffic over pedestrian and which prevented the expansion of the central area. The 1984 Central Area Local Plan had recognised that districts of distinctive character surrounded the inner zone (Jewellery Quarter, Entertainment Quarter, and a Heritage Quarter based around Digbeth, to name but three). However, the Inner Ring Road continued to isolate the central shopping zone from its surroundings. Many would rather not explore Birmingham's cultural riches than risk their own in a subway mugging. The lowering of Paradise Circus in 1989 to allow direct pedestrian access from Chamberlain Square to Centenary Square and the Convention Centre was the first indication of changed priorities.

The I.C.C., opened by the Queen in June 1991, was Birmingham's most high-risk gamble in its attempts to create an international business city. Consisting of 12 halls arranged around a central mall, it was the U.K.'s first purpose-built convention centre and cost around £180 million. Unlike the N.E.C. on Birmingham's outskirts, the city centre location of the new I.C.C. suggested that the benefits of business tourism would be felt directly by the shops, hotels and theatres of the city. And in Hall 2, generally known as Symphony Hall,

101. The new Birmingham of 1990s. Raymond Mason's sculpture *Forward* in the centre of Centenary Square reflected the determined optimism of a city regaining its international reputation.

Birmingham at last had a concert venue to match the reputation of its Symphony Orchestra. One of the Centre's early coups was as the location of the Euro-Summit of E.C. leaders in October 1992, during the crisis over ratification of the Maastricht Treaty.

The presence of the I.C.C. galvanised an area that had rarely been the subject of much attention, attracting ancillary developments from the 300-bed *Hyatt Hotel* and £60 million National Indoor Arena to a sequence of leisure/shopping/office proposals that were the hallmark of the early 1990s. In addition the city's commitment to a 'percentage for art scheme' in funding the Convention Centre saw the appearance of a host of new sculptures in and round Centenary Square, a tradition continued in the re-design of Victoria Square. The town that had waited 800 years for its first statue had by the mid-'90s become a veritable open-air art gallery.

Public art was one aspect of a 'physical enhancement strategy' begun in 1987 to rid the city of its reputation as a concrete jungle. Pedestrianisation, begun as early as 1972 in Union Street, advanced into John Bright Street and in 1992 took in major portions of New Street and Corporation Street. The canal network, too, long having ceased to be a part of the city's commercial life, now became a part of its leisure/commercial strategy. The Brindley Canal behind the I.C.C. and the Waterlinks developments at Aston became key factors in attracting new businesses to 'water-side locations', and the trees that had vanished with the Cherry Orchard in the 18th century began to re-appear in traffic-free streets at the end of the twentieth.

It was all a very curious journey, from a Saxon tribe that cut down trees to clear a space for their buildings to a modern tribe that put them back. But the city with the motto 'Forward' was never averse to looking backward as well.

Index

Adderley, Charles (Lord Norton), 141, 147
air raids, 193-4, 198-200
Afro-Caribbeans, 206-9
airport, 196, 212
Albert Street, 95
Alexandra Stadium, 172
Allin's Cabinet of Curiosities, 145
almshouses, 18
Anglo-Saxons, 3-4
arcades (shopping), 180, 185-6
Archer, Thomas, 37
Aris's Birmingham Gazette, see newspapers
Artisans' Dwellings Act, 152-3
Arts and Crafts movement, 146-7
Ash, Dr. John, 40, 60, 122-3
Ashted Estate, 45
Ashted Barracks, 56-7
Assay Office, 70
Aston, 4-6, 8-9, 20, 198, 207
Aston Expressway, 182, 201
Aston Hall, 20-1, 23, 117, 146, 170
Aston Hall & Park Company, 170
Aston Lower Grounds, 22, 170-1
Aston Villa Football Club, 171
Asylum for the Infant Poor, 40
Attwood, Thomas, 109-12, 113-5, 118
ATV, 132
Avery, W. & T., 77

Balsall Heath, 98, 105, 143-4, 170, 188, 190, 206-7, 209
Balti cuisine, 209
banks: Attwood & Spooner's, 110; Bank of England, 109; Midland, 179; Municipal Savings, 179, 194; Taylor & Lloyd's, 33, 179; TSB, 194
Banner Theatre, 134
Barrow's Stores, 156
Baskerville, John, 140
Bassano & Fisher, 99
Bartholomew Street, 102
baths, 143-4
BBC, 206
Beardsworth's Repository, 83, 112
bedsteadmakers, 29
Beehive Store, 185-6
Belgians, 193
Beorma, 3
Bestall, Alfred, 163
Betholom Row, 102
Bidlake, William Henry, 147
Big Top, 205
Bingley House, 33, 146
Bingley Hall, 129, 147, 179, 191, 210-1
Bird, Alfred (Bird's Custard), 80

Birmingham: Battle of, 24-7; canal navigations, 87-9, 91; City Football Club, 171; Concert Hall, 128; diocese of, 103; Dog Show, 129; Guild of Handicraft, 146; Heath, 136; Jewellers & Silversmiths Association, 101; manor of, 5-6, 9-12, 14-5; Metal Company, 89; Political Union, 112-3, 118; Royal Ballet, 127, 131
Birmingham, De, 5-6, 10-12, 14, 117
Birmingham & Midland Institute, 48, 125, 162
Black Patch, 149
Bloye, William, 65, 126
bombings, 105, 129-30, 212
Bordesley, 17, 55, 116, 158
Boult, Sir Adrian, 127
Boulton, Matthew, 58, 61, 63, 65-7, 71-7, 146
Boulton & Fothergill, 31, 66-8
Bournville, 1, 98, 143, 147, 157-8
Bournville Village Trust, 158, 200
brass, 29, 89-90
breweries, 168, 174, 210
Brindley, James, 87, 90, 92
Brindley Place, 92
Bristol Road, 85, 189
BRMB, 132
BSA, 176, 193, 199, 210
bull-baiting, 169
Bull Ring, 49, 80, 82, 119, 180-5
buses, 184, 189, 196-7, 206-7
buttons, 31-2, 65-6, 73, 107-8, 173-4

Cadbury's, 156-7, 193
Calthorpe, Lord, 147
Calthorpe Estate, 167-8
Camden, William, 12
Camp Hill Flyover, 201
canals, 61, 87, 90-1
Castle Bromwich, 196, 199, 204-5, 211
Castle Vale, 204-5
Catholics, 50, 103-4
CBSO, 126-7
cemeteries, 102, 138-41, 148-9
Centenary Square, 132
Central Television, 89, 132
Chamberlain: Austen, 192; Joseph 137, 139, 147, 150-2, 154, 163, 190-2; Neville 192-3, 198
Chamberlain & Martin, 148, 151, 157, 161-2
Chance, William, 160
Chance Bros., 98, 176
Chaplin, Charlie, 130
Charter of Incorporation, 116-7, 120-1
Chartism, 118-9
Chelmsley Wood, 205
Chinese community, 106
Church, Dr. William, 92

churches: Church of the Messiah, 149; Church of the Sav-
    iour, 149; Christ Church, New Street, 47, 116, 140; Holy
    Trinity, Bordesley, 18; St Agatha's, 147; St Bartholomew's,
    122; St Martin's, 5, 8, 15, 37, 80, 122; St Mary's,
    Handsworth, 65; St Paul's, 122-3; St Peter & Paul's, Aston,
    20; St Peter's catholic church, 103; St Philip's 37-9, 57,
    79, 116, 122-4
cinemas, 105, 129, 132-4, 201, 206
Civic Gospel, 149
Civil War see Wars
Clay, Henry, 173
coaches, 86-7
Coat of Arms, 117-8
Colmore Row (Newhall Lane, Ann Street), 38, 116, 145,
    150-1
Congregationalists, 167
Copy-press, 76
Corporation Street, 152-5
Council House, 124, 150, 154
Crescent, 108, 115, 165
cricket, 171-2
Crosskey, H. W., 149
Curzon Hall, 129, 131-2

Dale, Dr. Robert, 149
Dale End, 33, 52-3
Darwin: Erasmus, 58-9, 61, 63, 69; Charles, 146
Dawson, George, 139, 149
Deritend, 9, 12-14, 85, 107
Dickens, Charles, 89, 125, 162
Digbeth, 12, 14, 50, 85, 167
Dixon, George, 147, 161
Dobbs, James, 111
Domesday Book, 4-6
Duddeston: Hall, 21, 44; Viaduct, 97

East India Company, 110-1
Easy Hill, 47, 54-5
economy, 107, 109-11, 197, 212-3
Edgbaston, 60, 101, 116-7, 136, 194; Hall, 56, 60; Cricket
    Ground, 3, 171-2
Edge, Charles, 124
Edgehill, Battle of, 22
Edgeworth, Richard Lovell, 59, 61, 63-4, 92
Edmonds, George, 111-2, 118
education, 39, 58, 64, 159-63
Elan Valley, 137-8, 141, 200
electricity, 129, 152, 197-8
electro-plating, 121, 176
Elkington's, 176-7
Erdington, 4, 6, 188, 190, 199, 201
European Community, 185, 213
Exchange, 179
exhibitions, 146-7

Fair Hill, 54-5, 63
fairs, 15-16, 96, 169-70, 180-2
Farror, Joseph 82
Female Blondin, 139, 147, 170
Five Ways, 85
Floodgate Street, 4
football, 22, 170-1
Fort Dunlop, 178, 198
Fothergill, John, 67
Freeth, John, 88, 128
Froggary, 95, 100, 102

Galton: Mary-Anne, 76; Samuel 59
garden cities, 157
gas lighting, 69, 75, 107, 151-2
Gas Street Basin, 90-1
GEC, 177
General Hospital, 40-1, 122-3, 148, 164
Gillott, Joseph, 176
gipsies, 149
GKN, 151, 176
Graham Street chapel, 114, 149
Green's Village, 103
guilds, 9, 18-9
guns, 23, 31, 42, 59, 175-6

Hall, Thomas, 22
Hall Green, 196
Hall of Memory, 195-6
Hampden Club, 111
Handsworth, 5, 148, 190, 206-9
Hansom, Thomas, 124
Harborne, 39, 98, 115, 158, 190, 193
Harborne Tenants Ltd., 158
Hardy, Julius, 107-9
hawkers, 100, 103
Hay Mills, 176
health, 135-41
Heartlands, 94, 203, 213
Heathfield House, Handsworth, 76-7
Heaton Bros., 92
Hector, Edmund, 35
Highbury, 147, 194
Highwaymen, 87
Hill: Daniel, 143; Matthew Davenport, 142; Rowland, 142,
    160
Hollins: Peter, 121; William, 48, 121, 183
Holte, Sir Thomas, 120-1
Hopkins, Gerard Manley, 103
hospitals, 40-1, 122-3, 136-7, 148, 163-7
hotels, 78, 81, 86-7, 129, 153, 167-9, 206, 214
housing, 35-8, 108, 135-6, 141, 148-9, 152-8, 188, 195-6,
    203-5
HP Sauce, 174
Hwicce, 3

Ideal Village, 158
immigration see migration
Improvement Scheme, 105, 136, 152-5
Indian community, 206-9
industry, 14, 28, 38, 65-6, 89
Ing, William, 37
Inkleys, 103
International Convention Centre, 91-2, 127, 129, 132, 213-4
inventions, 71-7, 173, 176
IRA, 105, 212
Irish community, 103-6, 163, 191, 212
Irving, Washington, 117
Italians, 102-3

Jackson, Sir Barry, 132
Jeffs, Walter, 129
Jennens, John, 123
jewellery, 7, 13
Jewellery Quarter, 38, 111, 117, 140, 174-5, 193
Jewish community, 50, 100-2, 143

Keir, James, 58, 63, 67, 76

Kempson, James, 122
Kenrick, William, 147
Kettle's Steelhouses, 28
King's Hall, 154
Kings Heath, 1, 98
Kings Norton, 2-3, 6, 22, 24, 98, 190
Kingstanding, 24, 196
Kynoch, George, 177
Kynoch's, (IMI) 176-8, 193, 199

Ladywell, 4, 143
Ladywood, 116, 203
Lancastrian Schools, 159-60
law courts, 154
Lawrence Street chapel, 118
Leather Hall, 16, 18
Ledsam Street, 105
Leland, John, 12
Lench, William, 18
Lewis's Department Store, 185-6
libraries, 47-8, 144, 149, 205-6
Littler, Emile, 129
Lloyd, family, 28, 30, 32-3
Lloyd's bank see banks
Longbridge Motor Works, 178, 197, 210
Lucas, Joseph, 177, 210
Ludlow's Ammunition Works, 173
Lunar Society, 58-65, 67, 76, 92

Maccabe, Fred, 129
Maconochie, Capt., 142
Madin, John, 206
Manzoni, Herbert, 183, 203
markets, 6, 15, 17-8, 80, 180, 183, 185
Market Hall, 180-1, 183, 199
Mason, Josiah, 146, 162-3
Mason College see Universities
Masonic Hall, 133
Meeting House: Old, 50, 54; New, 50-1, 54
Mendelssohn, *Elijah,* 125
Metropolitan Carriage & Wagon Co., 98
Metchley Park, 2
Methodists, 43, 50, 132
migration, 14, 100, 102-3, 106, 206-9
mills, 6, 30, 33, 73-4, 108
Mint, 15-7, 75, 80-1
Moat, 9, 11, 14-15, 80
Moore, Joseph, 117, 123
Moseley, 56, 98, 102, 158
mosques, 106, 207
Mossel, Max, 125
motor racing, 172
munitions, 193, 199
Muntz, George Frederick, 112-3
Murdock, William, 74-5, 77, 92
Murphy, William, 104, 139
museums, 22, 88, 145-6
music halls, 129-30, 132, 189, 199
music festival, 37, 40-1, 121-6

nailmaking, 28, 30
National Exhibition Centre, 127, 210-2
National Indoor Arena, 91, 96, 127, 172, 214
National Schools, 160
Nechells, 188-9, 198, 203
Nelson, Horatio, 44, 81-2, 145

Nettlefold, John, 148-9
Nettlefold & Chamberlain, 151, 176
New Hall, 38-9
Newhall Hill, 84, 111-2, 114-5
Newman, Cardinal John, 103, 125
newspapers, 45-6, 53, 83, 86, 95, 107-8, 122, 129, 142
New Street, 16, 95
New Street station, 95-8, 102, 115, 141, 153
Newtown, 203-4
Nonconformists, 22-3, 28, 42, 50
Northfield, 1, 3, 5, 30, 190

Old Cross, 16, 31, 80-1
Old Crown, 9, 14
Old Square, 35-7, 86, 153-4
Oratory, 103
ormolu, 68
Ostler, Thomas, 146

Pakistani Community, 206-9
panoramas, 79
Pantechnetheca, 146
pantomime, 129, 131
papier-mâché, 173
parks, 14, 18, 115, 143, 147-9
Park Street, 18, 129-30
Paradise Circus, 205-6, 213
Paradise Street, 88-9
Parker, Charles, 134
Parson's Hill, 2
Peeky Blinders, 130
Peel, Sir Robert, 120-1, 176
Pemberton, John, 35
Perry Barr, 196
Phillips, Penelope, 37
Pickard's Mill, 73-4, 108
police, 119-20
Poor Law, 39-40, 108, 190
population, 14, 28, 78, 99-100, 111, 135, 153
Pratchet, Richard, 82-3
Price, Ald Frank, 203, 205
Priestley, Joseph, 51-6, 58, 62-3
Priory of St Thomas, 18, 35-6
Priory Estate, 35-6
prisons, 16-7, 83-4, 119, 142-3
Proof House, 31, 175
public houses, 14, 17, 49, 70, 95, 119, 122, 129, 134, 146, 168, 212
public offices, 83-4, 105, 112, 154
Pugin, Augustus, 103
Puritans, 22-3

Quakers, 32-5, 50, 59, 156
Queen's College, 162, 165

Ragged Schools, 160-1
railways, 45, 92-9, 102, 105, 115, 141, 144, 153, 201, 211
Rawlinson, Robert, 135, 137, 141, 152
Reformation, 18-19
Reform Movement, 111-5
ring road, 200-1, 205, 213
riots: Chartist, 118-9; Food, 73-4, 108; Handsworth, 209; Gordon, 50; Jacobite, 50; Murphy, 104; Navigation Street, 105; Priestley, 51-6; Rivers Rea 3-4, 12, 14, 30, 135; Tame, 6, 30, 137, 141
Roberts, Francis, 22, 25

Robey, George, 131, 189
Robin Hood Free Debating Society, 121-2
Roebuck, James, 72-3
Romans, 1-3
Rotton Park, 14, 90
Rotunda, 184
Roundabout House, 80
royal visits, 21-3, 154, 162, 166, 177, 201-2, 211, 213
rugby football, 171
Rupert, Prince, 24-6
Russian Mountains, 111
Russia, 28, 32
Ryan's Amphitheatre, 43
Ryland: John, 54; Louisa Anne, 148, 164

St Martin's Lane, 15
Saint Monday, 69, 167
Saltley, 98, 190, 199
Scholefield: Joshua, 30, 126; William 35, 115
schools, 19, 27, 39, 102, 159-62
School of Art, 146, 148
School of Jewellery, 146
sculpture, 39, 65, 77, 81-3, 115, 121-2, 176, 183-4, 202, 205, 214
Selly Oak, 4, 193
Serbians, 193
sewage, 141
Shambles, 80
Sheldon, 196
shops, 155, 185-7
Showell Green, 55-6
slavery, 30, 34
Small, William, 59-60, 63, 72, 92
Small Heath, 105, 176, 188, 210
Smeaton, John, 71, 90
Smethwick, 88, 90-1, 176
Snow Hill, 95, 172
Snow Hill Station, 96-8, 105, 153, 201
Soho, 67, 67-8, 70, 74-6, 107
Southall, Joseph, 147
Spaghetti Junction, 201
Sparkbrook, 30, 32-3, 54-5, 105, 115, 199, 206-7, 209
Sparkbrook Farm, 32-3
Sparkhill, 166
Spiceal Street, 15, 80, 83, 95
Spooner, Abraham, 28
steam, 67, 71-7, 92
steam cars, 63, 75, 92
steel, 28-9, 177
Stephenson, George, 94
Street Commissioners, 15, 17, 78-80, 95, 120, 124
strikes, 179, 197
Sturge, Joseph, 30, 126
Suffield, family, 145
Sumner, John, 169
Sutton Coldfield, 87, 117, 188
Sutton Park, 98
Swedenborgians, 50, 54
swords, 13, 30
Symphony Hall, 96, 127, 213-4
synagogues, 101

Tangye's, 176
Tanners' Row, 14

Taylor, John, 31-3, 43, 68
Telford, Thomas, 90-1
Temperance Movement, 156, 167-8
theatres, 42-4, 82, 122-3, 125, 127-32, 130, 145, 153-4, 170, 199
Thomason, Yeoville, 101, 150, 164
Tilley, Vesta, 129
Toldervy, William, 38
Tolkien, J.R.R., 103, 145, 163
Toqueville, Alexis de, 28, 42
Town Hall, 124-6, 144, 152, 191
toymaking, 31, 65-6
Toy Shop of Europe, 43
trams, 18-90
turnpikes, 85
Typhoo Tea, 90, 169

umbrellas, 174
Unett, Thomas, 36
Unionists, 190-3
Unitarians, 50-1, 54
universities: Aston, 155, 163; Birmingham, 144, 162-3, 194; Central England, 163

Van Wart, Henry, 117
Vaughton's Hole, 107, 169
Vauxhall Gardens, 44-5
Victoria Law Courts see Law Courts
Victoria, Queen, 21-2, 93, 154
Vietnamese Community, 106
visitors, 12, 28, 30-1, 38, 50, 83, 96
Volunteers, Loyal Birmingham, 108

Walker, Robert, 45
wars: Boer, 132, 191; English Civil 22-8; First World, 126, 130, 193-4; Second World, 183, 198-200
Washwood Heath, 55
Water Supply, 136-7
Waterhouse, 154
Watt: James, 58, 61, 70-7, 92; James Jnr., 21
waxworks, 49, 181
Webster & Horsfall, 177
Welch Cross, 17-18
Wellington, Duke of, 119
wells, 4, 137, 143
Wesley, Charles, 50
Westley, William, 5, 28
West Indians see Afro-Caribbean
Westmacott, William, 82
Whitehead, George, 105
Whitehurst, John, 59-61
Wilson, Jacob, 140
Winson Green, 136, 142-3, see also prisons
Winter Gardens, 154
Winteringham, Graham, 132
Witton, 6, 188
Wolverhampton, 23, 85, 91-2, 97
workhouses, 30, 40, 163-4
Wright, Joseph, 98-9
Wyatt, Samuel, 76

Yardley, 5, 190

zeppelin raids, 193-4
zoos, 170, 181

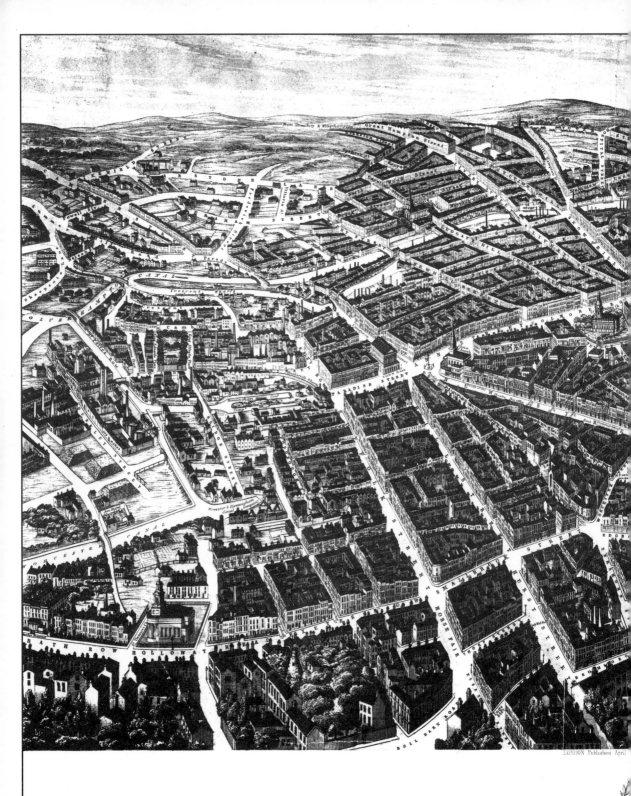

PANORAMIC VIEW